'*The Psychosis of Race* usefully intervenes upon contemporary theories of race and racism. By drawing attention to a psychotic structure that underlies the anxieties, delusions, and fantasies that spur racial violence in our present historical moment, this study takes Lacanian psychoanalysis in directions it has not fully explored.'
Sheldon George, *author of* Trauma and Race: A Lacanian Study of Race

'In arguing that our relationship to race is organized by the psychic structure of psychosis, Jack Black both aptly diagnoses our contemporary moment and puts forward an "ethical sensibility" for overcoming race and racism's psychic hold. Specifically, through an accessible exposition of key Lacanian concepts and original analyses of popular cultural artifacts, *The Psychosis of* Race sets us on the path to forging creative and agentic possibilities for overcoming our attachment to race as a futile attempt to secure our place within an unreliable socio-symbolic field.'
Jennifer Friedlander, *author of* Real Deceptions: The Contemporary Reinvention of Realism

'In this truly invigorating and critical analysis, Jack Black utilizes the vocabulary of terms developed by Jacques Lacan for the treatment and conceptualization of psychosis and applies them, in a distinctive cultural mode, to the psychical life of racialization, racism, and racial identity. In so doing, he moves us beyond the "post race" consensus and the shortcomings of equal representation as adequate responses to racist social structure. He highlights the distinctive analytical potential of thinking our psychical entanglements with race in terms that are uniquely illuminating.'
Derek Hook, *author of* Six Moments in Lacan *and co-editor of* Lacan on Depression and Melancholia

The Psychosis of Race

The Psychosis of Race offers a unique and detailed account of the psychoanalytic significance of race, and the ongoing impact of racism in contemporary society.

Moving beyond the well-trodden assertion that race is a social construction, and working against demands that simply call for more representational equality, *The Psychosis of Race* explores how the delusions, anxieties, and paranoia that frame our race relations can afford new insights into how we see, think, and understand race's pervasive appeal. With examples drawn from politics and popular culture—such as *Candyman, Get Out*, and the music of Kendrick Lamar—critical attention is given to introducing, as well as explicating on, several key concepts from Lacanian psychoanalysis and the study of psychosis, including foreclosure, the phallus, Name-of-the-Father, sinthome, and the *objet petit a*. By elaborating a cultural mode to psychosis and its understanding, an original and critical exposition of the effects of racialization, as well as our ability to discern the very limits of our capacity to think through, or even beyond, the idea of race, is provided.

The Psychosis of Race speaks to an emerging area in the study of psychoanalysis and race, and will appeal to scholars and academics across the fields of psychology, sociology, cultural studies, media studies, and the arts and humanities.

Jack Black is Associate Professor of Culture, Media, and Sport at Sheffield Hallam University and affiliated with the Centre for Culture, Media and Society, where he is Research Lead for the 'Anti-Racism Research Group'. An interdisciplinary researcher, working within psychoanalysis, media, and cultural studies, Jack is the author of *Race, Racism and Political Correctness in Comedy: A Psychoanalytic Exploration* (Routledge, 2021) and co-editor of *Sport and Physical Activity in Catastrophic Environments* (Routledge, 2022).

The Psychology and the Other Book Series
Series editor: David M. Goodman
Associate editors: Brian W. Becker, Donna M. Orange and Eric R. Severson

The *Psychology and the Other book* series highlights creative work at the intersections between psychology and the vast array of disciplines relevant to the human psyche. The interdisciplinary focus of this series brings psychology into conversation with continental philosophy, psychoanalysis, religious studies, anthropology, sociology, and social/critical theory. The cross-fertilization of theory and practice, encompassing such a range of perspectives, encourages the exploration of alternative paradigms and newly articulated vocabularies that speak to human identity, freedom, and suffering. Thus, we are encouraged to reimagine our encounters with difference, our notions of the "other," and what constitutes therapeutic modalities.

The study and practices of mental health practitioners, psychoanalysts, and scholars in the humanities will be sharpened, enhanced, and illuminated by these vibrant conversations, representing pluralistic methods of inquiry, including those typically identified as psychoanalytic, humanistic, qualitative, phenomenological, or existential.

Recent titles in the series include:

The Psychology and Philosophy of Eugene Gendlin
Making Sense of Contemporary Experience
Edited by Eric R. Severson and Kevin C. Krycka

Levinas for Psychologists
Leswin Laubscher

The Psychosis of Race
A Lacanian Approach to Racism and Racialization
Jack Black

For a full list of titles in the series, please visit the Routledge website at: https://www.routledge.com/Psychology-and-the-Other/book-series/PSYOTH

The Psychosis of Race

A Lacanian Approach to Racism and Racialization

Jack Black

LONDON AND NEW YORK

Designed cover image: La Cassette Bleue / Getty Images

First published 2024
by Routledge
4 Park Square, Milton Park, Abingdon, Oxon OX14 4RN

and by Routledge
605 Third Avenue, New York, NY 10158

Routledge is an imprint of the Taylor & Francis Group, an informa business

© 2024 Jack Black

The right of Jack Black to be identified as author of this work has been asserted in accordance with sections 77 and 78 of the Copyright, Designs and Patents Act 1988.

All rights reserved. No part of this book may be reprinted or reproduced or utilised in any form or by any electronic, mechanical, or other means, now known or hereafter invented, including photocopying and recording, or in any information storage or retrieval system, without permission in writing from the publishers.

Trademark notice: Product or corporate names may be trademarks or registered trademarks, and are used only for identification and explanation without intent to infringe.

Every effort has been made to contact copyright-holders. Please advise the publisher of any errors or omissions, and these will be corrected in subsequent editions.

British Library Cataloguing-in-Publication Data
A catalogue record for this book is available from the British Library

ISBN: 978-1-032-53897-6 (hbk)
ISBN: 978-1-032-53427-5 (pbk)
ISBN: 978-1-003-41420-9 (ebk)

DOI: 10.4324/9781003414209

Typeset in Times New Roman
by Taylor & Francis Books

In memory of Kim Hunt

Contents

Introduction   1

PART I
Race is (not) a social construction   23

1 Interrogating the social construction of race   25
2 The non-sense of race   35
3 Racial extimacy   47

PART II
Race and the structure of psychosis   61

4 Lacan and psychosis   63
5 The object *a* of race   85
6 Psychosis and lack: A nothing made something   100
7 Race and foreclosure   114
8 Psychosis and the Other   134
9 Paranoia and the racist fantasy   149

PART III
Ethics, lack, and doubt   173

10 A space for politics   175

11	Beyond race? The radical temporality of creative doubt	190
12	Kendrick Lamar and the psychosis of race	205
	Index	222

Introduction

There is no doubt that race exists. From defining and explaining one's athletic capability, to the medical statistics that populate news reports on cancer and COVID-19, references to race maintain a ubiquitous presence. We are, in this regard, routinely classified and delineated according to a racial arrangement that seeks to determine and characterise explicit racial differences. By categorizing the human population according to prescribed racial designations, race remains a distinctly synonymous classification, both appropriated and applied to a variety of situations, scenarios, and 'problems'. Indeed, while there are many who acknowledge the fact that race is nothing more than a social construction, its common usage suggests that it is unlikely to disappear. Today, race continues to be *constructed* by racists and anti-racists alike, maintaining a ubiquity that undermines any assertion that race no longer matters.

If anything, assumptions regarding race have proven adept at finding new ground for their expression. For both racists and anti-racists, one's race can prove fundamental to one's very being. While this is frequently asserted in examples of racism, for the anti-racist one's values, culture, and belief remain integral to one's prescribed racial identity—that is, one's inherent sense of self. As a consequence, it is one's *racial identity* that is both recognised and protected. Certainly, whereas examples of racism are, in most situations, socially policed through the adoption of 'correct' forms of address, ultimately, race maintains a cultural presence that explicitly sustains such racial distinctions. Though ascribed cultural affiliations and ethnic differences can prove just as essentialising as any ascription that seeks to identify biological differences between proposed racial groups, the effect of such cultural determination is that it readily assumes a 'dominant culture' as the norm: it is in relation to *this* culture that cultural differences are abjectly defined. What creeps into these discourses are more subtle, less obvious forms of racism that are often presented with the intention of expressing no racial hostility.

Take, for example, the widely-reported incident of Amy Cooper, who, while walking her unleashed dog in New York (U.S.), came into confrontation with a birdwatcher, Christian Cooper (no relation). After asking Amy to put her

DOI: 10.4324/9781003414209-1

dog on its lead, in an area where leads were required, a confrontation ensued between both Amy and Christian. Christian recorded the incident, which later went viral. In the video, Amy responds, 'I'm calling the cops … I'm gonna tell them there's an African American man threatening my life' (Aguilera 2020). On the phone to the police, Amy can be heard saying to the responder, 'There is an African American man—I am in Central Park—he is recording me and threatening myself and my dog. Please send the cops immediately!' (Aguilera 2020).[1] As Russell Sbriglia explains, what proves so 'jarring' about the incident:

> is that she [Amy] specifically says—both to the black man himself before she calls 911 and to the police dispatcher once she's on the phone with them—that 'an *African American* man' is threatening her life. It's almost as if, having mastered the proper, politically correct jargon ('African American,' not 'black'), what she's doing couldn't possibly be racist.
> (cited in Žižek 2020b, 39–40, italics in original)

In the days after, Amy would openly profess her non-racism, with the usual apologies ensuing (Black 2020). What is clear from the Cooper example, however, is that it is through a veneer of political correctness that we see a channel of racism maintained (Black 2021).

A similar occurrence would take place in the wake of a leaked draft judgement, which disclosed that the U.S. Supreme Court intended to reverse the *Roe v. Wade* ruling, thus ending women's right to abortion in the U.S. (the Supreme Court did in fact overturn the right on 24th June 2022). In response to the leak, U.S. actor, Amanda Duarte, tweeted: 'I do wonder how these white supremacist lawmakers would feel if their little white daughters were raped and impregnated by black men'. The tweet was later deleted, but what seemed to fly over the head of Duarte was the ease in which 'black men' became the crux of her 'anti-sexist' example, and the subsequent channel for her frustrations. It would seem that, for Duarte at least, the path to women's equality required a level of empathy that remained ignorant of the racism that she served to sustain.

What underscores the Cooper and Duarte examples is the evocation of race in scenarios that, on the face of it, bear no justification for its appearance. In fact, what each example reveals—and here we can assume that Duarte is fully aware of the moral impropriety surrounding racism if only on the basis that she later deleted her tweet—is that both Cooper and Duarte remained fully aware of the effects of racial discrimination, and the ongoing impact of racial inequality in the U.S. Presumably, if questioned, we can suppose that each would be cognizant of the impact of racial prejudice both within and outside the U.S., and, further still, would no doubt conceive of themselves as being non-racist. Instead, we can consider how it is the knowledge and the conviction that underscores their anti-racism which serves to maintain one's assumed 'racial empathy'.

This can be found in the bizarre case of Grace Halsell, a White journalist, who, in 1968, chose to undergo certain treatments that allowed her to 'physically' pass as a Black woman. Conducted in order to evidence the effect of racial injustice in the U.S., Halsell later documented her experiences in the book, *Soul Sister* ([1969] 1999). Halsell's attempts to build racial empathy remains unique, if only for the fact that changing her skin colour afforded her a level of racial appropriation that would, in some form or another, provide her a journalistic insight into the lives of Black women. Ultimately, the fact that Halsell's physical appropriations could help her understand the plight of Black communities, steers more towards a pathological obsession with the notion of Blackness as 'something' that can be obtained and displayed. Aside from the far more concerning assumption that a White woman could so easily appropriate the outward complexion of a Black woman, a form of racial dominance in and of itself, there nonetheless remains the contention within Halsell's actions that through the knowledge obtained in her experiences wider changes in racial inequality could be assured or, at least, highlighted.[2] If anything, it confirmed that one's racial identity could be *politicised*. Ultimately, in Halsell's fraught attempt to achieve racial empathy, it is the racial characteristics that Halsell sought to mimic which underlie the very distinctions and differentiations that prescribe the assumed racial differences that function to determine and fix one's racialization.

Approaching race

What is clear from these opening examples is the fact that they stand opposed to a political and cultural context that unrelentingly celebrates its racial diversity. In 2022, the short-lived U.K. prime ministership of Lizz Truss and her appointed cabinet, which included Kwasi Kwarteng as Chancellor of the Exchequer, Suella Braverman as Home Secretary, and James Cleverly as Foreign Secretary, was, aside from its brevity in office, remarkable for its racial diversity.[3] For the first time in U.K. history, the Great Offices of State were not held by a White man.[4] What is more, following Truss's brief prime ministership, on 24th October 2022, Rishi Sunak became the U.K.'s first prime minister of South Asian descent.[5]

Such 'celebration', however, would continue to be bound to the identity politics that it sought to proclaim. That is, by presenting a path of 'equality', based largely on symbolic representation and the politicization of one's racial identity and ethnic heritage, both the trickle-down diversity professed by Truss's cabinet, and the appointment of Sunak by Conservative MPs, remain miles apart from the structural inequalities that prevent such 'diversity' being achieved across the very society that both Truss and Sunak are responsible for.[6] Instead, these examples would, in the end, shed light on the racial anxieties that continue to underscore such diversity. In the weeks after Truss's cabinet appointments, Labour MP Rupa Huq was reported to have referred to Kwarteng as 'superficially' Black, highlighting instead his attendance at the elite Eton School (BBC 2022).[7] Though Huq's remarks rely upon the racist assertion that there must be a certain authenticity to being Black, a racial particularity that, presumably, Kwarteng was not capable of, her comments were followed by *The Mirror* newspaper, which mistakenly used a picture of Bernard Mensah, President of International for Bank of America, in a story pertaining to Kwarteng's mini-budget (Bryant 2022).

Evidently, it would seem that despite a proliferation of Black bodies within our visual, commercial, and political cultures (Gilroy 2000), the anxieties that abound one's confidence in openly decrying the legitimacy of one's race, or in mistakenly associating (again) one Black man for another, serve only to confirm and maintain the ubiquity of race as an unrelenting force that frames, but also constitutes, our reliance on racial forms of categorization and differentiation.[8] Indeed, the same can also be said for those examples where an enforced 'colour-blindness' works to enliven the very racial differences that are meant to be ignored. Like the anxieties that framed Kwarteng, such enforcement functions to mediate the visibility of racial difference. Whether or not these racial differences can be, on the one hand, disparaged for their non-significance, or, on the other, used to endorse the racial distinctions that they seek to dispel, we remain ill-equipped, or, perhaps, incapable, of upending the injustice, discrimination, and inequality that goes so far in preserving the hegemony of race as a principle of one's psychic and social organization. In effect, race does not simply reveal the inequalities embedded in society, but openly flaunts and propagates the very obscenities that maintain our social and political systems.

Of concern here is how easily the work of anti-racism can proceed to enact new forms of racial consequence that only exacerbate the division between the subject and the racial other. This occurs through the self-placation of obsessively identifying and finding new forms of racial prejudice. In such cases, the problem of racism resides in an anti-racism that succumbs to a level of virtue-signalling, whereby the valency of hate is merely redirected towards the racist other. Though guilt and confession become aligned in forms of self-humiliation and self-development, psychoanalytically, such diversions, and the sense of righteousness they convey, work to obscure the subject's lack just as much as they fixatedly maintain one's reliance on a set of racial distinctions that never go so far as dismantling the very discriminations that they rely upon (Black 2020).

The psychosis of race

Facing the fact that 'the term "race" conjures up a peculiarly resistant variety of natural difference' it is in 'the possibility of leaving "race" behind' (Gilroy 2000, 29) that the task of approaching the inequalities that sustain the racial worldview maintain a critical significance. To this end, the opening sections to this Introduction have taken a familiar path. Elucidating on the significance of race while also highlighting its ongoing role in shaping and framing our discussions on race, racism, and racial difference, it is now customary to assert the well-trodden explanation that race is a phenomenon both historically and socially constructed. Part I will seek to upend this common trajectory. By taking to task the assertion that race remains a social construction, it will consider how such debates can just as easily reify racial distinctions as much as they seek their critique. In the end, deferring to race as a mere social construction serves only to infix its social embeddedness, so that the very nonsense of race continues to prescribe the external differences that constitute one's sense of racial being.

It is on this basis, however, that the significance of race, as a form of thinking, works to presuppose examples of racial division. Indeed, elsewhere, Asare has referred to the need to 'exorcise' our reliance on race, revealing how 'the language of exorcism speaks to the harm associated with the race framework, and also of the need to battle this affliction in multiple realms' (2018, 23). These realms comprise Gilroy's (2000) account of raciology and the racial hierarchies it helps to erect and maintain. Referring specifically to the work of Frantz Fanon, Gilroy points to the very ways in which 'race-thinking' works to both subordinate certain racial groups, while also prescribing Whites with 'the alchemical magic of racial mastery' (2000, 15). Echoing the work of Sheldon George (2014; 2016; 2022), it is this apparent mastery which masks and obscures the very lack that constitutes the racialized subject, whether they be Black, White, Brown, Red, or Yellow. While Gilroy does not follow the psychoanalytic path that underscores George's work, Gilroy undoubtedly aligns with George when asserting that 'Black and [W]hite are bonded together by the mechanisms of "race" that estrange them from each other and amputate their common humanity' (Gilroy 2000, 15). While the latter 'may not have been animalized, reified, or exterminated, … they too have suffered something by being deprived of their individuality, their humanity, and thus *alienated* from species life' (Gilroy 2000, 15, italics added).

It is in accordance with such deprivation that a psychoanalytic approach can prove helpful. Whether it be in delineating the very *jouissance* that racism expounds (Hook 2018; McGowan 2022; Miller 2017; Zalloua 2020), or through a fantasy of race that both constrains and delimits the subject's sense of being as well as that of the other (George 2016), in each case, it is the effects of one's racial 'enjoyment', or one's fantasy relation to the object *a* of race, that disavows or outright prevents a level of universality grounded in the inconsistencies of the human subject (Flisfeder 2022; Gilroy 2000; Zalloua 2020).

Accordingly, amid the pernicious work of race—which continues to systematically expel forms of racial inequality, discrimination, and injustice—this book argues that it is in our reliance on race to demarcate, divide, and differentiate the human population that our understanding of race is both secured and perpetuated through acts of racism (Fields and Fields 2012). In fact, when race is conveyed and maintained just as much through one's assumed racial identification, as it is in the capacity to remain cognisant of a range of racial improprieties, then our reliance on race can best be expressed through what this book will refer to as the 'psychosis of race'. Specifically, this will consider how our seeing and thinking about race elicits and relies upon a psychotic structure that frames and shapes our social relations and institutions.[9] This includes examples of racism and racial hatred as well as the anti-racist agendas that seek to critique the prejudices, inequalities, and discriminatory practices that racism relies upon. Bringing together key concepts and texts in the study of race, racism, and psychosis—such as extimacy; fantasy; lack; master-signifier; *jouissance; objet a*; the phallus; and foreclosure—it will be argued that Lacan's (1997) theory of psychosis provides a critical insight into the ongoing effects of racialization. In so doing, this book details how racial anxiety, paranoia, delusion, and fantasy maintain a constitutive significance in examples of racialization that serve to mark and prescribe the human subject *their* race.

Importantly, the following discussion and analysis will seek to focus on the ongoing significance of 'race' in contemporary society. More importantly, by directing attention towards the effects of race, we do not ignore racism. Referring explicitly to the work of Karen and Barbara Fields, and their key text, *Racecraft* (2012), McGowan argues that to '[t]alk about race instead of racism is always ideological and has the effect of ensconcing us in the trap of attempting to tolerate difference instead of focusing on eradicating racism' (2022, 24–25).[10] Whereas the ideological effects of racism underscore the need for its eradication, it is important not to ignore the very 'craft' that racism achieves, especially in propagating a reliance on race, both as a point of reference, and as an assumed cause of racial difference. Accordingly, while the following discussion stands opposed to liberal requirements that posit the need for greater forms of tolerance in our relations with the other (requirements that simply rely upon increasing representational forms of racial equality [Black 2021]), it is in elaborating upon the trap of race—the 'craft' that racism so persuasively achieves—that the eradication of racism can be asserted (McGowan 2022).[11]

As will be explored in Part I, and while drawing specifically from Lacan's Symbolic order and the Real, race and racism are, in the analysis that follows, entwined. That is, insofar as our understanding of the Symbolic and the Real cannot be separated, equally, the same can also be said for race and racism. To discuss, think, see, or conceive of race is to be on the path of racism, and, thus, in sight of the Real. Inevitably, this book follows such a path, arguing that our capacity to tackle racism rests upon our ability to understand, and, therefore critique, our reliance on race—here, psychosis can help us navigate such a predicament.

Why psychosis?

By introducing the psychosis of race, this book will not defer to some form of psychological reductionism, which ultimately locates the analysis of race and racism in the subject's individuality and their own internal pathologies. Instead, the benefits of undertaking a psychoanalytic interpretation is made clear when we consider how our unconscious investments in race indelibly require a psycho-sociological approach. In fact, if there remains a political project to psychoanalysis, then it stems from a level 'of analysis which has always had an intrinsically social character' (Zupančič 2008, 38). Identifying this 'intrinsically social character' can allow us to examine the social pathologies that provide a path towards increasing forms of particularization and individuality. What it also points towards is the benefits afforded to Lacan's account of the (big) Other. As Lacan posits, '[f]rom the moment the subject speaks, the Other, with a big O, is there' (1997, 41). Consequently, it is only by 'grasping the unconscious as the subjective locus of the Other ... that we avoid falling into the routine dualism of private versus public domains—a dualism that typically risks de-politicizing racism' (Hook 2008, 69). Though our unconscious relies upon the Other as the structure which helps organize and maintain the Symbolic order, equally, it is in accordance with the Other's signifiers that the unconscious connects the subject to the process of signification and to the Symbolic order itself.

Indeed, while this emphasizes how our unconscious investments remain at the behest of the Other, and, specifically, 'the Other's discourse' (Lacan 2006a, 10), what is of greater concern is that one's social and psychical development emerges from the questions that arise when we consider the very gaps, inconsistencies, and antagonisms that mark our social existence. While it is in view of these questions that the existence of the unconscious can be averred, it is with regard to the Other that our social relations, as well as our relation to reality, can be interrogated.

It is on the back of such interrogation that we can trace the importance of the Other in studying the effects of racism. Hook summarises:

> What the Lacanian concept of the Other makes possible is that we may retain a form of explanatory reference to the unconscious—so crucial in fathoming racism—without reducing it either to the inner depth of repressed emotions or to an ostensibly a-social sphere of primal instincts *within* the singular subject.
>
> (2008, 68, italics in original)

Today, the effects of retaining this 'explanatory reference' are compounded by the contention that our public discourses and relations to 'truth', as well as what is conceived as either 'right' or 'wrong', are increasingly framed by an absence of authority, or, at least, by a decline in respect and trust towards those institutions that once served as sources of authority (i.e., political parties, public services, the church). One noticeable example of this is how our reliance on race, and the ongoing perpetuation of racism, convey a lack of moral anchorage. The violent shooting of unarmed Black civilians in the U.S.; the enduring systemic reproduction of racial violence and abuse; and the flagrant propagation of hate speech by politicians, journalists, and social commentators, each seeking to exacerbate domestic tensions in the guise of public interest, are all repeated, reproduced, and accepted as part of our day-to-day reality, laying seed to the hatred, violence, and 'us' and 'them' hostility that underscores our social and political relations. In this context, the promulgation of racial paranoia and anxiety echoes Frederic Jameson's (1995) contention that, amidst a demise in Symbolic efficiency, the turn to conspiracy theories and other forms of 'cognitive mapping' compels a psychotic aesthetic that is increasingly brought forth under the totalizing logic of postmodern late capitalism (see also Jameson 1992).[12] Identifying the *they* and *them* 'responsible' for this decline becomes dependent upon a process of racialization that seeks to frame and position the racist and anti-racist subject as well as the racial other.

Though it may seem that our capacity to determine the truth and to trust the information that we are provided with serves only to cement the declining efficiencies of a Symbolic order slowly eroding under a lack of public trust, it is here that our reliance on racial forms of differentiation, and the ongoing perpetuation of racism in both its psychical and structural forms, functions to reveal the contradictions, antagonisms, and ambivalences that underscore the psychosis of race. In fact, while the decline in Symbolic authority does not confirm the complete and utter collapse of the big Other—indeed, to postulate such a collapse would itself require an Other with which this collapse could be perceived against—what it does suggest is that our relations to race continue to bear a psychotic character.[13] Accordingly, by permitting 'to break with a deficit model of psychosis' (Vanheule 2011, 147), Lacan was able to situate an understanding of psychosis that was focused upon the subject's relation to the Other, which, in the context of the present study, can allow us to explore the ongoing effects of race, racism, and racialization today.

As will be argued, it is through employing Lacan's (1997; 2006f) theory of psychosis that we can identify and approach the anxieties, paranoias, fantasies, and delusions that frame our reliance on race. To appreciate this importance, it is appropriate to remember that, for Lacan:

> the idea of psychotic structure is not a presumed mode of psychological organization that is hidden in the mind or the brain. It concerns the *logic of subjective functioning as expressed in relation to the Other, which entails a specific position of the subject.*
>
> (Vanheule 2019, 78, italics in original).

This book will consider how it is with regard to this 'relation to the Other' that a specific racial position is prescribed to the subject, and that it is from a psychotic structure that our orientations to race and racism, as well as an array of racial practices (stereotyping, racist fantasies, racial paranoia, racial anxiety, racial segregation, etc.), can be explored.

Furthermore, whereas for Lacan the very nature of reality is phantasmatic, by extension psychosis cannot be reduced to a simple loss of reality on behalf of the psychotic. Rather, it is in accordance with a perceived lack of authority in the Other that our social relations, popular cultural formations, and public discourses exhibit a psychotic structure. Insofar as 'the psychotic is without the primary, or fundamental, (symbolic) link to anchor the structure of psychical reality' (Fimiani 2021, 104), it is without the Other's perceived authority that we are left in a position of 'non-sense' that race helps to shape and define. Where psychosis expresses 'a fundamental difficulty in articulating one's position as a subject' (Vanheule 2011, 94), the appeal of *race* stems not only from the assurances that it affords but from the very difficulties that these assurances create and maintain. As will be explored in Part I, race makes 'meaning', but it remains a meaning that is tied to a level of non-sense that is both fixed and intrusive.

The subject of race

In the proceeding chapters, Lacan's theory of psychosis will 'provid[e] a framework to reflect on the ways in which subjectivity takes shape' (Vanheule 2011, 80); a framework in which the effects of the subject—primarily, its inherent lack (the gap which constitutes being)—undergo a process of racialization. Echoing Seshadri-Crooks, it is argued 'that to be a subject of race is a pathological state' (2000, 60), in which the psychosis of race can help to take seriously 'Lacan's view [that] pathological formations like neuroses, psychoses and perversions have the dignity of fundamental philosophical attitudes towards reality' (Žižek 2006, 3–4).

Certainly, by exploring race as a pathology, we do not lose the importance of the Symbolic order or Lacan's focus on language, the Other, and the Real. In fact, as Seshadri-Crooks explains, 'where race is concerned, it is the signifier itself that is the symptom' (Seshadri-Crooks 2000, 60). Yet, as Part I will consider, rather than conceiving of race as discursively constructed and reconstructed—an approach that ignores the limits of the Symbolic and, thus, the Real—the following analysis will consider how the psychosis of race both shapes and frames our subjectivity through 'the individual's ability to articulate a subjective position via the signifier' (Vanheule 2011, 77). Thus, it is in accordance with the signifier and, hence, the Symbolic order, that our investments in race—specifically, how we make use of race and relate to race—remain both socially and psychically significant. This posits that the psychosis of race is not beholden to the racist subject, but instead frames, positions, and structures the processes of racialization that interdependently involve both the racist subject and racial other. It is in this way that the exclusions promulgated by Whiteness are neither ignored nor disavowed. Rather, what the psychosis of race affords is a consideration of race's inherent non-sense, as well as the irrationality that underscores the subject's racialization.

This bears some resemblance to Andrews (2016) account of the psychosis of Whiteness, which he relates to the discursive significance of Whiteness as grounded in systemic forms of racial inequality. Set against critiques of White privilege and unending calls for further education and more dialogue, the psychosis of Whiteness examines how such efforts propose a decentring of Whiteness that, in Andrews's account, are resigned to failure. Instead, for Andrews, 'if we see Whiteness as a psychosis, then we understand that it is hallmarked by irrationality and a distinct inability to see reality in any other way than the distorted view it creates' (Andrews 2016, 439). As a result, any attempt to decentre Whiteness is ultimately undermined by the hallucinatory effects that the psychosis of Whiteness induces.

Certainly, the assertion that Whiteness 'can be addressed, dismantled, or overcome ... through rationale dialogue' (Andrews 2016, 436) is a falsity that will ring true in the argument that follows. Where this argument will diverge, however, is in drawing attention to the underlying contentions that Andrews exposes. Ultimately, if examples of Whiteness remain 'rooted' in social structures that bear no opportunity for correction or critical engagement, then efforts to dispel, undermine, or even destroy the social conditions underpinning hegemonic Whiteness remain, in Andrews's case, beyond the act of reason. While this sense of fated failure posits 'a discursive psychosis that cannot be tamed through reason' (Andrews 2016, 442), it is not '[u]ntil the conditions that create Whiteness are destroyed' that the psychosis of Whiteness can be challenged and effaced (Andrews 2016, 451).

In this respect, it is difficult to determine how such destruction can ever be enacted when one's ties to the social conditions remain under the 'spell' of psychosis, and where the very act of 'reason' is itself nullified. Indeed, to seek a path of identifying or revealing some 'truer' reality or form of reason, outside of that which the subject envisions, is to ignore the structural significances that position, orientate, and locate the subject's psychosis. Instead, in the case of reason, we can ask how it is that the contradictions and inconsistencies inherent to reason serve to compound an irrational, yet no less determining, reliance on race.

Therefore, as the focus of this book will confer, to move beyond the very idea of *race* is to think through the 'ontological structure' that race prescribes (Lacan 2006b, 76).[14] Though Andrews's account does not explicitly refer to psychoanalytic theory, the analysis that follows will explore how the psychosis of race maintains its resilience through an obfuscation of the subject's constitutive lack (George 2016). Whatever one's racial determination, the psychosis of race delimits a form of racial being that irrationally positions and ultimately fixes one's relation to lack, the signifier, and the racial Symbolic order.

Is that a Jew or a crocodile hiding under the bed?

By drawing from Lacan's work on psychosis, this book will not seek to prescribe race an *a priori* existence. Nor will it suppose that acts of racism cannot be challenged or resisted. Instead, as Seshadri explains, it is in accordance with the psychoanalytic approach that 'the production of racial group attachment as a historical and psychological construct' can allow us to consider how race has come to 'generat[e] powerful effects of biological embodiment' (2022, 302). Importantly, these effects have a significant psychic component, grounded in a level of extimacy that socially positions the subject's perception of race as well as their own racial embodiment (see Chapter 3 for an extended discussion on race and extimacy).

To help explain this perception, we can turn to the following tale involving an analyst and their analysand:

> A patient comes to see him complaining that a crocodile is hiding under his bed. During several sessions the analyst tries to persuade the patient that this is all in his imagination. In other words, he tries to persuade him that it is all about a purely 'subjective' feeling. The patient stops seeing the analyst, who believes that he cured him. A month later the analyst meets a friend, who is also a friend of his ex-patient, and asks him how the latter feels. The friend answers: 'You mean the one who was eaten by a crocodile?'
> (Zupančič 1998, 67).

For Zupančič, the underlying question that abounds this tale is that which asks: what is it 'that killed [... and] "ate" the subject?' (1998, 67). Her answer: 'Nothing other than: "I have the *objet petit a* under my bed, I came too close to it"' (Zupančič 1998, 67).

Accordingly, there remains a psychotic dimension to this tale, one revealed by the fact that the analysand comes 'too close' to their *objet petit a*. In psychosis, whatever may underscore one's delusion, be it a crocodile, or some other malignant force, 'there is a solidity to the meaning ascribed to their situation' (Leader 2012, 77). Leader elaborates upon this meaning by highlighting how in examples of psychosis '[l]ibido is localized outside: in the persecutor or in a fault in society or the order of the world. ... There is a "badness" out there that has been situated and named' (2012, 77). What is unique, however, is that '[t]he content of the paranoiac delusion here may be absolutely true' (Leader 2012, 77). Therefore, what remains *essential* to examples of psychosis and paranoia is the conviction that sustains the 'delusion' occupying the subject's life—that is, the *certainty* of the crocodile hiding under the bed.

Here, our reliance on race follows a similar form to that of the poor analysand and their crocodile. For instance, consider the following example from Žižek, who notes that:

> [i]t's not enough to say anti-Semitism is factually wrong, it's morally wrong; the true enigma is: why did the Nazis *need* the figure of the Jew for their ideology to function? Why is it that if you take away their figure of the Jew their whole edifice disintegrates?
>
> (1999, italics added)

It is here that we can draw a connection between the convictions (the *need*) upholding the figure of the Jew and the certainty that supports the crocodile under the bed. For the analysand, it was not enough to declare to them that the crocodile was nothing more than a figment of their imagination, a feeling which they themselves were creating. Rather, the underlying enigma, which compounded the analysand's predicament, was why was there a *crocodile* to begin with? What was it about this *objet a* that proved too much for the analysand? Along the same lines we can echo Zizek's inquiries, and ask: why does the fascist need *the Jew* in order to function? What is it about the Jew's *objet a* that proves 'too much' for the Nazi? What both examples reveal is the importance of the fantasy *objet a*, which, in examples of racism, cannot simply be expunged or ignored. What constitutes the other in the racist fantasy, and what underlies our perceptions of race, *is* the other's *objet a*—that very object which prescribes and denotes one *their* race. It is what fuels and exacerbates the paranoias, anxieties, and delusions that underpin how we see and think about race.

In either case, for the poor analysand, consumed by their crocodile, or the unfaltering Nazi, consumed by the Jewish intruder, their convictions cannot be approached by simply considering their personal failings. On the contrary, what is required is a consideration of the position that such convictions sustain in their relation to the other. Yet, this begs the question: to what extent do we take the analysand's fears and the Nazi's racism 'seriously'? To discount the analysand's concerns or to ignore the Nazi's racism is to fall foul of the reasoning, the certainty, and the expelling of doubt that underlies both positions.

Ultimately, it remains too easy to discredit examples of racism as merely the thoughts and beliefs of an uneducated, uncultured 'working class'. In fact, in the case of antisemitism, 'we cannot simply distinguish between "real" Jews and the way they are perceived by others' (Žižek 2022, 198). To do so would suggest that the racist does not understand, or rather, does not accept, the Jew's 'real' identity; a problem that can be easily fixed with better understanding, more 'dialogue', and further education. Instead, as Žižek notes: 'thousands of years of the exclusion and persecution of the Jews, and all the fantasies projected onto Jews, have inevitably also affected their identity which is formed in reaction to the fantasies grounding their persecution' (2022, 198). In the case of racism, one must always take the racist fantasy seriously, especially when, in the psychosis of race, such fantasy underpins the subject's 'reality'.

Therefore, in order to challenge and resist our convictions in race we must take seriously the very certainties that frame one's knowledge *of* race. To do so is to engage with an account of psychosis that approaches the reality of race in all its psychotic complexity. Better knowledge and more education cannot dispel race's most disparaging effects if only because it is in accordance with our racial fantasies, paranoias, anxieties, and delusions that our reliance on race is lived.

The veracity of race

Evidently, this Introduction proposes a path that sits outside any clinical examination of psychosis towards exploring how forms of racism, racial prejudice, and racial discrimination can be read through 'a cultural mode of psychosis' (Samuels 2001, 141, fn.14). This requires perceiving psychosis as a form of social orientation that dictates our very reliance on race. Only by locating Lacan's approach to psychosis in a critical and interpretative account of culture, can we begin to conceive how the psychosis of race works to frame and shape the subject's relation to and perceptions of the racialised other.

What psychosis provides therefore is a 'logic' through which our understandings of race and racism can be conceived (Fernandez 2014). It can, for example, allow us to unpick 'the scientific point of view', which confidently proclaims 'race ... as a false epistemology of human difference', while all the while ignoring or disavowing the very fact that race continues to provide 'powerful social and ontological effects' (Seshadri 2022, 300). Though race 'markedly invests identity and shapes the psyche's fundamental fantasy' it remains 'deeply buried and intricately imbricated ... in the constitution of the western subject' (Seshadri 2022, 300).[15] To this end, any form of anti-racism must itself be aware of the 'subjective complicity' that draws together the social and the psychic (Cheng 2001, 298). It is for this reason that 'to properly have and be a race, it is necessary that the discourse be inscribed at a fundamental level of subject constitution' (Seshadri 2022, 302).

Consequently, at the heart of this study will be the consideration that the presence of race—indeed, the fact that it remains, despite its criticisms, a constant feature of our contemporary societies—is due to the very way in which the psychosis of race seeks to fix and determine one's sense of being. It is to fully appreciate what the Fields refer to as the 'marrow-deep certainty that racial differences are real and consequential, whether scientifically demonstrable or not' (Fields and Fields 2012, 198). In effect race's 'intransigence' can be conceived as 'an outcome of the fact that the visible reference of race makes a claim to nature—it is about "telling," like "sex," who is this or that' (Seshadri-Crooks 2000, 19). Accordingly:

> [u]nlike other forms of socially constructed difference, such as class or ethnicity, 'race,' like sex, appears as a fundamental and normative factor of human embodiment, something that one inherently is from birth. Thus, despite historicist arguments about its social construction, which may or may not be valid, there is a powerful *semblance* of necessity built into race that makes it ultimately intractable to constructionist claims.
> (Seshadri-Crooks 2000, 19–20, italics in original).

Though Seshadri-Crooks cautions against 'analogizing race with sex', race nonetheless succeeds in inserting itself into the constitution of the subject (2000, 20). That is, while 'there is no denying the fact that race is, after all, a historical invention, and that like most inventions it veils the artifice of its origins', this is, for Seshadri-Crooks, 'not interesting' (2000, 20). Instead, '[w]hat is confounding about race is its successful grafting to nature' (Seshadri-Crooks 2000, 20), or, what comes to be perceived, through a psychotic form, as fixed, determined, and prescribed by the inconsistencies, disruptions, and failings that constitute one's very nature.[16] Following this, Part II will explore how the role of the *objet a* in psychosis—the object *a* of race—becomes attributed to the subject's sense of being in such a way that it's assumed 'essence' serves to fix the subject to their prescribed racial identity. Here, ethnic determinants, cultural heritage and genetic determination become co-aligned in one's racial identity. Indeed:

> [w]hen identity refers to an indelible mark or code somehow written into the bodies of its carriers, otherness can only be a threat. Identity is latent destiny. Seen or unseen, on the surface of the body or buried deep in its cells, identity forever sets one group apart from others who lack the particular, chosen traits that become the basis of typology and comparative evaluation.
> (Gilroy 2000, 103–104)

It is in accordance with the fact that racial identity is conceived as destiny—that race is perceived to elicit a truth about the subject conveyed by either the body or its cells—that race comes to determine, and, thus separates, one subject from another. In so doing, race's very significance remains determined by acts of racialization that work to both define one's racial prescription as well as marking and defining one's racial identity. In the case of the latter, race can often appear in subtle forms, such as the apparently neutral definition of a crime statistic, educational attainment, or national demographic.

However, what we see in these examples is the extent to which '[r]acialization establishes an illusory essence of identity according to which unique individuals are relegated to one or another fictive race, membership in which is determined by ludicrous and arbitrary criteria (e.g., the rule of hypodescent for blacks)'

(Hoyt 2016, 134). Though the veracity of one's racial identity confines one to the very definitions that prescribe this racial identification, through the process of psychosis, one's very racialization is predetermined by one's sense of racial being—a fact determined just as much by one's social affiliations as it is in the significance that is given to one's racial visibility. It is in this way that the psychosis of race can speak to how an apparent racial essence underlies the various forms of seeing and thinking about race that both create and sustain its ongoing significance. Indeed, while '[r]ace structures human subjectivity in ways largely ignored by Jacques Lacan in his psychoanalytic reading of the subject' (George 2022, 241), and while '[t]he work of theorizing the role of race in the constitution of the subject has only just begun' (Seshadri 2022, 303), it is through exploring and applying the psychosis of race that this book will proceed.

Accordingly, whereas Part I, 'Race is (Not) a Social Construction', will lay the groundwork for conceiving how it is in accordance with the signifier, and, thus, the Symbolic order, that our investments in race—specifically, how we make use of race as well as relate to race—bestow a social and psychic significance, Part II, 'Race and the Structure of Psychosis', will bring together key concepts in Lacan's approach to psychosis (such as extimacy; fantasy; lack; master-signifier; *jouissance; objet a*; the phallus; and foreclosure). This will explore how examples of racial anxiety, paranoia, delusion, and fantasy come to constitute the racialization that marks and prescribes the human subject *their* race.

In Part III, 'Ethics, Lack, and Doubt', the social importance embedded in our capacity to doubt, and, hence, to know, will be examined. Drawing from Lacan's (2018) account of the sinthome, Part III will develop an ethical praxis that traces the possibility of confronting the psychosis of race, a central aspect of which will be the reinterpretation of 'post-race' debates. By focusing specifically on the 'post-' prefix, it is argued that the relevance of any 'post-race' assertion speaks not to our present moment (and to a misguided assumption that we have overcome racism) but to a future 'yet-to-come' (Gilroy 2000). Indeed, from this future position, an introduction of doubt, which questions and undermines our present certainties in race, racism, and racialization, will be asserted.

To help elucidate on this approach, the concluding chapter pays critical attention to the songs, 'Sing About Me, I'm Dying of Thirst' and 'Mortal Man', both performed by the Compton-born, hip-hop musician, Kendrick Lamar. By highlighting how Lamar presents a critical perspective on the act of representation, as performed through his adoption of a unique temporal structure and lyrical form, it is argued that Lamar's work offers a space in which both his lyrics and music can confront the psychosis of race. It is here that a re-structuring of our relation to language and new forms of mediation will be used to critique the psychosis of race.

Notes

1. The incident involving Amy and Christian took place on the same day that Derek Chauvin, a Minneapolis police officer, used his knee to slowly suffocate and kill George Perry Floyd Jr. during a routine arrest.
2. What this ignores is the 'fictional nature of social reality [which] undermines most attempts to counter forms of prejudice by simply pointing to the distortions on which they are based' (Samuels 2001, 11, see also Žižek 2008).
3. Appointed on 6th September 2022, within 45 days Kwarteng had been fired and both Braverman and Truss had resigned.
4. In the U.K. government, the Great Offices of State refer to the Prime Minister, Chancellor of the Exchequer, Foreign Secretary, and Home Secretary.
5. Under Sunak, Braverman was reinstated as Home Secretary (she had previously resigned from the position after sharing official documentation using her personal email account and, thus, was in breach of the ministerial code) and Cleverly was re-appointed as Foreign Secretary.
6. Reports by the Runnymede Trust (Edmiston et al. 2021) and The Centre for Social Justice (2020) continue to identify declines in racial equality across the U.K., especially in education, health, criminal justice, and work. This decline is compounded by research that reveals how, amidst the cost-of-living crisis, Black and minority ethnic groups are more likely to live in poverty due to a highly regressive and racialised tax and social security system (Edmiston et al., 2021).
7. In keeping with the arguments of this book, Huq's remarks can be read as displaying the paranoid conviction that there are 'authentic' ways of being Black.
8. As will be discussed in Chapter 6, my decision to stick with the term 'racialization' stands opposed to McGowan (2022), where, in referring to the racialized other, McGowan argues that the term fails to account for those instances where the racial other is perceived as not having a race (such as, the Jew in Nazi anti-Semitism). What Chapter 6 will highlight, however, is that even in cases where a particular group is defined by their racial non-particularity, it is, nonetheless, their very *non-particularity* that becomes the abiding feature of *their* racialization.
9. References to structure, and, specifically, 'psychotic structure', will be used throughout this book. In accordance with Lacan, such use does not assume 'a negation of the subject' (Marini 1992, 43). On the contrary, as Marini explains, Lacan's reference to structure reflected 'his dependency on an order that went beyond him and that was at his origin—the Symbolic' (Marini 1992, 43). All subjects are dependent upon this order, as it is this same Symbolic order that structures the subject's relation to race, and which, over the course of this book, will allow us to investigate the effects of a psychotic structure in examples of racialization.
10. A discussion on 'racecraft' will be returned to in Chapter 3.
11. I would argue that what the Fields so brilliantly demonstrate in their account of racecraft is the ability to perceive and critique this 'trap' in discussions on race and racial difference (Fields and Fields 2012). What an understanding of racecraft exposes, therefore, is *the racism* that our references to 'race' inevitably rely upon.
12. Here, Kornbluh summarises how '[a]ttenuated efficacy of the symbolic entails the relativization and fragmentation of meaning; the proliferation of "alternative facts," of that which is "posttruth," and the like; and the lack of common social institutions and practices for coordinating stable signification' (2022, 409). In light of this, the relation we hold to these examples helps to emphasise the critical and cultural importance of psychosis.
13. It is also in this context that we can refer to Lacan's Name-of-the-Father and to the importance of foreclosure in examples of psychosis (these are both discussed in Chapter 7). Elsewhere, Svolos considers the decline of the Name-of-the-Father and

the personal and social/political ramifications this establishes (Svolos and Rouselle 2022). Indeed, amidst 'the decline of the symbolic as the dominant domain and the decentering or overthrow of the name-of-the-father as universal, the corollary for that in the social world is certainly the decline in dominance of universalism and, in the West, the church, in particular, and authorities and traditions, in general' (Svolos and Rouselle 2022). Importantly, this bears a psychotic significance, wherein the prevalence of a 'generalized foreclosure' means that '[t]he symbolic is no longer dominant' (Svolos and Rouselle 2022). Chapter 7 will serve to explore this contention by conceiving how such a decline in dominance denotes a disrupture in Symbolic mediation.

14 Appearing in Lacan's, 'The Mirror Stage as Formative of the *I* Function as Revealed in Psychoanalytic Experience', the full quote reads, '[i]n my view, this activity has a specific meaning up to the age of eighteen months, and reveals both a libidinal dynamism that has hitherto remained problematic and an ontological structure of the human world that fits in with my reflections on paranoiac knowledge' (2006b, 76). The 'activity' in question refers explicitly to the child's identification with the specular image, the founding of its identification in an assumed image. McGowan's (2020) criticisms of Lacan's 'mirror stage' will be considered in Chapter 4; for now, it is helpful to conceive how this 'ontological structure' can be conceived in accordance with the topological structure of the Mobius strip. With regard to Lacan's (2004) later work on the Real (and the gaze), 'the two sides [of the Mobius strip] representat [sic] the imaginary and the symbolic, with the real functioning as the cut. As an effect of the torsion of the strip, the real becomes structurally inherent to the figure, rather than "having a place." The cut designates the impossibility that the imaginary and the symbolic will meet the real, while at the same time the real is inherent in representation as negativity' (Herzogenrath 2010, 21). It is through this 'ontological structure' that the dialectic between subject and reality is conceived for Lacan (Žižek 2020a).

15 Notably, Seshadri (2022) attributes race's imbrication within the western subject as attributable to the ignorance of psychoanalytic accounts of race. This is exacerbated when we consider Hsiao's contention that '[Frantz] Fanon's mention and application of the mirror stage in the colonial situation ... exemplif[ies] an early encounter, or missed encounter, between Lacanian psychoanalysis and decolonization or post-colonial theory' (2010, 162). Despite this 'missed encounter', since Seshadri-Crooks's, *Desiring Whiteness: A Lacanian Analysis of Race* (2000), there has been Robert Samuels's, *Writing Prejudices: The Psychoanalysis and Pedagogy of Discrimination from Shakespeare to Toni Morrison* (2001); Shannon Winnubst's, "Is the mirror racist? Interrogating the space of whiteness" (2004); Stephen Frosh's, *Hate and the 'Jewish Science': Anti-Semitism, Nazism and Psychoanalysis* (2005); W.J.T. Mitchell's, *Seeing Through Race* (2012); Azeen Khan's "Lacan and Race" (2018); and, Sheldon George's, *Trauma and Race: A Lacanian Study of African American Racial Identity* (2016). Pre-dating Seshadri-Crooks, there is Christopher J. Lane's edited collection, *The Psychoanalysis of Race* (1998), and, more recently, George and Derek Hook's *Lacan and Race: Racism, Identity and Psychoanalytic Theory* (2021). Further still, in studies of colonialism and post-colonialism, Hook's, *A Critical Psychology of the Postcolonial: The Mind of Apartheid* (2012); Jamil Khader's *Cartographies of Trans-nationalism in Postcolonial Feminisms: Geography, Culture, Identity, Politics* (2014); Robert Beshara's, *Decolonial Psychoanalysis: Towards Critical Islamaphobia Studies* (2019); Gautam Basu Thakur's, *Postcolonial Lack: Identity, Culture, Surplus* (2020); and Zahi Zalloua's, *Žižek on Race: Toward an Anti-Racist Future* (2020), all provide a Lacanian approach to race and racism.

16 Seshadri-Crooks clarifies this approach in relation to the following questions, each of which will help guide the proceeding analysis: '[t]hus we must ask how race

appears as the logic of human difference itself. Why do we allocate difference along certain conventional lines of looking? How do we come to be racially embodied? What is the structure of racial difference, and what insights can psychoanalysis offer in the study of the raced subject?' (2000, 20).

References

Aguilera, Jasmine. 2020. "White woman who called police on a Black man at Central Park apologizes, says 'I'm not a racist'." *TIME*, May 26. https://time.com/5842442/amy-cooper-dog-central-park/.

Andrews, Kehindre. 2016. "The psychosis of Whiteness: The celluloid hallucinations of *Amazing Grace* and *Belle*." *Journal of Black Studies* 47, no. 5: 435–453.

Asare, Abena Ampofoa. 2018. "Exocising 'racecraft': Toward the RaceSyllabus." *The Radical Teacher* 112: 16–26.

BBC. 2022. "Rupa Huq MP's Kwasi Kwarteng remarks were racist – London mayor." September 29. https://www.bbc.co.uk/news/uk-england-london-63052522.

Beshara, Robert. 2019. *Decolonial Psychoanalysis: Towards Critical Islamophobia Studies*. London, UK: Routledge.

Black, Jack. 2020. "On reflexive racism: disavowal, deferment and the Lacanian subject." *Diacritics* 48, no. 4: 76–101.

Black, Jack. 2021. *Race, Racism and Political Correctness in Comedy – A Psychoanalytic Exploration*. Abingdon, UK: Routledge.

Bryant, Miranda. 2022. "Mirror apologises for using picture of wrong person in Kwasi Kwarteng story." *The Guardian*, October 1. https://www.theguardian.com/politics/2022/oct/01/mirror-apologises-for-using-picture-of-wrong-person-in-kwasi-kwarteng-story.

The Centre for Social Justice. 2020. "Facing the facts: ethnicity and disadvantage in Britain: disparities in education, work, and family." November. https://www.centreforsocialjustice.org.uk/wp-content/uploads/2020/11/CSJJ8513-Ethnicity-Poverty-Report-FINAL.pdf.

Cheng, A.C. 2001. *The Melancholy of Race: Psychoanalysis, Assimilation, and Hidden Grief*. Oxford, UK: Oxford University Press.

Edmiston, Daniel, Shabna Begum, and Mandeer Kataria. 2021. "Falling faster amidst a cost-of-living crisis: Poverty, inequality and ethnicity in the UK." *Runnymede*, October.

Fernandez, Hilda. 2014. "Ideology, clinical structures and the ethical challenge to the analyst." *Contours Journal* 5. https://www.sfu.ca/humanities-institute/contours/LaConference/page9.html.

Fields, Karen E. and Barabara J.Fields. 2012. *Racecraft: The Soul of Inequality in American Life*. London, UK: Verso.

Fimiani, Bret. 2021. *Psychosis and Extreme States: An Ethic for Treatment*. Champagne, CH: Palgrave Macmillan.

Flisfeder, Matthew. 2022. "Are we human? Or, postmodernism and the subject of modernity." In *Understanding Žižek, Understanding Modernism*, edited by Jeffrey R. Di Leo and Zahi Zalloua (196–210). New York, NY: Bloomsbury.

Frosh, Stephen. 2005. *Hate and the 'Jewish Science': Anti-Semitism, Nazism and Psychoanalysis*. Basingstoke, UK: Palgrave Macmillan.

Frosh, Stephen. 2016. "Studies in prejudice: theorizing anti-Semitism in the wake of the Nazi Holocaust." In *Psychoanalysis in the Age of Totalitarianism*, edited by Matt Ffytche and Daniel Pick (29–41). London, UK: Routledge.

George, Sheldon. 2014. "From alienation to cynicism: race and the Lacanian unconscious." *Psychoanalysis, Culture & Society* 19, no. 4: 360–378.
George, Sheldon. 2016. *Trauma and Race: A Lacanian Study of African American Racial Identity*. Waco, TX: Baylor University Press.
George, Sheldon. 2022. "The Lacanian subject of race: sexuation, the drive, and racial subjectivity." In *Lacan and Race: Racism, Identity, and Psychoanalytic Theory*, edited by Sheldon George and Derek Hook (241–262). Abingdon, UK: Routledge.
George, Sheldon, and Derek Hook. 2022. *Lacan and Race: Racism, Identity, and Psychoanalytic Theory*. London, UK: Routledge.
Gilroy, Paul. 2000. *Against Race: Imagining Political Culture Beyond the Color Line*. Cambridge, MA: The Belknap Press of Harvard University Press.
Halsell, Grace. 1969/1999. *Soul Sister*. Washington, DC: Crossroads International Publishing.
Herzogenrath, Bernd. 2010. *An American Body | Politic: A Deleuzian Approach*. Hanover, NH: Dartmouth College Press.
Hook, Derek. 2008. "Absolute Other: Lacan's 'Big Other' as adjunct to critical social psychological analysis?" *Social and Personality Psychology Compass* 2, no. 1: 51–73.
Hook, Derek. 2018. "Racism and jouissance: evaluating the 'racism as (the theft of) enjoyment' hypothesis." *Psychoanalysis, Culture & Society* 23: 244–266.
Hook, Derek. 2012. *A Critical Psychology of the Postcolonial: The Mind of Apartheid*. London, UK: Routledge.
Hoyt, Carlos A. 2016. *The Arc of a Bad Idea: Understanding and Transcending Race*. Oxford, UK: Oxford University Press.
Jameson, Fredric. 1992. *Postmodernism Or, The Cultural Logic of Late Capitalism*. London, UK: Verso.
Jameson, Fredric. 1995. *The Geopolitical Aesthetic: Cinema and Space in the World System*. Bloomington, IN: Indiana University Press.
Khader, Jamil. 2014. *Cartographies of Transnationalism in Postcolonial Feminisms: Geography, Culture, Identity, Politics*. Lanham, MD: Lexington Books.
Khan, Azeen. 2018. "Lacan and race." In *After Lacan: Literature, Theory, and Psychoanalysis in the Twenty-First Century*, edited by Ankhi Mukherjee, 148–166. Cambridge, UK: Cambridge University Press.
Kornbluh, Anna. 2022. "Imagined communities 2.0." *Rethinking Marxism* 34, no. 3: 406–412.
Lacan, Jacques. 1997. *The Seminar of Jacques Lacan, Book III, 1955–56: The Psychoses*, edited by Jacques-Alain Miller. London, UK: Routledge.
Lacan, Jacques. 2004. *The Four Fundamental Concepts of Psycho-Analysis*, edited by Jacques-Alain Miller. London, UK: Karnac.
Lacan, Jacques. 2006a. "Seminar on 'The Purloined Letter'." In *Écrits. The First Complete Edition in English*, translated by Bruce Fink, in collaboration with Heloise Fink and Russell Grigg (6–50). London, UK: W. W. Norton & Company.
Lacan, Jacques. 2006b. "The mirror stage as formative of the *I* function as revealed in psychoanalytic experience." In *Écrits. The First Complete Edition in English*, translated by Bruce Fink, in collaboration with Heloise Fink and Russell Grigg (75–81). London, UK: W. W. Norton & Company.
Lacan, Jacques. 2006f. "On a question preliminary to any possible treatment of psychosis." In *Écrits. The First Complete Edition in English*, translated by Bruce Fink, in

collaboration with Heloise Fink and Russell Grigg (445–488). London, UK: W. W. Norton & Company.
Lacan, Jacques. 2018. *The Seminar of Jacques Lacan, Book XXIII: The Sinthome,* edited by Jacques-Alain Miller. Cambridge, UK: Polity.
Lane, Christopher, ed. 1998. *The Psychoanalysis of Race.* New York, NY: Columbia University Press.
Leader, Darian. 2012. *What is Madness?* London, UK: Penguin.
Marini, Marcelle. 1992. *Jacques Lacan: The French Context,* translated by Anne Tomiche. New Brunswick, NJ: Rutgers University Press.
McGowan, Todd. 2020. "The object of cinema." *Crisis & Critique* 7, no. 2: 229–243.
McGowan, Todd. 2022. *The Racist Fantasy: Unconscious Roots of Hatred.* New York, NY: Bloomsbury.
Miller, Jacques-Alain. 2017. "Extimate enemies." Translated by Frédéric Baitinger, Azeen Khan, and Roger Litten. *The Lacanian Review: Hurly-Burly,* no. 3: 30–42.
Mitchell, W.J.T. 2012. *Seeing Through Race.* Cambridge, MA: Harvard University Press.
Ruti, Mari. 2012. *The Singularity of Being: Lacan and the Immortal Within.* New York, NY: Fordham University Press.
Samuels, Robert. 2001. *Writing Prejudices: The Psychoanalysis and Pedagogy of Discrimination from Shakespeare to Toni Morrison.* New York, NY: State University of New York Press.
Seshadri, Kalpana R. 2022. "Afterword: there is only one race…" In *Lacan and Race: Racism, Identity, and Psychoanalytic Theory,* edited by Sheldon George and Derek Hook (299–304). Abingdon, UK: Routledge.
Seshadri-Crooks, Kalpana. 2000. *Desiring Whiteness: A Lacanian Analysis of Race.* London, UK: Routledge.
Svolos, Thomas, and Duane Rouselle. 2022. "Psychoanalysis and politics: Duane Rouselle interviews Thomas Svolos." *European Journal of Psychoanalysis.* https://www.journal-psychoanalysis.eu/articles/psychoanalysis-and-politics-duane-rouselle-interviews-thomas-svolos/.
Thakur, Gautam Basu. 2020. *Postcolonial Lack: Identity, Culture, Surplus.* Albany, NY: State University of New York Press.
Vanheule, Stijn. 2011. *The Subject of Psychosis: A Lacanian Perspective.* Basingstoke, UK: Palgrave Macmillan.
Vanheule, Stijn. 2019. "On ordinary psychosis." In *Lacan on Psychosis: From Theory to Praxis,* edited by Jon Mills and David L.Downing (77–102). London, UK: Routledge.
Winnubst, Shannon. 2004. "Is the mirror racist? Interrogating the space of whiteness." *Philosophy & Social Criticism* 30, no. 1: 25–50.
Zalloua, Zahi. 2020. *Žižek on Race: Toward an Anti-Racist Future.* London, UK: Bloomsbury.
Žižek, Slavoj. 1999. The Superego and the Act: A Lecture by Slavoj Žižek." *LiveJournal: Zizek,* August. https://zizek.livejournal.com/1101.html.
Žižek, Slavoj. 2006. *How to Read Lacan.* London, UK: Granta Books.
Žižek, Slavoj. 2008. *The Sublime Object of Ideology.* London, UK: Verso.
Žižek, Slavoj. 2020a. *Sex and the Failed Absolute.* London, UK: Bloomsbury.
Žižek, Salvoj. 2020b. *Pandemic! 2: Chronicles of a Time Lost.* New York, NY: OR Books.

Žižek, Slavoj. 2022. *Surplus Enjoyment*. London, UK: Bloomsbury.
Zupančič, Alenka. 1998. "The subject of the law." In *Cogito and the Unconscious, Sic 2*, edited by Slavoj Žižek (41–73). Durham, NC: Duke University Press.
Zupančič, Alenka. 2008. *Why Psychoanalysis? Three Interventions*. Aarhus, DK: Aarhus University Press.

Part I

Race is (not) a social construction

Chapter 1

Interrogating the social construction of race

Race elicits a certain investment on behalf of the subject. Such a line is taken up by Seshadri-Crooks when she considers that 'even as the scientific untenability of race is ever more insisted upon by scientists and anthropologists ... race itself shows no evidence of disappearing or evaporating in relevance' (2000, 4). Ultimately, '[i]t is common sense to believe in the existence of race' (Seshadri-Crooks 2000, 4), which '[t]he liberal consensus' seeks to manage by 'celebrat[ing] difference' (Seshadri-Crooks 2000, 8). Such celebrations do not necessarily undermine the prevalence of race, and, thus, one's racial identity, but instead seek its perpetuation. This remains, however:

> a 'baby and the bath water' syndrome, in which the dirty water of racism must be eliminated, to reveal the cleansed and beloved 'fact' of racial identity. This rather myopic perspective refuses to address the peculiar resiliency of 'race,' the subjective investment in racial difference, and the hyper-valorization of appearance. It dismisses these issues or trivializes them because race seems a historical inevitability.
>
> (Seshadri-Crooks 2000, 8–9)

What seems to underpin such an historical inevitability, which seeks the subject's investment in the 'hyper-valorization' of racial difference, is the very banality of racism. Notwithstanding acts of racism that involve assault or derogatory language, often examples of racism exist within routine social practices that are so fundamentally embedded in our relations to the world that they have become omnipresent. In fact, it can be argued that the banality of racism stands opposed to, and thus is maintained in, its distinction towards overt forms of racist violence. This works alongside the concern that racism cannot be tackled through better knowledge and enlightened appeals to curtail one's racial ignorance. In effect:

> one can repeatedly challenge racists with the proof of (biological/genetic) racial non-difference in all the ways that matter, without making the slightest dent in their racist perceptions, because, after all, they have already

DOI: 10.4324/9781003414209-3

> acknowledged that race makes no difference; they just opt anyway to act as if it does.
>
> (Hook 2012, 181)

For the racist, they know very well that race 'makes no difference', but, nevertheless, they continue to act as if it does.

Instead, the belief that racial non-difference can be achieved through better knowledge underscores much of the discourse concerning 'unconscious bias'. For McGowan, the reference to '*[b]ias* suggests a distortion of knowing and suggests that the problem is confined to how we know. This term indicates the belief that racism represents a failure to know accurately' (2022, 20, italics in original). Along such lines, racism remains an 'epistemological problem' (McGowan 2022, 20); something that can be easily rectified once one has completed the relevant unconscious bias training.

In the case of the liberal celebration of difference (which just as easily reifies forms of racial differentiation), the racist's fetishistic disavowal ('I know very well that racial differences do not matter, but nevertheless...'), or the misconceptions underlying one's unconscious understanding, there insists a pursual of racism that belies a fundamental consideration of the effects of race, both as an idea and as a social practice that works to maintain racial hierarchies (Gilroy 2000). Since Seshadri-Crook provided an 'interrogation of the mystique of "race"', and, specifically, 'what race is and why we need it' (2000, 3), it seems that the ubiquity of race intreats a return to such interrogation.

What is constructed?

To begin, we can consider how the mystique of race continues to find form in the social habits it maintains. For Fanon (2008), these habits are maintained through institutions that systematically embed race in social practices that dehumanize the racialized subject, both spatially and psychically. In so doing, Black inferiority becomes naturalized. Through fear and imitation, inferiority and dependency, the violence of these learned habits are constructed and reproduced through complex social formations that delimit one's identity along racial lines.

To say that race can be learnt, imitated, and habitualized is to uphold the opinion that race remains a 'social construction', which can subsequently be re-signified, reinterpreted, and deconstructed. George notes:

> [w]hat resignification today entails is an ambivalent scholarly desire to maintain race that is actively facilitated by conceptualizations of agency and identity as discursive, a desire to uphold race while also depriving it of a lethal essentialism that is often the core of racism.
>
> (2016, 36)

Indeed, as is clear in George's account, the problem with such a position is the paradox it enacts. That is, while race is considered to be socially constructed, determined by hegemonic groups and social institutions, it is, nonetheless, the degraded and disenfranchised who are required to 'reinterpret' such constructions as well as resign their debilitating effects. On the one hand, forms of racial discrimination serve to locate and marginalize a particular racial group, while, on the other, these same groups are conceived as the very liberators endowed with the agency to 'freely' reinterpret their position.

Thus, what is ignored in the social construction thesis is 'the subject's paradoxical relationship to the signifier' (Ruti 2012, 77). Here, Ruti explains how:

> [a]s much as the subject is subjected to the symbolic, it also needs the tools offered by this symbolic—particularly the all-important tool of signification—to cope with this subjection. Even though the subject can never claim full agency over the signifier, it can have a more or less empowered relationship to it.
> (2012, 77)

There is, for Ruti, certain conditions where the subject 'may be able to borrow some of its [the signifier's] creative spark to devise ideals, values, and nuggets of meaning that offer it an (always inadequate) antidote against traumatization', but the capacity to gain 'full agency', or to apply the signifier in whatever manner the subject wishes, is impossible (2012, 77). Though this 'degree of resistance' underscores what Ruti refers to as 'poststructuralist theories of subversion', its impact goes much further in examples of social theorizing that proffer the capacity to resist and redetermine hegemonic forms. What is elided in such accounts is the assumed subjective agency that such resistance requires. In fact:

> those who have been particularly badly traumatized can find it extremely difficult to access the agency of the signifier. When the subject is surrounded by signifiers that carry the hegemonic messages of the tyrant, and that do not consequently grant it any opportunity for affirmative self-constitution, the signifier itself can become an enemy of insurmountable proportions.
> (Ruti 2012, 78)

In effect, those subjected to structural forms of racial inequality and discrimination are often simply required to express the symbolic endowment that allows them to resist and reconstruct their racial position. While this speaks to wider linguistic reinterpretations of race, eliciting the power of the signifier to incite social change can prove just as debilitating for those groups where the fundamental structural requirements needed to elicit social and political change, let alone resistance, are neither available nor accessible. Despite the falsity of race, racial fictions still maintain a grammatical and socio-symbolic significance, and, thus, whether affirming or resisting one's racial prescription, one is required to assert its validity. In the end, '[u]sing the language of race to escape from the confines of race only results in so much banging up against its invisible walls' (Hoyt 2016, 8).

Moreover, it is difficult to determine what exactly is being 're-constructed'. While we can assure ourselves that it is the harmful effects of a discourse predicated on racial disparities that lies at the crux of any endeavour seeking to reconstruct our relations to and perceptions of race, in the end, it is the actual significance of 'race' that remains ignored. What we are left with is a multiplicity of 'racial constructions'—all of which assume and uphold the legitimacy of 'race' in conjunction with the racial differences it requires.[1]

To this extent, we can consider how attempts to re-signify race locate one's racial identity as a 'choice' that one can easily make. Despite Rich's contention that '[w]e should not have to be slaves to the biological definition of identity, and we should not use race or gender identities as weapons to punish one another' (2015), the fact that one's identity can be 'weaponized', serves only to relay the suggestion that identity is something that can, and, thus, should be, 'capitalized' upon. Furthermore, while any advocation of the social construction of race would stand apart from the assertion that race bears a biological legitimacy founded upon genetic differentiation, such claims are nonetheless embroiled in a fetishization of race, most notable in references to skin colour and other prescribed markers of racial differentiation and demographic interpretation.

This correlation can be found in the extent to which one's genetic make-up assumes a racial inheritance that casually overlooks the incompatibility between genes and social categories (Seshadri-Crooks 2000). Here, the very act of differentiating groups on assumed, internal differences is apparent in the extent to which we categorize and sort national populations. There remains a long history of linking racial affiliation to one's national identity, whereupon biology and ethnic heritage become embroiled in certain (re)interpretations of the nation-state's history and its civic inclusivity. Determining one's ancestry is, in most instances, a subtle determination of how far back one's location in a specific nation-state can be traced. In such instances, one's familial lineage can serve to mark one as a 'racial' minority set against the assumed characteristics of a national majority. While assumptions are drawn between one's national heritage and the essence of one's genes, such 'genetic' characteristics are very easily insnared in debates on national purity. This can be seen in the legal principles that upheld the adoption of the 'one-drop rule' in U.S. racial classifications during the 1900s, and, in contemporary, secular, colourblind societies, such as France, where determining one's national heritage can function as a smokescreen for latent debates on, and arguments for, the racialization of national identity along the lines of genealogy (Knox 2016). Accordingly, whether subscribing or denouncing a biological conception of race, what matters is whether it is the *concept* of race that is being rejected or not (Hoyt 2016).

Naturalising a construct

By drawing on the above claims, there is no intention of ignoring the importance of establishing race as a social construction, especially when it reveals 'how racism is linked to processes of social, political and economic domination and marginalisation' (Hook 2004, 673). What is apparent, however, is that '[t]he right-minded teaching that "race has nothing to do with biology, but is merely a social construction," is true but misleading' (Fields and Fields 2012, 193). As the Fields assert, what is required is a consideration of 'social construction itself, as thought and as action' (Fields and Fields 2014, 193).

It is 'as thought and as action' that race becomes fixed to one's (racial) identity. Here, the fluidity of identity is grounded in a subjective sense of self-awareness, marked just as much by one's understanding of the immorality of racism, and the inadequacy of race, as it is in the racial determinants that have historically and culturally defined one's race. There are important conclusions to be drawn from such assertions, including the proposals for a liberally-progressive, multi-racial future, or conservative-led projects which seek to decentre the centrality of race in favour of the rational individual, determined by their very own means. In both cases, we see a '[c]hampioning [of] one's particularity', a position which 'always leaves one where one is, and where one is is necessarily the contingent result of one's social situation' (McGowan 2019, 187).

Unfortunately, such contingency underscores the concern that one can present a positive racial identification; a form of liberation that seeks to discursively promote greater forms of racial recognition, thus subverting and/or resisting the racial inequalities that frame and position the human population. These criticisms are required and laudable, but, as George asserts, '[t]he problem with contemporary theoretical and political approaches to the aggression and racism that still plague race relations today is that their frequent reliance upon the concept of race precludes engagement with this fundamental aggressivity produced by the concept itself' (2014, 370). This aggressivity can be seen in an unending pursuit—an 'obsessive pursuit of the Real' (George 2014, 369)—that both fuels and maintains a process of deconstruction and re-signification that shows no sign of stopping.[2] In effect, what such a pursuit encourages is the continuation of race as a concept that instils racial difference.

More importantly, such aggression points to the very contradiction that race requires. As Jackson argues, with regard to anti-racism literature, 'there cannot be an anti-racist canon that does not crystallize the very sense of things it proposes to undermine' (2020). What is more, such a perpetuation of *that* which is sought to be undermined is played out in the determination of one's social being by and through the very racial categories that one seeks to upend. In other words, in order to reinterpret one's racial subjectivization, one is required, in the first instance, to subject oneself to a racial classification that also determines and restrict one's action (Copjec 1994).³ Thus, in any anti-racist project one is, for better or worse, racially named and determined, so that 'the more one attempts to render race as merely a social construct, the more it contributes towards the naturalization of that construct' (Seshadri-Crooks 2000, 17).

This is evidenced in Thakur's critique of postcolonialism, whereupon 'postcolonial strategies of identity construction rely on the mechanism of Othering already established by colonial Europe' (2020, 179). In so doing, 'post-/anti-/de-colonial demands for rehabilitation or recognition of particular identities structurally mimic or resurrect the mechanisms of Othering' inherent to colonialism (Thakur 2020, 180). What such demands require is the act of racism itself, a racism which, although critiqued, is reinterpreted and repeated in new forms of hostility and aggression. In effect, what we encounter is a proliferation of racisms, a repetition and multiplication of its very trauma that in no way targets or dislodges the malevolence that is maintained *in* and *through* the act of racism.

Therefore, what the social construction of race results in, indeed, what is left at the crux of its endeavour, is a subject torn between the lack of agency prescribed by one's socially-constructed position and an endowed capacity to identify and upend the very social constructions that restrict one's agency through some 'essential' realization. If socially constructed, then the very construction of race can just as easily reassert and further entrench the subject's desubjectivization, with the subject conceived as nothing more than the product of their social circumstances.

Certainly, the argument here is not against promoting forms of anti-racist resistance—any form of resistance requires, at the most basic level, the understanding that new forms of belonging and ways of living must be 'socially' reconstructed. Yet, to assume that this path is so readily available within a structure that views prescribed deficiencies as the constructed consequence of one's objective circumstances or social conditions is to look too quickly to a Symbolic order that simply requires re-arrangement and renewal. At worse, it lends credit to the racist to carry on *constructing* their racism. In either case, there is the 'failure to acknowledge and account for influences upon race and the racial subject that lie outside of the structure imposed by discourse' (George 2016, 14).

Cause and negativity

This points to the importance of undertaking a psychoanalytic perspective, for what '[p]sychoanalysis … gives precedence to [is] that which throws into question the self-confirming nature of its own axioms: the real, the impossible, that which does not work' (Fink 1997, 140). To grasp this significance, we can turn to Lacan's understanding of 'cause' and, specifically, how it differs to common uses. For example, in the scientific method, 'events […] are] understood as leading smoothly, in accordance with well-known "laws," to other events' (Fink 1997, 31). In contrast, 'Lacan understands cause in a more radical sense, as that which disrupts the smooth functioning of lawlike interactions', or, the link *between* cause and effect (Fink 1995, 64). Fink notes:

> [c]ausality in science is absorbed into what we might call structure—cause leading to effect within an ever more exhaustive set of laws. A cause as something that seems not to obey laws, remaining inexplicable from the standpoint of scientific knowledge, has become unthinkable, our general tendency being to assume that it will just be a matter of time before science can explain it.
> (1995, 64)

Denoting that which does not follow the laws of cause and effect, the Lacanian Cause can be conceived 'as that which is found only in what does not work' (Copjec and Chubbs 2020, 200). That is, by indicating 'the unassimilable points of failure and trauma, around which signifiers weave a protective net' (Friedlander 2022, 112), Lacan sought to draw attention away from the passivity of a cause, awaiting scientific explanation, towards its negativity, thus conceived 'as a break or interruption' (Copjec and Chubbs 2020, 200). Importantly, Lacan 'doesn't ask what causes the break[, ...] so much as he defines the break as an eruption of a negativity, a gap, from which eruption a new fantasy must be woven to sustain living' (Copjec and Chubbs 2020, 200).

When applied to race we can begin to consider how Lacan's focus on the negativity of the Cause can help to undermine social constructionist accounts. In particular, Friedlander (2022) draws upon the work of George (2016) to emphasize how '[r]ather than envision[ing] the field of signifiers as random and open to manipulation (and resignification), the [Lacanian] notion of "Cause" reminds us that the Symbolic is organized through the incessant haunting of negativity' (Friedlander 2022, 112). Consequently, what is ignored in the social construction of race is this very negativity: a negativity that both upholds as well as undermines the smooth functioning of the Symbolic order.

Furthermore, what this notion of 'Cause' posits is that there is no 'complete' Symbolic order or symbolic structure that could adequately circumscribe our social conditions. Representation is not a complete process and identity does not function as an already-constituted 'tool' that can be used to redefine and resist one's subjectification: if this was true, then it would have to be assumed that one's identity was already freely available, 'ready-made', and determined. Equally, could any identity ever be 'new'? Here, the capacity to construct, create, and establish one's identity would inevitably be drawn from a repertoire of existing identities. In either case, there remains the *a priori* assumption that there is an inherent, 'essential' basis to the subject—the very ground from which any social construction is based upon (Black 2020).

Though the very act of construction may denote a level of hysteria that forces us to continually define and redefine our symbolic coordinates, our social positions, and our social relations, what belies such hysteria is the failure to accept and/or acknowledge the negativity, or the lack, that constitutes any symbolic system and the structure of language itself. This in no way ignores the importance of the signifier, of the act of social construction, and of the symbolic systems that are erected and thus work to maintain certain groups in positions of power. Rather, what a Lacanian psychoanalysis points towards is the incompleteness, inconsistency, and undecidability—i.e., the inherent lack—that constitutes both the subject and the Symbolic order. To account for this lack in understandings of race is to ascertain that defining and promoting one's agency and responsibility relies upon acknowledging the relative impotency that is shared in our relation to the signifier, the Symbolic order, and the Other.

Accordingly, while we remain 'doomed', within the process of signification, 'to suture what is ultimately unsuturable' (Daly 1999, 76), this is not to give-up on the act of social resistance itself or to betray the importance of anti-racism struggles—now, more than ever, this is an importance that can only ever be socially and collectively achieved. Instead, it is to fully appreciate that our '[social] relations are always both fluctuating and creating flux, stabilized and stabilizing' and 'what is most important about them, what makes them susceptible to analysis, is that they are mediated' (Rothenberg 2010, 17). For race, this requires a consideration of the very ways in which it is mediated through forms of articulation that construct our relation to race as both fixed and inherited. As Seshadri-Crooks notes, while examples of 'kinship', 'ethnicity', and 'culture' all conspire to endow the subject with a racial inheritance, which determines the subject a racial particularity, 'the emotional force of an *ethnos* that race so effectively and resiliency enables' allows race to 'deriv[e] its power not from socially constructed ideologies, but from the dynamic interplay between the family as a socially regulated institution, and biology as the site of essences and inheritances' (2000, 17, italics in original). It is in this confluence that 'race attaches to individual bodies and psyches (the imaginary), while simultaneously operating through a trans-social logic (the symbolic)' (Winnubst 2004, 43, fn.2). What is clear, however, is that this relation is not one in which 'race is historically and socially constructed *and* ... individually embodied' (Winnubst 2004, 43, fn.2, italics added), but, rather, is founded upon the *negativity* that exists between our historical/social constructions and individual embodiment.

Notes

1 Such multiplicity compels a 'hyper-visibility [that now] supplies the signature of a corporate multiculturalism in which some degree of visible difference from an implicit white norm may be highly prized as a sign of timeliness, vitality, inclusivity, and global reach' (Gilroy 2000, 21).

2 My divergence from George can be signalled at this point. To help clarify, George elaborates upon such aggression in the following: '[i]t is this obsessive pursuit of the Real, thus encouraged by race, that can lead to the violence and frustration of racism. This frustration arises because whiteness can never reconstitute being. In truth, whiteness functions only as the *object a* that merely *promises* wholeness by simultaneously masquerading as the phallus, the castrated object that manifests the illusory site of bliss in the Imaginary form of the subjective-self' (2014, 369, italics in original). My reflections on the significance of the object *a* and its ties to Whiteness are considered further in Chapter 5. This discussion centres upon the location of the object a and the phallus in psychosis.
3 This is considered further by Copjec (1994), where she differentiates psychoanalytic anti-racism and the impact of democracy to the work of Foucault.

References

Black, Jack. 2020. "On reflexive racism: disavowal, deferment and the Lacanian subject." *Diacritics* 48, no. 4: 76–101.
Copjec, Joan. 1994. *Read My Desire: Lacan Against the Historicists*. Cambridge, MA: The MIT Press.
Copjec, Joan, and Colby Chubbs. 2020. "Psychoanalysis and consequences." *Chiasma* 6, no. 1: 189–203.
Daly, Glyn. 1999. "Politics and the impossible: beyond psychoanalysis and deconstruction." *Theory, Culture & Society* 16, no. 4: 75–98.
Fanon, Frantz. 2008. *Black Skin, White Masks*. New York, NY: Grove Press.
Fields, Karen E. and Barabara J. Fields. 2012. *Racecraft: The Soul of Inequality in American Life*. London, UK: Verso.
Fink, Bruce. 1995. "Science and psychoanalysis." In *Reading Seminar XI: Lacan's Four Fundamental Concepts of Psychoanalysis*, edited by Richard Feldstein, Bruce Fink, and Maire Jaanus (55–64). Albany, NY: State University of New York Press.
Fink, Bruce. 1997. *The Lacanian Subject: Between Language and Jouissance*. Princeton, NJ: Princeton University Press.
Friedlander, Jennifer. 2022. "In medium race: traversing the fantasy of post-race discourse." In *Lacan and Race: Racism, Identity, and Psychoanalytic Theory*, edited by Sheldon George and Derek Hook (105–120). Abingdon, UK: Routledge.
George, Sheldon. 2014. "From alienation to cynicism: race and the Lacanian unconscious." *Psychoanalysis, Culture & Society* 19, no. 4: 360–378.
George, Sheldon. 2016. *Trauma and Race: A Lacanian Study of African American Racial Identity*. Waco, TX: Baylor University Press.
Gilroy, Paul. 2000. *Against Race: Imagining Political Culture Beyond the Color Line*. Cambridge, MA: The Belknap Press of Harvard University Press.
Hook, Derek. 2004. "Racism as abjection: a psychoanalytic conceptualisation for a post-apartheid South Africa." *South African Journal of Psychology* 34, no. 4: 672–703.
Hook, Derek. 2012. *A Critical Psychology of the Postcolonial: The Mind of Apartheid*. London, UK: Routledge.
Hoyt, Carlos A. 2016. *The Arc of a Bad Idea: Understanding and Transcending Race*. Oxford, UK: Oxford University Press.
Jackson, Lauren Michele. 2020. "What is an anti-racist reading list for?" *Vulture*, June 4. https://www.vulture.com/2020/06/anti-racist-reading-lists-what-are-they-for.html

Knox, Katelyn E. 2016. *Race on Display in 20th- and 21st-Century France*. Liverpool, UK: Liverpool University Press.

McGowan, Todd. 2019. *Emancipation After Hegel: Achieving a Contradictory Revolution*. New York, NY: Columbia University Press.

McGowan, Todd. 2022. "The bedlam of the lynch mob: racism and enjoying through the other." In *Lacan and Race Racism, Identity, and Psychoanalytic Theory*, edited by Sheldon George and Derek Hook (19–34). Abingdon, UK: Routledge.

Rich, Camille Gear. 2015. "Rachel Dolezal has a right to be black." *CNN* June 16. https://edition.cnn.com/2015/06/15/opinions/rich-rachel-dolezal/index.html

Rothenberg, Molly Anne. 2010. *The Excessive Subject: A New Theory of Social Change*. Cambridge, UK: Polity.

Ruti, Mari. 2012. *The Singularity of Being: Lacan and the Immortal Within*. New York, NY: Fordham University Press.

Seshadri-Crooks, Kalpana. 2000. *Desiring Whiteness: A Lacanian Analysis of Race*. London, UK: Routledge.

Thakur, Gautam Basu. 2020. *Postcolonial Lack: Identity, Culture, Surplus*. Albany, NY: State University of New York Press.

Winnubst, Shannon. 2004. "Is the mirror racist? Interrogating the space of whiteness." *Philosophy & Social Criticism* 30, no. 1: 25–50.

Chapter 2

The non-sense of race

In commenting upon the analysis of race, Seshadri-Crooks makes clear the following concern:

> [e]xploring the structure of race requires a toleration of paradox, an appreciation of the fact that it is an inherently contradictory discourse, and a willingness to see beyond relations of power in order to mine the depth of subjective investment in it.
>
> (2000, 9).

The effect of these paradoxes and contradictions can be considered in the very way that race sits *outside* of discourse. This is not to suggest that race holds no symbolic or discursive value, but that what it achieves is a semblance of support that obscures and occludes the subject's relation to being. As a result, what our 'subjective investment' in race provides is a level of stability that underpins the subject's racialization.

According to Lacan, 'all being is discursive', but, as Zupančič highlights, 'the discursive is not-all' (2017, 129). The fact that discourse is not-all—or, rather, 'not whole'—helps draw attention to the fundamental negativity that comprises the Symbolic order as well as that which serves as the genesis of the Lacanian 'Cause'. This suggests that all Symbolic mediation is a mediation of the Real: that traumatic, impossible element which disrupts but also constitutes the Symbolic order. It is the Real's 'extimate' presence (an internal exclusion), which exposes the very limits of discourse, revealing that in order for something to be defined in discourse there must remain an Other for it to be defined against (Miller 2017). If race is to be found in discourse, then it is at the limits of discourse that the effects of race can be conceived.

The peace of the evening

But how can this limit be conceived, let alone exposed? For Lacan, all Symbolic expression is marked by a limit, or, by what he refers to as the signifier in the Real. This can be identified in a unique example that Lacan describes in Seminar III:

> [y]ou are at the close of a stormy and tiring day, you regard the darkness that is beginning to fall upon your surroundings, and something comes to mind, embodied in the expression, *the peace of the evening*. I don't think anyone who has a normal affective life is unaware that this is something that exists and has a completely different value from the phenomenal apprehension of the close of the clamor of the day, of an attenuation of contours and passions. There is in *the peace of the evening* both a presence and a choice from everything that surrounds you. ... What does this being, or not, of language, this *the peace of the evening*, mean? To the extent that we're not expecting it, or wishing for it, or haven't even thought about it for a long time, it's essentially as a signifier that it presents itself to us. No experimentalist construction can justify its existence, there is a datum here, a certain way to take this time of the evening as a signifier, and we can be open to it or closed to it. And it's precisely insofar as we have been closed to it that we receive it through this peculiar echo phenomenon, or at least the start of it, which consists in the appearance, at the limit of the phenomenon's grip on us, of what will most commonly be expressed for us by these words, *the peace of the evening*.
>
> (1997, 138 and 139, italics in original)

The experience—or, rather, the astonishment—that Lacan describes suggests a level of utter confoundment that bears no sense or justification. The effect of 'the peace of the evening' is that it does not reveal, nor does it suggest, any meaning, yet it presents itself as a signifier. The experience that Lacan describes is clearly marked by a limit that impedes any comprehension, beyond its very occurrence, so that:

> [w]e have now come to the limit at which discourse, if it opens onto anything beyond meaning, opens into the signifier in the real. We shall never know, in the perfect ambiguity in which it dwells, what it owes to this marriage with discourse.
>
> (Lacan 1997, 139)

There is a 'perfect ambiguity' that finds itself in that which defies meaning. What opens into the 'signifier in the real' is what the peace of the evening evokes: an opening that bears no sense or explanation, but which nonetheless occurs, and, when it does occur, provides a presence that proves undeniable (a sense of meaning in and of itself).[1]

What encompasses the peace of the evening is that its sudden presence is internally established and inherently produced within the Symbolic order. In evoking what remains extimate, it reveals that the Symbolic is neither fixed nor determined, but rather posed by the Real. The Real, in all its various contradictory manifestations, remains:

> *nothing but* this impossibility of its inscription: the Real is not a transcendent positive entity, persisting somewhere beyond the symbolic order like a hard kernel inaccessible to it, some kind of Kantian 'Thing-in-itself'—in itself it is nothing at all, just a void, an emptiness in a symbolic structure marking some central impossibility.
>
> (Žižek 2008, 195, italics in original)

It is this 'nothing at all' which marks the Real's impossible materiality, posing as the limit of the Symbolic order in which it is inscribed. Moreover, it is the very 'emptiness' evoked in the signifier in the Real that suddenly and unexplainably materialises *in* the Symbolic order. In experiencing the peace of the evening, a fundamental distinction is educed, which, when it undoubtedly occurs, leaves one in the impossible position of determining whether the experience *reveals* the limits of the Symbolic order or whether it remains an unexplainable *effect* of the Symbolic order, a mark of its own inconsistency. What this ultimately draws attention to is the difficulty of meaning when faced with the enigmatic status of the Real.

We can begin to conceive of this ambiguity in relation to the paradoxes and contradictions that race upholds (Seshadri-Crooks 2000). Following the above, is race something that is simply experienced, thus bearing no existence *within* the confines of the Symbolic order? Or, is its very expression an *effect* of the Symbolic order's limitations? What we can assert, for now, is that race relies upon a certain disruption that is extimately located as part of the very limit that underwrites our turn to (and our reliance on) discourse.

In fact, for Lacan, the visual and physical differences that determine one's race means that 'races are, in effect, effects of discourse' (Khan 2018, 149). As both Millar (2017) and Khan (2018) make clear, as 'effects of discourse' Lacan links race to the 'subjective position' that his conception of discourse permits, one that is determined by the subject's relation to the signifier (Miller 2017, 80, cited in Khan 2018, 157). We can, however, go further here and ask: what 'effect' does this subjective position have when faced with the limits of the signifier, as that which is both of and beyond the Symbolic order? By way of approaching this question, we can link Lacan's account of racism 'to the problematic of segregation, which is intensified as a consequence of the decline of the Name-of-the-Father in an age when the discourses of science and capitalism are bringing about fundamental shifts' (Khan 2018, 149). Here, race functions much like the causality that science affords.

Indeed, as noted by Fink (1997), and as discussed in the previous chapter, it is scientific knowledge that mutes any Cause in a series of law-like effects that work to establish and maintain structures of knowledge, wherein any disruption and/or irregularity can be, or will be, accounted for.[2] Insofar as 'science rearranges social groupings at the same time as it introduces a universalizing principle that, in turn, accentuates processes of segregation' (Khan 2018, 150), we end-up confronting the very limit that it evokes—the fact that any arrangement serves to establish and include what at the same time it excludes. It is here that race bears a similar logic: organizing human differences and delineating racial groups based upon prescribed categories of (racial) meaning that fundamentally rely on the exclusions they enact. Such forms of racial classification are 'constructed', and this is widely acknowledged, but the 'support' that such classifications assert emanates from the effect that race generates as well as the apparent knowledge it establishes. The evidence for this knowledge is clearly visible: in plain sight of one's racial visibility the disruptions of the (Lacanian) Cause can be displaced; a semblance of support can be found.

The basis of this support can thus be seen in the very naturalization that race achieves. While this in no way ignores the effects of racism, as evident by the fact that examples of racial discrimination become tied to the body's arbitrary features, it is in being perceived as 'natural' that there remains 'no possibility of interrogating the structure and constitution of the subject of race' (Seshadri-Crooks 2000, 31). Any critique of race is subsequently foreclosed and left unanswered. Here, the support that race upholds is equivalent to post-structuralist accounts that seek to endow the construction of race with a sense of agency that in no way challenges the racial foundations that underpin the Symbolic order (George 2016). In such instances, race remains nothing more than an epistemological limit, tasked with filling in the gap of the Real (Thakur 2020). There remains no acknowledgement of the 'limit' as ontologically dependent on the subject assuming its inherent lack; or, as Thakur explains, 'lack … as the irrevocable condition of being—I, the subject, *am* lack' (2020, 189, italics in original).

Race, the signifier, and non-meaning

To achieve such an acknowledgement, requires, in part, a re-conception of race not as a constructed phenomenon, but as a 'resilient non-sense' (Seshadri-Crooks 2000, 2). While race remains 'distinctive as a belief structure and evokes powerful and very particular investments in its subjects' (Seshadri-Crooks 2000, 4), it is the condition of these investments which proves important. In considering this importance, it is helpful to remember that in any psychoanalytic interpretation, it is the 'kernel … of *non-sense*' that underpins the subject's self-division—the split subject (Lacan 2004, 250, italics in original).[3] It is the task of psychoanalysis to 'isolate' the very non-sense that irreducibly posits the subject. All interpretation is thus directed 'towards an original non-sense' (Benvenuto 2020, 113); indeed, 'the precise point at which sense is produced in non-sense' (Lacan 2005, 120).[4]

Drawing from Ferdinand de Saussure and Roman Jakobson, Lacan's approach to non-sense followed a number of important corrections which he sought to make, both to the work of Freud, but also within philosophy. Specifically, 'Lacan hoped to correct, not only Freud who failed to problematize language, but also philosophers like Immanuel Kant who reduced nonsense to the simple absence of meaning and Martin Heidegger who dismissed the value of "small talk" (*Gerede/Unsinn*)' (Ragland 1995, 74). These corrections would underpin Lacan's (1997) work on psychosis, where, in his analysis of the delusional Judge Schreber, he outlined 'a positive value to nonsense' (Ragland 1995, 74).[5]

In fact, for Lacan, the task of psychoanalysis is to interpret what remains at the level of non-sense for the subject, an assertion predicated on the fact that 'one's basic identifications have no meaning at all, they simply *are*' (Laurent 1995, 31, italics in original). Certainly, '[o]ne can explore the meanings they have, but one must not neglect the fact that, in the end, they make no sense' (Laurent 1995, 31). In locating this non-sense, Lacan followed the task of isolating the master-signifier (S_1): that which affords the subject its subjectivization due to its link with other signifiers (S_2) (Fink 1997). Here, '[e]ach isolated S_1, is, when it appears, nonsensical' (Fink 1997, 78). The isolated S_1 'may very well be a word or name the analysand has used every day of his or her life' (Fink 1997, 78), but, in its isolation, it carries no immediate sense. Equally, '[n]onsense may ... [also] appear in an incomprehensible slurring of words to which no meaning whatever can be attributed, as the resulting sounds suggest nothing in the way of a play on words' (Fink 1997, 78). In either case, for Lacan, '[i]nterpretation is directed not so much at the meaning as towards reducing the non-meaning of the signifiers, so that we may discover the determinants of the subject's entire behaviour' (2004, 212). This involves taking non-sense, and its subsequent disruption, and framing it within a Symbolic framework that 'isolates' the very kernel of non-sense. Importantly, this is not a preconceived framework, complete with meaning, but one in which the very form of the signifier—and its significance for the subject—has been grasped; where the signifier in the Real has been encountered.[6]

On this basis, it is possible to deduce 'the nonsensical nature of the signifier' as evident by the fact that 'the signifier's very existence exceeds its significatory role, that its substance exceeds its symbolic function' (Fink 1997, 119). What is key, however, is that '[t]his excess is the product of sense, not its external limit or subversion. ... Even as the excess resists signification, it does so within a world of signification—or else we would not even be able to register it' (McGowan 2007, 27). Furthermore, if, '[t]he signifier is what founds the subject; the signifier is what wields ontic clout, wresting existence from the real that it marks and annuls', then, it is clear that what the signifier 'forges is ... in no sense substantial or material', instead, the subject is always marked by a non-sense, by the 'nonsensical substance' that is the signifier (Fink 1997, 52–53). Thus, it is in the nonsense of the signifier that the subject's kernel of non-sense can be found.

What this points towards is how 'sense is not the experience of a determinate sense, but the absence of sense, more precisely: the frustrating experience of being sure that something has a sense, but not knowing what it is' (Žižek 2010, 378).[7] Žižek's remarks closely echo Lacan's (1997) reference to the 'peace of the evening', wherein '*[t]his vague presence of a non-specific sense is sense "as such," sense at its purest*' (Žižek 2010, 378, italics in original). What this alludes to is the generative absence that underscores all Symbolic communication—the very lack which nonetheless perpetuates the act of communication. The paradox here is that the meaning of any communication 'is a non-sense strictly internal to the field of meaning', that which 'delimits it *from within*' (Žižek 1999, 29 italics in original).[8]

Race and the delimitation of racial difference relies on such non-sense. Race exists as a signifier that bears no meaning—no material substance—beyond the act of racialization. As a signifier, drawn from a Symbolic order of racial signifiers, race provides an 'irreducible, traumatic, non-meaning' from which '[the subject] is, as a subject, subjected' (Lacan 2004, 251).[9] It is in this way that we can conceive how race functions to fill the gap in causality (Žižek 2004). Žižek politicizes such a gap via conceptualizing a '*positive* notion of lack, a "generative" absence' (2004, 32, italics in original) that avers the 'irreducible crack in the edifice of Being' (2004, 37). In effect, the causality that race relies upon, indeed, 'the point of non-sense sustaining the flow of sense' (Žižek 2004, 25), is essentially a depoliticization of this very gap; one in which the lack that constitutes both the subject and the Symbolic order remains obscured. Consequently, while race functions on the forms of labelling it prescribes, as well as the classifying and designating of racial groups, it nonetheless insists at the level of the signifier's non-sense: 'racial signifiers do not mean anything in the strong sense of having "no sense"' (Seshadri-Crooks 2000, 155).

Whereas the above discussion has sought to question the limits of discourse and the effects of race within this discourse, we can now concede an answer: race insists as the very non-sense that bears no truth nor meaning. While race clearly and irrevocably 'exists', its existence remains predicated on the functionality of the non-sense it conveys. Here, it is in relation to the meaningless of the signifier that race works from the inconsistencies of the Symbolic order, providing a support in non-sense that posits and upholds the subject's racialization. It is this support that undercuts the very 'knowledge' that the social construction of race seeks to profess. By asserting that race is socially constructed, one's knowledge of race—its constructed nature—is thus known, understood, and brought into existence. It is in the construction of race that race's permanence is discursively maintained.

Separated from the inherent non-sense of the signifier, race is endowed with a fullness—a comprehensive racial meaning—that finds itself expressed in a range of racial interpretations, stereotypes, and discriminations. Indeed, what this obscures is the non-sense that race relies upon. By seeking a complete delineation of racial difference, race diverts attention away from its very meaninglessness. The task, therefore, is not to make race meaningful—to re-signify it so that it affords some better meaning—but to acknowledge and interpret the meaninglessness it conveys.

Race and the master-signifier

In *Desiring Whiteness: A Lacanian Analysis of Race* (2000), Seshadri-Crooks effectively details the unconscious attachments that underscore our relations to race as both structured and organized by the master-signifier, 'Whiteness'. For this, she locates our investment in racialization as correlated to 'the unconscious signifier Whiteness, which founds the logic of racial difference, [and] promises wholeness' (Seshadri-Crooks 2000, 21).[10] In fact, what remains implicit to this study is the structure of relations that the master-signifier establishes: 'a signifying chain that through a process of inclusions and exclusions constitutes a pattern for organizing human difference' (Seshadri-Crooks 2000, 3). Acting as 'an ideal rather than an empirical biological attribute', Whiteness functions as a master-signifier that 'organizes human difference in terms of an opposition between white and people of color', and, thus, 'discloses a discriminatory logic at its kernel' (Seshadri 2022, 301). This affects all racialized subjects by pre-determining each subject to a racial categorization that shapes and frames the subject's assumed racial difference via a regime of racial visibility.

George extends this line of inquiry by examining how, in accordance with the master-signifier, 'race grounds the fantasies that promise the subject access to being' (2016, 22). Here, 'the master signifier of whiteness seeks to recover this being for the white subject but more often denies it to blacks' (George 2016, 136). It is Whiteness that relies on such fantasies, proposing a level of transcendence that goes beyond the visibility of race (its phenotype distinctions) towards an access to being where the subject's constitutive lack is elided. Accordingly, while 'Whiteness attempts to signify being, or that aspect of the subject which escapes language' (Seshadri-Crooks 2000, 21), we can also conceive how such attempts either deny a relation to being, on behalf of Blacks, or indoctrinates Black struggle to the resignification of the master-signifier's values, thus compounding Black fantasies of being (indeed, both appear in George's [2016] account). In either case, it is 'the pre-existence of "black" and "white" as if these were natural and neutrally descriptive terms' that works to maintain the master-signifier's significance (Seshadri-Crooks 2000, 36). What this significance ignores is that in order 'to trouble the relation of the subject to the master signifier … One must throw into doubt the security and belief in one's identity, not promote more fulsome claims to such identity' (Seshadri-Crooks 2000, 36).

Indeed, if one is to trouble this relation, as well as doubt the belief that one's racial identity prescribes, then it is in the *containment* of the master-signifier—as present within a logic of embodiment that essentially marks and delineates the human body as racially defined—that such 'fulsome claims' regarding one's race are implied. What any racial marking or delineation prescribes is a level of containment, a form of particularity, that racially fixes, determines, and essentializes one's prescribed racial identity, whether White, Black, Brown, Red, or Yellow. It is on this basis that the master-signifier bestows a sense of 'wholeness' upon the racialized subject—prescribing them *their* race. In so doing, race functions as the very object which constitutes one's (racial) being. Consequently, while the significance of the master-signifier resides in it being unconsciously tied to Whiteness, its effects can be found in the extent to which it works to maintain as well as structure racial difference. It is thus the master-signifier 'Whiteness' which 'remains outside the play of signification even as it enables the system' (Seshadri-Crooks 2000, 20), bestowing it a *transcendental significance*, especially in the domain of orchestrating and structuring racial difference.

This universal significance is played out via the process of signification, which the master-signifier endeavours to sustain; ultimately, '[w]e cannot do without it and remain within the signifying field' (McGowan 2018, 200). Yet, as McGowan highlights, 'the master signifier is not a meaningful signifier' (2018, 200), adding:

> [w]e cannot invest our hopes in it as the site of emancipation, but neither should we fear that it will contaminate all universality. While the master signifier grounds the signifying field, it does not have any significance within that field. *To imbue this signifier with significance by treating it as a universal apes the conservative error, which reveres the master signifier as the source of substantial identity.* In both cases, the error lies in seeing significance in an empty structural necessity.
>
> (2018, 200, italics added)[11]

In this respect, it is not the 'promise' that the master-signifier holds which underwrites the system of racial difference, but the act of endowing the master-signifier a certain mastery ('Whiteness') which leads to the acceptance of racial identity and racial difference (George 2014; 2016; Seshadri-Crooks 2000). It is in this way that racial differences are perceived—and, by extension, the master-signifier is perceived—as natural and taken-for-granted, with the delineation of racial variances viewed as *a priori* markers of human difference. This reveals that any act of critique, which is directed at the master-signifier, finds itself imbricated in the continuation of the master-signifier—as *that* which becomes the target of such critique.

This is not to ignore the fact that for both Seshadri-Crooks and George the significance of the master-signifier can be undermined via a traversal of the fantasy (Seshadri-Crooks 2000), or through establishing a level of cynical distance towards the racial Symbolic order (George 2016). In both instances, an acknowledgement of the subject's inherent lack is procured. Nevertheless, what the Whiteness as master-signifier overlooks is the potential to consider how the delineation of racial differences occurs not from the authority of the master-signifier (its ability to proffer a promise), *but from its very lack of authority*. As will be discussed in Chapter 7, the path taken in this study will be to argue that our investment in race is upheld via an act of foreclosure, and, specifically, from the foreclosure of the master-signifier in psychosis. This foreclosure corresponds with what has been referred to as the demise of Symbolic efficiency (Žižek 2000), and the subsequent lack of authority that is attributed to the master-signifier.

Notably, what the act of foreclosure establishes is a paranoid proclivity that is brought to light in examples of racial paranoia. Here, paranoia 'stems from its ability to close the gap in the social field of meaning, its ability to be a guarantor that authorizes our social interaction … develop[ing] in response to the inherent inconsistency of social authority' (McGowan 2013, 45). Though it is '[t]he subject [who] occupies the position of the gap in social authority' (McGowan 2013, 48), it is through the foreclosure of the master-signifier that the inherent inconsistencies of the Symbolic order are obscured and the subject's inherent lack— 'the gap in social authority'—is 'filled' with their prescribed racial classification. It is on this basis that the subject's very lack is elided, with our subsequent investment in race predicated on the racial demarcations it consistently provides.

Consequently, what the foreclosure of the master-signifier enacts is an obfuscation of its inherent emptiness. It is because there is no signifier that can fully comprise the subject that our subjectivity can emerge and develop. There is, therefore a 'missing signifier'—'a signifier of lack that is itself necessarily lacking'—which is fundamentally obscured in examples of race (McGowan 2020, 231). The effects of this obfuscation will be returned to and elaborated upon in Chapter 5; for now, we can begin to determine how our investment in race stems from the 'emptiness' it omits. This locates the significance of race not simply in the Symbolic order that racially delineates and defines one's racial classification, but at the point of the subject's Symbolic castration. In effect, it is by foreclosing the opportunity to conceive of race as lacking—as non-sense—that examples of racial difference are both registered and upheld.[12]

Notes

1 It is appropriate therefore that this example appears in Lacan's (1997) seminar on psychosis. As will be discussed further in Chapter 4, Lacan's approach to psychosis is one that critically considers the subject's relation to meaning. Nobus explains, '[w]hen Lacan conjured up the image of "the peace of the evening", he mainly intended to exemplify how psychotic patients experience the antinomy between meaning and being in a radically different way, up to the point where for them meaning becomes being in itself' (2021, 155). Therefore, for Lacan, there is significance in the meaning that psychosis avails. In fact, where we may usually consider a psychotic delusion to be meaningless, what psychosis can help us ascertain

is the effects of the signifier and its relation to meaning for both the psychotic and the non-psychotic subject.
2 Importantly, 'genuine scientific work does not exclude the cause, as that which interrupts the smooth functioning of lawlike activity, but rather attempts to take it into account in some way, as in the case of Heisenberg's uncertainty principle' (Fink 1997, 141).
3 The full quote from Lacan reads, '[t]he fact that I have said that the effect of interpretation is to isolate in the subject a kernel, a *kern*, to use Freud's own term, of *non-sense*, does not mean that interpretation is in itself nonsense' (2004, 250, italics in original). Whether referred to as the 'split subject', the 'divided subject', or the 'barred subject', ultimately, the Lacanian subject is nothing but the split that occurs due to the subject's alienation in language (this is discussed more in Chapter 4) (see Fink 1997, 45).
4 I have interpreted Lacan's (1997; 2006) use of the hyphen in 'non-sense' as denoting the ambiguity in 'sense' itself; that is, its own negativity. In 'The Instance of the Letter in the Unconscious', the line is translated as 'the precise point at which meaning is produced in nonmeaning' (Lacan 2006, 423).
5 See Chapter 4 for further discussion on the Lacan's analysis of Judge Schreber.
6 Similarly, 'the analyst, in the analytic setting, listens for the real (impossibilities) in the analysand's symbolic and attempts to hit that real with interpretation' (Fink 1997, 143).
7 We can compare this experience 'to Hegel's famous formula "the secrets of the ancient Egyptians were also secrets for the Egyptians themselves"' (Žižek 2006, 234). Here, Žižek notes that 'when ... confronted with a mysterious religious ritual from some "primitive" culture, my first experience is that of a mystery which is impossible to penetrate ("If only I possessed enough information to unravel the secret meaning of what I am now observing!"); what, however, if the "meaning" of this ritual is also a mystery for its participants themselves? *What if the primordial form of meaning is such an alienated meaning—"it must mean something, although I do not know what"?* What if this resistant core of frustrating non-sense is what transforms mere meaning (simple denotative reference of a statement or a practice) into a deeper Sense?' (2006 234, italics in original).
8 The argument here runs similar to Ferdinand de Saussure's account of the signifier, wherein the meaning of a signifier stems from its relation to (its difference to) other signifiers in a series. As a result, 'there is no positivity in a signifier, it "is" only a series of what it is *not*' (Žižek 2016, 42, italics in original). Yet, Žižek asks: '[a]t this point, an obvious commonsense reproach arises which should be given all its weight: if all signifiers are just the combination of difference from other signifiers, why then does not the entire network of signifiers collapse into itself? How can such a system retain a minimum of stability? One should introduce here self-reflexivity into the signifying order: if the identity of a signifier is nothing but the series of its constitutive differences, then every signifying series has to be supplemented—"suture"—by a reflexive signifier which has no determinate meaning (signified), since it stands only for the presence of meaning as such (as opposed to its absence); in a further dialectical twist, one should add that the mode of appearance of this supplementary signifier which stands for meaning as such is non-sense (Giles Deleuze developed this point in the *Logic of Sense*)' (2016, 42).
9 Connections can be drawn here with Gilroy who highlights how race 'articulates reason and unreason' (2000, 53) as well as denoting a 'rational irrationality' (2000, 69).
10 In effect, for Seshadri-Crooks, Whiteness is desire insofar as 'Whiteness attempts to signify being, or that aspect of the subject which escapes language' (2000, 21).

11 This is echoed by Thakur, who highlights that 'an intriguing fact about the master signifier [... is that] while it plays an anchoring role in signification, it is free of a signified. Or, the master signifier is always empty; it does not attach to a signified' (2020, 192). Accordingly, while 'the master signifier functions to stitch together (*point de capiton*) free-ranging signifiers into a meaningful whole (a fantasy of wholeness repressing the constitutive antagonism between signifiers), its own incompleteness or disjunction from a signified must remain concealed' (Thakur 2020, 192).
12 Chapter 5 elaborates on the effects of foreclosure with regards to the object a, paranoia, and the lack of a lack (i.e., racial anxiety).

References

Benvenuto, Sergio. 2020. *Conversations with Lacan: Seven Lectures for Understanding Lacan*. London, UK: Routledge.

Fink, Bruce. 1997. *The Lacanian Subject: Between Language and Jouissance*. Princeton, NJ: Princeton University Press.

George, Sheldon. 2014. "From alienation to cynicism: Race and the Lacanian unconscious." *Psychoanalysis, Culture & Society* 19, no. 4: 360–378.

George, Sheldon. 2016. *Trauma and Race: A Lacanian Study of African American Racial Identity*. Waco, TX: Baylor University Press.

Gilroy, Paul. 2000. *Against Race: Imagining Political Culture Beyond the Color Line*. Cambridge, MA: The Belknap Press of Harvard University Press.

Khan, Azeen. 2018. "Lacan and race." In *After Lacan: Literature, Theory, and Psychoanalysis in the Twenty-First Century*, edited by Ankhi Mukherjee (148–166). Cambridge, UK: Cambridge University Press.

Lacan, Jacques. 1997. *The Seminar of Jacques Lacan, Book III, 1955–56: The Psychoses*, edited by Jacques-Alain Miller. London, UK: Routledge.

Lacan, Jacques. 2004. *The Four Fundamental Concepts of Psycho-Analysis*, edited by Jacques-Alain Miller. London, UK: Karnac.

Lacan, Jacques. 2005. *Écrits: A Selection*, translated by Alan Sheridan. London, UK: Routledge.

Lacan, Jacques. 2006. "The instance of the letter in the unconscious, or reason since Freud." In *Écrits. The First Complete Edition in English*, translated by Bruce Fink, in collaboration with Heloise Fink and Russell Grigg (412–444). London, UK: W. W. Norton & Company.

Lacan, Jacques. 2007. *The Seminar of Jacques Lacan, Book XVII: The Other Side of Psychoanalysis*, edited by Jacques-Alain Miller, translated by Russell Grigg. New York, NY: W. W. Norton & Company.

Laurent, Éric. 1995. "Alienation and separation (II)." In *Reading Seminar XI: Lacan's Four Fundamental Concepts of Psychoanalysis*, edited by Richard Feldstein, Bruce Fink, and Maire Jaanus (29–38). Albany, NY: State University of New York Press.

McGowan, Todd. 2007. *The Real Gaze: Film Theory after Lacan*. Albany, NY: State University of New York Press.

McGowan, Todd. 2013. *Enjoying What We Don't Have: The Political Project of Psychoanalysis*. Lincoln, NE: University of Nebraska Press.

McGowan, Todd. 2018. "The absent universal: from the master signifier to the missing signifier." *Problemi International* 2, no. 2: 195–214.

McGowan, Todd. 2020. "The mask of universality: politics in the pandemic response." *Crisis & Critique* 7, no. 3: 228–243.

Miller, Jacques-Alain. 2017. "Extimate enemies." Translated by Frédéric Baitinger, Azeen Khan, and Roger Litten. *The Lacanian Review: Hurly-Burly*, no. 3: 30–42.

Nobus, Dany. 2021. "Book review: when words fail – a review of Wittgenstein and Lacan at the limit: meaning and astonishment, Maria Balaska." *Continental Thought & Theory* 3, no. 1: 154–157.

Ragland, Ellie. 1995. *Essays on the Pleasures of Death: From Freud to Lacan*. New York, NY: Routledge.

Seshadri, Kalpana R. 2022. "Afterword: there is only one race..." In *Lacan and Race: Racism, Identity, and Psychoanalytic Theory*, edited by Sheldon George and Derek Hook (299–304). Abingdon, UK: Routledge.

Seshadri-Crooks, Kalpana. 2000. *Desiring Whiteness: A Lacanian Analysis of Race*. London, UK: Routledge.

Thakur, Gautam Basu. 2020. *Postcolonial Lack: Identity, Culture, Surplus*. Albany, NY: State University of New York Press.

Žižek, Slavoj. 1999. "The undergrowth of enjoyment: how popular culture can serve as an introduction to Lacan." In *The Žižek Reader*, edited by Elizabeth Wright and Edmond Wright (11–36). Malden, MA: Blackwell Publishing.

Žižek, Slavoj. 2000. *The Ticklish Subject: The Absent Centre of Political Ontology*. London, UK: Verso.

Žižek, Slavoj. 2006. *The Parallax View*. Cambridge, MA: The MIT Press.

Žižek, Slavoj. 2008. *The Sublime Object of Ideology*. London, UK: Verso.

Žižek, Slavoj. 2010. *Living in the End Times*. London, UK: Verso.

Žižek, Slavoj. 2016. *Disparities*. London, UK: Bloomsbury.

Žižek, Slavoj. 2022. *Surplus Enjoyment*. London, UK: Bloomsbury.

Zupančič, Alenka. 2017. *What Is Sex?* Cambridge, MA: The MIT Press.

Chapter 3

Racial extimacy

We can now begin to determine how the very perpetuation of race, as well as the act of racial classification, continues to be maintained across a variety of day-to-day uses, despite the widely-recited claim that race is socially constructed and bears no biological importance. Indeed, with race obscuring the subject's inherent lack (George 2016), we can observe how the gap between the enunciated and the position of enunciation is elided (Black 2020). Conveying the distinction between the content of what is said (enunciated) and the position from which this content is made (enunciation), it is the gap between the enunciated and enunciation that underscores the impossibility to ever say it all or to speak literally (often, Žižek refers to this distinction in variations of the phrase: 'you are saying this to me, but what do you mean?'). However, when the distinction between the enunciated and enunciation is foreclosed, we see an investment in the enunciated, without any attention given to the position of enunciation. It is in this way that certain statements can be made, without any acknowledgement or further consideration given to the effects of what is said and to the fact that it is being said. We can, it seems, openly acknowledge the construction of race, while, at the same time, and often in the same breath, 'construct' the very 'racial' distinctions that one would seek to renounce. It is here that the social construction of race does not dislodge or undermine the prevalence of race, but, instead, secures its proficiency.

This goes someway to identifying the paradoxes inherent to race. Indeed, as the above sections have explained, race remains a phenomenon that bears no 'real' significance, but which nonetheless proves particularly pervasive in structuring human relations and the societies they form. Equally, when studying race, one is also on the verge of creating that which the very act of critique seeks to undermine. For this reason, race posits a distortion in how we relate to other subjects as well as how our perspective on reality, and our relationship to reality, is both created and shaped. This requires remaining critical of the social construction of race, without maintaining its very construction. To return to Seshadri-Crooks, it requires:

DOI: 10.4324/9781003414209-5

> confound[ing] racial signification by stressing the continuity, the point of doubt among the so-called races, to the extent that each and every one of us must mistrust the knowledge of our racial belonging. ... Such practices can only be, and must be representational, as what they necessitate is a radical intervention into language and signification.
>
> (2000, 159)

This 'radical intervention' can begin with an acknowledgement of the non-sense of race and how such non-sense poses a mediation of the Real. Typically, it is in encountering the Real that the inconsistency of the Symbolic order—its inherence nonsense—is made apparent for the subject. This can occur, for example, after a traumatic incident that suddenly engenders a collapse in meaning for the subject. This collapse in meaning is analogous to the Lacanian maxim: there is no big Other (and, equally, there is no Other of the Other). In contrast, race serves as the very 'medium' in which confrontations with the Real return in examples of racism; indeed, as signifiers in the Real (Black 2021; Mitchell 2012). More importantly, it is through this return in the Real that examples of Symbolic mediation work to determine and fix the subject *their* race.

Race and the extimacy of the Real

The subject is subjected to a socio-symbolic order that positions and locates them in relation to a variety of symbolic determinants ('man', 'woman', "Black', 'White', etc.). It is in this sense that forms of social oppression, and, more specifically, examples of racialization and racism, reside within the relation between the Symbolic and the Real—that is, in their non-separation. Insofar as the Real of racism returns in social conventions and shared meanings that relay as well as require the signifiers that delimit one's 'racialized' being, the subject is, to a certain extent, 'trapped' by the signifiers that infiltrate and confine the subject to a particular racial prescription. At the same time, it is these very signifiers that are required to elicit the 'resignification' of one's racial prescription as well as the trauma it enacts. Accordingly, while such signifiers psychically and corporally determine the subject, they underscore the relative despondency that the subject experiences in relation to a Symbolic structure of signification that relies upon the Real as much as it seeks the neutralization of its most disruptive effects. Thus, it is in the relation between the Symbolic and the Real that the effects of racism continually 'reappear' in the social construction of race.[1] Here, the invention of race, and its subsequent critique, requires a deferment to the Symbolic restrictions that its very signification provides.

It is along these lines that we confront the paradoxes that race relies upon, as well as the effects of racism, which help to maintain forms of racial difference. As noted by Copjec, it is important to remember that:

for the symbolic to evict the real and thereby establish itself, a judgment of existence is required; that is, it is necessary to *say* that the real is absented, to *declare* its impossibility. The symbolic, in other words, must include the negation of what it is not. This requirement is not without its paradoxical effects, for it means ultimately that the symbolic will not be filled with only itself, since it will also contain this surplus element of negation.

(1994, 121, italics in original)[2]

This underscores how examples of anti-racism cannot rely entirely on the capacities of the Symbolic order to help render a re-signification of race. Instead, within the Symbolic, there remains an element of negation that avers the Real. Ultimately, in order to tackle examples of racism, a re-politicization of this negation—the Symbolic order's inherent gap—is required. As Zalloua asserts, anti-racist 'politics begins by insisting on the *gap* between the existing administered social order and the ontological lack that bolsters it' (2020, 16, italics in original).

Thakur (2022) goes further here, drawing from the work of Fanon, to emphasize how a decolonization of the colonized requires an inherent negation. He notes:

for Fanon the problem of social and racial inequality in colonialism is not simply a matter that can be resolved through the restoration of the colonized's rights, voice and identity, but it is a symptom of the impossible deadlock or antagonism structuring colonial social relations. This impasse is the *inherent nonlogic* structuring colonial society and colonial politics. And for this reason, it is not enough that the colonized defy or escape her racially and socially inferior position to the colonizer: the colonized must recognize her being as irrevocably divided between negations— what it is not (black) and what it cannot be (white). Fanon's brilliance lies in this identification of the colonized as (ontological) void.

(Thakur 2022, 286–287, italics in original)

It can be added that the 'brilliance' which Thakur observes stems in part from an acknowledgment of the Real as extimately related to the subject's lack and to the impasses and impossible deadlocks that structure the Symbolic order. Consequently, it is with regard to the Real that the inherent exclusions of the Symbolic discursively establish the racial categories that come to function as part of the Symbolic order. These categories render the imposition of the signifier that subsequently prescribes and designates the subject *their* race. This posits how it is in accordance with the signifier that examples of racism underwrite the subject's racialization.

As a form of extimacy, it is important to note that the Real is not expungable and cannot simply be ignored or removed. Instead, the Real bears its significance through the 'referential value' that race procures (George 2016, 39). We can draw connections here with what Gilroy has referred to as 'raciology': 'the lore that brings the virtual realities of "race" to dismal and destructive life' (2000, 11); indeed, 'a shorthand term for a variety of essentializing and reductionist ways of thinking that are both biological and cultural in character' (2000, 72). What Gilroy's raciology prescribes is a discourse of racial difference that binds the racial Symbolic order to the extimacy of the Real. This can be seen when racial identity becomes fixed to certain traits, such as when visible markers (skin colour, etc.) are tied to particular attributes that are perceived to denote one's (racial) character. In so doing, it is the racial prescription that extimately ties the raced subject to the Real. This underscores the non-sense inherent to race and how it works to uphold certain definitions that rely upon a set of attributes that cannot be easily defined. Race seems to both assist as well as resist signification, exceeding the very Symbolic structure that delimits its effects.

In elaborating upon these effects, while also drawing links between race, extimacy, and the Real, we can identify how examples of racism, as well as acts of racial hatred, are tied to a racial Symbolic order that remains grounded in examples of racial difference. To do so requires a return to the topology that extimacy prescribes, one in which traditional boundaries—inside–outside, Black–White—are redefined. Upon reflection, it becomes apparent that examples of extimacy underscore the entirety of Lacan's work, such as, in the relocation of the gaze in the object (not the subject); in the assertion that the subject's desire remains the desire of the Other; and in the Real that 'ex-ists' as part of the Symbolic order.[3] Indeed, what this final contention allows us to consider is how '[t]he Real is ever present as a limit of the Symbolic, not external but *extimate* to the Symbolic' (Kornbluh 2017, 37, italics in original). This proposes that we do not separate race from racism or assume that without racism we can obtain a better relationship to race. In the case of the latter, racial distinctions would be maintained, with race continuing to function as a form of segregation (Field and Fields 2012). Instead, by conceiving of the Real as extimate, we can consider how examples of racism sit at the interstices of a racial Symbolic, from which the signifier of race impedes upon the subject and where the Real is confronted. In fact, whereas Johnston highlights how 'the extimate is frequently referred to', in Žižek's work, 'as "the little piece of the Real," what is "in you more than you,"' (Johnston 2005, 113), it as the intersection of what is extimate that the Real resides. This can be identified in the very way in which our biology and the Symbolic intersect. George explains:

> [e]merging from the intersection of biology and the Symbolic, race does not manufacture difference but instead structures a prescribed mode of interpretation that grants forms of existent biological difference more critical Symbolic value. The biological fact of phenotypic variations functions in racial discourse as race's alibi, masking the inherent arbitrariness of racial distinction by internalizing and eternalizing difference

as an embodied permanency. Because phenotypic differences in pigmentation and morphological variations in bone and hair are often traceable through ancestral lines, these visible differences provide an ostensive basis for a biological notion of race as defined by inheritable characteristics. ... Though, by grounding itself in the biology of phenotype, race comes to imply deeper dissimilarities in such things as morality, intellect, degrees of licentiousness, violent proclivities, and so on, it is the system of the Symbolic itself that grants race and these implied dissimilarities their value, establishing a differential status that has meaning only within a chain where black adopts its Symbolic significance through its interrelation with and distinction from white.

(2016, 40)

Reading Gilroy's (2000) 'raciology' alongside George's 'prescribed mode of interpretation', we can determine how the existence of racial values and beliefs are not simply learned, obtained, and reproduced by the subject, but that such values rely upon an extra-discursive level that fundamentally affords one's phenotypic differences 'an embodied permanency' (2016, 40). Consequently, while it is only 'by grafting itself onto biology, ... [that] race presents itself as pre-dating the system of the Symbolic, masquerading as an inherent component of nature indicative of visible, natural variations in groups of humans' (George 2016, 40), such 'permanency' achieves its grounding due to the 'intimate exteriority' that race prescribes (Lacan 1997, 139). One's very being is thus racialized through that kernel of the Real which marks one's racialization and the racism therein.

'Now you see it, now you don't': racecraft and racism's mental tricks

What the above discussion has sought to afford, is an approach to race that is not separated from the racism it relies upon. Indeed, to separate the two would be tantamount to presenting a separation of the Real from the Symbolic. To help elaborate upon this relationship we can turn to the Fields account of 'racecraft' (Fields and Fields 2012). Working from the contention that '*Race* is the principal unit and core concept of *racism*' (Fields and Fields 2012, 17), racecraft denotes a 'busy repertoire of strange maneuvering' that underscores how we think about, relate to, and ultimately, navigate, our relations to race (Fields and Fields 2012, 16). That is:

[racecraft] refers ... to mental terrain and to pervasive belief. ... [R]acecraft originates not in nature but in human action and imagination; it can exist in no other way. The action and imagining are collective yet individual, day-to-day yet historical, and consequential even though nested in mundane routine.

(Fields and Fields 2012, 18)

The analogy to 'witchcraft' is deliberately employed by the Fields in order to stress the commonalities between the two. Through 'circular reasoning, prevalence of confirming rituals, barriers to disconfirming factual evidence, self-fulfilling prophecies, multiple and inconsistent causal ideas, and colorfully inventive folk genetics' (Fields and Fields 2012, 198), they draw a connection between the characteristics of witchcraft and the certainties that racecraft affords. In fact, when '[t]aken together, such traits constitute a social world whose inhabitants experience (and act on) a marrow-deep certainty that racial differences are real and consequential, whether scientifically demonstrable or not' (Fields and Fields 2012, 198). While '[o]bviousness is the hallmark of such a world' (Fields and Fields 2012, 198), such certainty is established through the assurances that race's visibility provides. In so doing, '[r]acecraft creates the easy false certainty of seeing and defining group membership to provide kinship, security, and pleasurable aggression without acknowledging one's manipulation of social reality' (Reynoso 2021, 63).

For Reynoso, racecraft has a demonstrable impact on psychoanalysis, whereby through 'its associative allusions to witchcraft, the term calls to mind specific historical, group, magical, moral, violent, and oppressive qualities that must be recognized as central to all of racism's manifestations' (2021, 52–53).[4] We can go further here and locate these qualities as inherent to the workings of a racial Symbolic order, the very underpinnings of which remain tethered to the Real. Indeed, by 'ex-isting' within the system of signification, it is at the point of extimacy that the effects of racecraft can be confirmed: for, if the Real bears no definition, beyond the fact that it cannot be defined, then '[t]he racecraft of racism is omnipresent though illusive' (Reynoso 2021, 72)—it bears an extimate presence that underwrites one's everyday existence, while also shaping our actions and imaginations.

By racially prescribing where one's sense of ancestry and community can be defined and located, racecraft elicits a whole set of ideas that manipulate and underscore our relations to reality. Importantly:

> [t]hese ideas do not exist purely in the mind, or in only one mind. They are social facts—like six o'clock, both an idea and a reality. Because racecraft exists in this way, its constant remaking constantly retreats from view. This 'now you see it, now you don't' quality is what makes racism—the practice of a double standard based on ancestry—possible.
>
> (Fields and Fields 2012, 25)

It is in the act of 'remaking' that the effect of racism resides in a number of 'mental tricks' (Fields and Fields 2012, 27). The key here is not to perceive these 'mental tricks', and the racism they evoke, as 'an emotion or state of mind, such as intolerance, bigotry, hatred, or malevolence' (Fields and Fields 2012, 17). Instead, '*[r]acism* is first and foremost a social practice, which means that it is an action and a rationale for action, or both at once'; its 'trick' lies in the fact that '*[r]acism* always takes for granted the objective reality of *race*, as just defined' (Fields and Fields 2012, 17, italics in original). For example:

> [c]onsider the statement 'black Southerners were segregated because of their skin color'—a perfectly natural sentence to the ears of most Americans, who tend to overlook its weird causality. But in that sentence, segregation disappears as the doing of segregationists, and then, in a puff of smoke—*paff*—reappears as a trait of only one part of the segregated whole. In similar fashion, enslavers disappear only to reappear, disguised, in stories that append physical traits defined as slave-like to those enslaved.
>
> (Fields and Fields 2012, 17)

In effect, what this weird causality permits is the elicitation of a perceived racial difference as an inherited characteristic of the particular group. The transformation that occurs here is one in which the act of racism becomes *a characteristic of the racialised*... something they *are* as opposed to the actions of what the racist *does*.

Similar effects can be identified in how any reference to 'genes' is often tied to one's race and, specifically, one's 'blood'. Here, Fields and Fields note the following:

> [o]nly as metaphor may one speak of 'black genes' and 'white genes,' or of 'white' and 'black' blood. But once invoked, the metaphor launches a logical program of its own: If 'blood' is synonymous with 'race,' and 'DNA' is synonymous with 'blood,' then 'DNA' is synonymous with 'race.' Although spurious, that synonymy engages a powerful logic in its turn. Invoke a race, and the notion of a distinguishing blood stands to reason. In the folk lexicon, that is precisely what *race* means. ... The power of this ancient metaphor reveals itself fully when news articles identifying a genetic basis for this or that medical condition are read, and even written, as if 'genetic' and 'racial' were one and the same. At that point, 'gene' is no longer a scientific notion. It is a folk notion traveling incognito.
>
> (2012, 52–53, italics in original)[5]

As a result, 'race' comes to certify, as well as explain, a whole range of genetic factors, including one's medical conditions and one's 'racial heritage'. Insofar as, 'the signifier establishes race at the same moment that genetics establishes kinship, ... it is this synchrony that enables the simultaneous articulation of genes and identity/destiny, though not causally' (Seshadri-Crooks 2000, 17). Ultimately, it is this lack of linear causality that racecraft ensures.

The effect-cause of racism

What this discussion allows us to revisit is the fundamental relation between race and racism.[6] Indeed, as evident in the above examples, it seems as if the significance of racecraft confirms a strange causality, an 'effect-cause', whereby it is racism that presumes and, in no uncertain terms, prescribes, one's racial origin as the foundation to one's very being. What this reveals is the extent to which race serves as the justification for racist beliefs as well as for the exploitation, marginalization, and violent discrimination of large proportions of the earth's population. While accounts of race remain dependent on one's cultural, historical, and geographical location, and whereas many remain fully cognizant of the fact that race is better conceived as a myth, such arguments tend to make little headway in undermining or combating racist perceptions. This is not simply an ignorance on behalf of those who openly and candidly acknowledge examples of racism, but, rather, speaks to a more fundamental concern in how race occupies a reified form in our social world that frames both its perpetuation and critique. Thus, when criticizing the invalidity of 'race', one remains tethered to a line that follows the (racist) presuppositions that one wishes to admonish (Gilroy 2000). It is '[t]he very visibility of race, ... [that] attests to the predominance of racism' (McGowan 2020, 187), and, furthermore, if '[r]acism always takes for granted the objective reality of race' (Fields and Fields 2012, 17), then, it is through the perpetuation of race that examples of racism are sustained via a backward causality that prescribes the justification of racial classifications. It is in this way that racism works as an effect-cause that frames, organises, and upholds racial difference (Black 2021; Gilroy 1993; Mitchell 2012).

The power of this effect-cause—a reversal of the common cause-effect relation—is that it bears no relation to the actuality of one's visible physical differences. Instead, these differences are, after the fact, assumed a racial connotation that works as the very cause and explanation for the presence of racial difference. Accordingly, while 'the social alchemy of racecraft transforms racism into race, disguising collective social practice as inborn individual traits', it is the *effects* of racism that are disguised through the individualization that race assumes (Fields and Fields 2012, 261). In such instances '[t]he invisible aspect of race becomes apparent', so that 'the focus of racecraft is not the outward, visible color of a person's skin (hair type, bone structure, etc.) but the presumed inward, invisible content of that person's character' (Fields and Fields 2012, 207). Ultimately, 'through the transforming power of racecraft, an individual becomes a race, roommates become an "interracial pairing," and the outcome, whether friction or friendship, becomes "race relations"' (Fields and Fields 2012, 40).

Therefore, while '[w]e see race in order not to see racism' (McGowan 2020, 187), it is nonetheless clear that examples of racism bear an extimate presence within the act of racecraft itself. That is, if we conceive of racecraft as determining the navigation of a racial Symbolic order that impacts upon both our actions and imaginations, then what the Real extimately reveals is those 'parts of racecraft's inner horizon that inhabit perception itself' (Fields and Fields 2012, 72). What racism sustains is the very limits that structure this 'inner horizon', the effect of which is that it bears witness to 'the decisive role of the signifier's hidden cause as a nodal point for the subject's psychic constitution' (Friedlander 2022, 112). Such a 'hidden cause' serves as the break that defines the subject's constitution, or the 'gap' that sustains the subject (Copjec and Chubbs 2020). What this fundamentally reveals is how the 'Cause is the traumatic and eruptive core around which the signifiers of consciousness ever assemble themselves, if only in the defensive act of establishing for the subject a protective distance from this core' (George 2016, 16). Subsequently, while Cause maintains an 'extimate relation to the subject' (George 2016, 16), it nonetheless maintains and structures the Symbolic order, bound as it is to the excesses of the Real.

The contradiction in race

This points to the very fact that while there is, for Lacan (2006), 'no metalanguage', equally, there remains no neutral position from which an assessment of race can be provided. In contrast to 'post-race' assertions, the position from which one speaks (the position of enunciation) remains tied to the 'hidden cause' that extimately structures the subject's racialization (Friedlander 2022). We can follow this in relation to the fact that, as noted by Friedlander, when one asserts that '"race no longer matters," the very attestation functions to negate the validity of the statement—if race really did not matter anymore then there would be no need to make the enunciation' (2022, 108). The paradox at play here is that any act that may critique or even promote examples of racial articulation is itself located in the position from which this articulation is made: a position that effectively reinstates the very racial differences that underscore one's articulation of race. It is also what propagates the double-standards that racism relies upon: evident in the contention that it is 'race' that results in one's inequality, poor health, or untimely death. It is for this reason that the Symbolic structuring of race is, at the same time, an intercession of the Real: indeed, an 'immanent impossibility' (Žižek 1990, 252) that permits race a point of Symbolic reference from which the 'reality' of racial difference is constructed.

It is on basis that the Fields contend that racism does not require a racist (Fields and Fields 2012). Instead, the racial Symbolic remains bound to the Real via a structure of seeing that frames and shapes our perspectives of race and racial difference. What is more, we can begin to see how these perspectives chime with the very ways in which race has become, for Gilroy (2000), 'ordinary'. This is not to suggest that race is unremarkable or that examples of racism have in some sense been overcome; rather, it is that the problems and positives of living with race and racism now constitute an ordinary part of our day-to-day lives. Indeed, while we may seek a diminishment of the very values that are attributed to race, this can also expose how the 'mundanity' of perceiving racial difference is itself a site of inequality and contradiction (Gilroy 2000).

It is in the presence of these inherent contradictions and inconsistencies that one's racial identity works to occlude as well as compound the effects of racism. Following the Žižekian contention that '[t]he task of philosophy is not to solve problems but to redefine them; not to answer questions, but to raise the proper question' (Žižek 2006, 141), Zalloua emphasizes 'that how we perceive or conceptualize the problem of racism may in fact be part of the problem' (2020, 9). Over the course of Part I, the task has been to examine this problem in accordance with a racial Symbolic order that works to produce the inherent exclusions that engender the very excesses it seeks to manage. As a result, the Real forever maintains a presence within the Symbolic, often by returning to this order through forms of otherness that comprise, but also threaten and dislodge, our Symbolic coordinates. The relative success of these coordinates can be seen in examples of language and meaning, but also in the fantasies that both affirm and explain our relations to reality as well as other subjects. Here, 'narrative fantasy organizes the mind's experience into a network of formal signifying elements structured as relationships of cause and effect within a larger symbolic network of language and cultural discourse' (Zornado 2017, 7). There is, however, no clear-cut relation between cause and effect, with the return of the Real proving to be the very distortion that undermines the linearity between cause and effect. Key here is that the 'craft' of 'racecraft' does not require 'race' to exist, in much the same way that witchcraft did not require witches to exist; instead, 'racecraft creates a closed system that allows its own consequences to be taken as its verification and cause for further reproduction of racial belief that resists learning from experience' (Reynoso 2021, 54).

The effect of such a system is that while it remains closed, it also remains empty. That is, when '[r]ace produces unconscious effects, and as a hybrid structure located somewhere between essence and construct, it determines the destiny of human bodies', then it remains 'our ethical and political task to figure out how destiny comes to be inscribed as anatomy, when that anatomy does not exist as such' (Seshadri-Crooks 2000, 56). Moreover, the inscription of a destiny onto an anatomy that does not exist allows us to identify how race enacts its very illusion. The success of this illusion is that it remains paradoxically effective. Consigned to a racial Symbolic order that precedes the subject, while also prescribing and delimiting the subject's racialization, the effect of race bears no inherent truth, and thus remains, much like Lacan's *objet petite a*, an 'object, … which is … simply the presence of a hollow, a void' (2004, 180). The presence of such a hollow object bears witness to the contradictions that race relies upon, insofar as by remaining 'empty' race can discursively define what one's supposed biological 'essence' is assumed to be. It is in its very ex-sistence therefore that race helps to engender powerful group attachments, based on racial difference and an assumed racial identity. On this basis alone, any attempt to identify a 'post-racial' future remains fraught: to imagine a future beyond the presence of race, requires, at least, a conception of race which we can then move beyond (this task will be taken-up in Part III).

A turn to psychosis

It is clear from this opening section that the effects of racism continue to persist, despite the widely-heralded claim that race remains nothing more than a social construction. In short, racism and racial prejudice cannot be tackled by simply highlighting the social construction of race.[7] Certainly, if approached, there are many who would openly deride the existence of racism, as well as the inequalities that it sustains. Yet, none of this seems to have any impact upon the racism that we regularly witness and/or experience. Across daily news-cycles, we are routinely made aware of the institutional effects of racism in public services, as well as the impact this has on local communities and the victims themselves. Further still, on digital and social media platforms it seems as if we are only ever a few clicks away from engaging with racist provocations and outright racial harassment. For McGowan, '[t]he contemporary proliferation of racism in spite of our knowledge about its wrongs suggests that we have an unconscious investment in racism that continues and multiplies' (2022, 19). He adds:

> [t]he unconscious investment is the central pillar of racism's intransigence. Unless one takes the unconscious as the starting point for making sense of racism's appeal, the mystery of the enduring power of racism is almost impossible to decipher. ... The struggle against racism requires an engagement with the unconscious, but deciphering the unconscious appeal of racism places us on the difficult terrain of psychoanalytic interpretation.
>
> (McGowan 2022, 19)

Alongside a critique of the social construction of race, the above sections have traced the beginnings of this psychoanalytic interpretation. The remainder of this book will seek to expand upon this interpretation, where, in Parts II and III, specific attention will be given to examining what will be referred to as the psychosis of race.

Notes

1 I conceive of this relationship between the Symbolic and the Real in accordance with Pluth's assertion that 'the real persists within the symbolic, and the symbolic has effects on the real' (2007, 93).

2 In fact, Copjec adds that it is 'through the signifier's repeated attempt—and failure—to designate itself [... that] [t]he signifier's difference from itself, its radical inability to signify itself, causes it to turn in circles around the real that is lacking in it. It is in this way—in the circumscription of the real—that its nonexistence or its negation is signified *within* the symbolic' (1994, 121, italics in original).
3 Much of this finds its crowning culmination in the essential Lacanian principal that the unconscious lies not within the confines of the subject but in language (Lacan 2004).
4 In particular, Reynoso (2021) considers the effects of racecraft on the treatment of a psychotic patient. What is unique to Reynoso's (2021) account, and what will prove fruitful to the discussion in Chapter 9, is that the effects of racecraft are not beholden to the psychotic patient or the racist. Indeed, '[f]or the target of racist abuse, the intense paranoia that drives the racism and infuses the scene of it (Did that just occur?; What is happening?; What's just been done to me?) demands language and ideas that expressively situate it within the societal lineage and history of generational group oppression' (Reynoso 2021, 53).
5 In so doing, 'the notion of a race dovetails with the folk notion that different races of people have differently constituted bodies and correspondingly different susceptibilities to illness' (Fields and Fields 2012, 67–68).
6 This is noted by Gilroy, who laments the fact that, for some, 'racial differences are just natural things, and racism comes along and messes them up[.] ... A lot of anti-racist work is of that type. It says: "Nature gives us racial differences, look around the room, some of the differences you see are racial; others are not". It's just racism makes those differences bad' (Gilroy et al. 2018, 188). In contrast, Gilroy perceives 'racism as a system assembling races in the world. ... It is not something that grows from racial difference. It creates racial difference' (Gilroy et al. 2018, 188).
7 In fact, when such assertions are fully taken-up they can result in examples of 'reflexive racism'. This is explored further in 'On Reflexive Racism: Disavowal, Deferment and the Lacanian Subject' (Black 2020).

References

Black, Jack. 2020. "On reflexive racism: disavowal, deferment and the Lacanian subject." *Diacritics* 48, no. 4: 76–101.
Black, Jack. 2021. *Race, Racism and Political Correctness in Comedy – A Psychoanalytic Exploration*. Abingdon, UK: Routledge.
Copjec, Joan. 1994. *Read My Desire: Lacan Against the Historicists*. Cambridge, MA: The MIT Press.
Copjec, Joan, and Colby Chubbs. 2020. "Psychoanalysis and consequences." *Chiasma* 6, no. 1: 189–203.
Fields, Karen E. and Barabara J. Fields. 2012. *Racecraft: The Soul of Inequality in American Life*. London, UK: Verso.
Friedlander, Jennifer. 2022. "In medium race: traversing the fantasy of post-race discourse." In *Lacan and Race: Racism, Identity, and Psychoanalytic Theory*, edited by Sheldon George and Derek Hook (105–120). Abingdon, UK: Routledge.
George, Sheldon. 2016. *Trauma and Race: A Lacanian Study of African American Racial Identity*. Waco, TX: Baylor University Press.
Gilroy, Paul. 1993. *The Black Atlantic: Modernity and Double Consciousness*. London, UK: Verso.
Gilroy, Paul. 2000. *Against Race: Imagining Political Culture Beyond the Color Line*. Cambridge, MA: The Belknap Press of Harvard University Press.

Gilroy, Paul, Tony Sandset, Sindre Bangstad, and Gard Ringen Høibjerg. 2018. "A diagnosis of contemporary forms of racism, race and nationalism: a conversation with Professor Paul Gilroy." *Cultural Studies* 33, no. 2: 173–197.
Johnston, Adrian. 2005. *Time Driven: Metapsychology and the Splitting of the Drive*. Evanston, IL: Northwestern University Press.
Kornbluh, Anna. 2017. "Reading the Real: Žižek's literary materialism." In *Everything You Always Wanted to Know about Literature but Were Afraid to Ask Žižek, Sic 10*, edited by Russell Sbriglia (35–61). Durham, NC: Duke University Press.
Lacan, Jacques. 1997. *The Seminar of Jacques Lacan, Book VII, 1959–1960: The Ethics of Psychoanalysis*, edited by Jacques-Alain Miller and translated by Dennis Porter. New York, NY: W. W. Norton & Company.
Lacan, Jacques. 2004. *The Four Fundamental Concepts of Psycho-Analysis*, edited by Jacques-Alain Miller. London, UK: Karnac.
Lacan, Jacques. 2006. "On a question preliminary to any possible treatment of psychosis." In *Écrits. The First Complete Edition in English*, translated by Bruce Fink, in collaboration with Heloise Fink and Russell Grigg (445–488). London, UK: W. W. Norton & Company.
McGowan, Todd. 2020. *Universality and Identity Politics*. New York, NY: Columbia University Press.
McGowan, Todd. 2022. "The bedlam of the lynch mob: racism and enjoying through the other." In *Lacan and Race Racism, Identity, and Psychoanalytic Theory*, edited by Sheldon George and Derek Hook (19–34). Abingdon, UK: Routledge.
Mitchell, W.J.T. 2012. *Seeing Through Race*. Cambridge, MA: Harvard University Press.
Pluth, Ed. 2007. *Signifiers and Acts: Freedom in Lacan's Theory of the Subject*. New York, NY: State University of New York Press.
Reynoso, Joseph S. 2021. "The racist within." *The Psychoanalytic Quarterly* 90, no. 1: 49–76.
Seshadri-Crooks, Kalpana. 2000. *Desiring Whiteness: A Lacanian Analysis of Race*. London, UK: Routledge.
Thakur, Gautam Basu. 2020. *Postcolonial Lack: Identity, Culture, Surplus*. Albany, NY: State University of New York Press.
Zalloua, Zahi. 2020. *Žižek on Race: Toward an Anti-Racist Future*. London, UK: Bloomsbury.
Žižek, Slavoj. 1990. "Beyond discourse-analysis." In *New Reflections on The Revolution of Our Time*, by Ernesto Laclau (249–260). London, UK: Verso.
Žižek, Slavoj. 2006. "Philosophy, the 'unknown knowns' and the public use of reason." *Topoi* 25, no. 1–2: 137–142.
Zornado, Joseph. 2017. *Disney and the Dialectic of Desire: Fantasy as Social Practice*. Champagne, CH: Palgrave Macmillan.

Part II

Race and the structure of psychosis

Chapter 4

Lacan and psychosis

The term psychosis has been used to define and collate a number of interrelated pathologies, including schizophrenia, manic depression, paranoia, and narcissism. Amongst these categories, hallucinations and delusions are frequently cited as examples of psychosis. While diagnoses of psychosis remain ill-defined and, at times, contradictory, Lacanian interpretations emphasize the universal significance of psychosis: a subject position that effects all individuals to varying degrees.

Indeed, Lacan's interest in psychosis would form the basis of his doctoral thesis, where, in treating the patient Aimée, he sought to draw from psychoanalytic theory in order to move beyond explanations that located psychosis in the individual's brain functioning.[1] In his subsequent Seminars, Lacan explored the relationship between the subject and the Other, approaching psychosis as a structure of unconscious identification. What would remain essential to Lacan's work was his focus on examining psychosis, not as a biological condition or illness, but as a phenomenon related to language and the structural position that language enacts for the subject.

Much of this would continue Lacan's task of developing the ideas of Freud, where, in his seminar on psychosis, Lacan (1997) draws extensively from Freud's account of the German Judge, Daniel Schreber. While suffering from violent delusions, Schreber chose to detail his disorders in the publication, *Memoirs of My Nervous Illness* (2000). Here, the vivid descriptions of Schreber's delusions and paranoid experiences would prove crucial to Freud's (1981) later interpretation of psychosis. However, for Lacan, Freud's error was that he did not 'problematize language' (Ragland 1995, 74)—an error that was to be rectified by Lacan in his own account of Schreber. Specifically:

> [by] [a]rguing that Schreber's articulations exhibit organization and a kind of rational thought, Lacan taught … that speech is a field of meaning where certain signifiers are organized, or not. The absence of normal grammatical language in Schreber's articulations indicates his inability to screen out the unconscious. His capacity to repress has ceased, which is typical of

DOI: 10.4324/9781003414209-7

> psychotic discourse where the ego ceases to serve as a screen between the Other and the speaking subject.
>
> (Ragland 1995, 74)

More broadly, what Lacan's focus on language and the signifier bring attention to is the fact that we live not simply in a world, but, rather, a world of language. Even before the subject is born, language 'exists prior to each subject's entry into it' (Lacan 2006d, 413). It was by considering how language fundamentally structured the position of the subject—including how they relate to, as well as move within, the structures of the world—that it became possible for Lacan to trace the psychic symptoms relevant to neurosis, perversion, and psychosis.[2]

Lacan's understanding of psychosis would develop throughout his seminars, with Vanheule (2011a) identifying four distinct eras in Lacan's approach.[3] While these eras span the breadth of Lacan's theoretical and conceptual developments, they also point to a number of key Lacanian concepts that elucidate on the significance of Lacan's account. One notable concept is Lacan's *objet petit a* (object *a*).

Developing upon his early seminars, which focused specifically on the effects of language for the subject, Lacan's object *a* draws attention to those aspects of human experience that reveal the limits of the signifier—specifically, the disruptions that occur as part of the Symbolic order that language fails to define or curtail. Encapsulated in the object *a*, such distortions prove integral to psychosis, wherein a separation from this primary object has failed to take place. Following his seminar on anxiety, Lacan (2014) traces the effects of these disruptions and distortions as inherent to the Symbolic's failure to fully account for the subject's being, as well as the subsequent lack of authority that the psychotic attributes to the Other.

Later, Lacan (2018) would consider instances where psychosis is either managed by the subject or even avoided. This can be identified in Vanheule's reference to Lacan's 'fourth era' (1975–1976), 'where knot theory is used to operationalize the interrelations between the real, the symbolic and the imaginary' (Vanheule 2020, 165). Drawing upon the work of James Joyce, Lacan (2018) examines how Joyce's writing allowed the writer to stave-off psychosis through his development of the sinthome. Occupying a topological significance, Lacan emphasizes the sinthome's creative capacity in affording the subject a level of identification with their symptom. According to Lacan, it was Joyce's 'destructive' use of language that allowed him to creatively invent new ways of applying language in his work.[4]

Such examples pose a novel approach to psychosis—one in which the distinction between what we would typically consider 'normal' and 'psychotic' requires a renewed focus. For Lacan (2006e), all subjectivity is reliant on fantasy, with the 'delusional' forming a constitutive part of social life. It is on this basis that Kunkle asserts that 'normality is really just a special form of psychosis' (2008, 17).⁵ This is not to suggest that to be 'normal' one has to be psychotic, but that the formal structure underpinning psychosis bears a unique relation to what can be considered 'normal'. McGowan elaborates on this line of thinking by highlighting how '[t]he normal subject, conceived in the properly psychoanalytic sense, has no external entity by which to measure its own deviation from the norm', insofar as 'to become a normal subject is to recognize that there is no authorized social authority, no guarantee for normality' (2013, 125).⁶

Certainly, while Lacanian psychoanalysis would suggest that there is no 'normal' subject, with all subjects varying between the hysterical, neurotic, and perverse positions, what both Kunkle and McGowan draw attention to is the relationship between psychosis and authority—in particular, the 'guarantee' that is afforded to such authority. As outlined by Vanheule, when 'the only fundament of our belief in the world is an act of faith, which carries no truth value whatsoever' (2011a, 160–161), then it becomes suddenly apparent that the functionality of our everyday existence rests upon a certain level of 'madness'. Accordingly, for our experiences of reality to be conceived as meaningful, and for our lives and the relations we form to mean something, then a certain belief in the fiction (i.e., the values and norms) that we attribute to the world, as well as the moral authorities who uphold them, is required.

Therefore, to live 'normally' is, in most instances, a subscription to a 'special form of psychosis' that gives some level of credibility to an authorization that could delimit what is 'normal' (Kunkle 2008, 17). Indeed, while the purpose of Lacanian analysis is to reveal to the subject that all authority is inherently baseless and marked by lack—that there is no external justification for authority; no set of norms or values that would lend it complete credibility; in short, there is no big Other—in psychosis, there is no realisation of this fact. Instead, whether one can be conceived as psychotic or not depends largely on their position to the Other and the Symbolic order.

This underscores an important aspect of Lacanian psychosis: primarily, psychosis is not an 'illness' or 'biological' deficiency, beholden to the individual, but a structural position grounded in the Lacanian claim that there is no real self or ego that constitutes the subject. Instead, the 'I is an other' (Lacan 2006b, 96) forged in 'socially elaborated situations' (Lacan 2006b, 79). Importantly, this is not to say that there is no ego-development. In fact, while no one is born with an 'ego', equally, no one is born a psychotic. Consequently, '[r]ather than view[ing] ego development from a Freudian lens, which situates intrapsychic activity as the locus of mental life', we can, following Lacan, conceive of 'the ego [… as] a fantasy of self-relation defined by the Other' (Mills 2019, 16).

For any subject—psychotic or not—one's subjectivity is predicated on various external images that are both idealized and used by the subject in order to establish an 'inherent' sense of self. It is on this basis that madness can be conceived as 'the direct effect of an identificatory structure' (Vanheule 2011a, 27), where 'the risk of madness is gauged by the very appeal of the identifications on which man stakes both his truth and his being' (Lacan 1947, 143 cited in Vanheule 2011a, 27). What remains significant about these claims is the contention they propose: indeed, if one's identity and sense of self is derived from external causes, outside the psyche, then all forms of 'self-knowledge' present '[a]n imaginary mode of relating to the world [which] is fundamental to psychosis' (Mills 2019, 16).

Life as madness

We can now begin to approach the everyday relevance of psychosis, drawing attention to the fact that examples of psychosis may not occur because someone is 'mad', but, rather, that their ability to live with 'madness' may have, in some form or another, been disrupted. Leader's account of 'quiet madness' undertakes such an approach, with him considering how examples of a psychotic structure do not necessarily require obvious forms of disruption. For Leader, 'people can *be* mad without *going* mad' (2012, 11, italics in original).[7] Echoing the above, this suggests that 'madness' and 'normality' are not opposed but related. Burnham notes:

> we come across a person talking in an animated fashion, perhaps waving his arms, but no one else is around. Here the 'stupid first impression' is that someone is talking to himself, is walking around gesticulating like a madman. But we correct that impression when we realize that, no, he is on his phone, he has that triangular thing hanging off his ear. He is using Bluetooth technology. And then that second impression itself is corrected, and we go back to the first representation, which now includes wireless technology in the larger picture of daily life as madness.
>
> (2018, 161)

This 'life as madness' is also echoed in other contemporary examples. Referring to psychiatry work from the 1950s, Leader highlights how psychotic subjects were often analyzed for the very way in which they 'learnt' emotion, 'as if their feelings could be turned on or off according to the needs of the situation' (2012, 201). Indeed:

> [t]he creation of these surface emotions chimes with the social imperatives of our culture today, which see emotion less as the authentic sign of our inner life than as a set of behaviours to be learned. If we are trained properly, we will learn emotional skills and so be able to show the 'appropriate' emotion. What was seen by the analysts and psychiatrists of the 1950s as a sign of psychosis has now become a norm of healthy subjectivity.
>
> (Leader 2012, 201)

While Leader's example refers explicitly to the learning of emotions, we can draw attention to the fact that all subjects are required to conform to certain identifications, if only on the basis that any identity, whether conformist or radical, involves some external standard through which to judge it by. For Miller (2013), however, there remains a certain emptiness to these identifications.

With regard to those who may not have suffered any explicit psychotic triggering, Miller (2013) outlines how a fixity to a particular identification can offer some hope of stabilization and compensation, which he refers to as 'ordinary psychosis'.[8] Echoing the psychotic's display of 'surface emotions' (Leader 2012, 201), such forms of compensatory (over-)identification are discussed in Lacan's (1997) account of Hélène Deutsch's (1942) 'as-if mechanisms'. These identifications display a blind acceptance on behalf of the subject towards certain identities and forms of behaviour which are copied from the surrounding environment—for example, notable individuals. Uncritically accepted, these learnt behaviours allow the psychotic to act 'as if' they are fully aware of the social requirements that are associated with a variety of social positions. Importantly, it is these 'as if' identifications that provide an opportunity for the psychotic *not* to question their position, or, rather, their *relation to* specific social positions. It is in this way that certain surface emotions and learned identities provide a level of stabilization for the subject, allowing one to live and function within society.

What this suggests is that examples of psychosis can rely upon an 'a-subjective attitude' that can subsequently 'manifes[t] itself in relation to others (daily life and transference), where no close connections seem to be made' (Vanheule 2019, 84). In fact, 'since the imaginary mechanism is what gives psychotic alienation its form, but not its dynamics' (Lacan 1997, 146), it is due to the lack of mediation afforded by the Symbolic order that psychotic estrangement occurs. This is underlined by the fact that, amidst the ingressions of the Symbolic order, 'the subject fails to take shape' (Vanheule 2019, 99).

This posits a certain regression on behalf of the psychotic, from which there is a failure to differentiate between the ego and their own image, resulting in paranoia. Consider the following example:

> Paranoia is passionate madness in the etymological sense of passion: pathos, what we suffer. Let's imagine I'm in front of a mirror and don't recognize it as such: if I stretch my hand towards the gentleman facing me, I will see him stretching his hands towards—or against?—me. In short, I, a paranoiac, do not recognize that the other—my persecutor, sexual cheater, unreachable lover—is my image, and for this reason I misunderstand his or her intentions.
>
> (Benvenuto 2020, 132)

While any relationship is marked by a sense of ambivalence and the possibility of aggression, in psychosis there is no mediation and no third party who can manage this relation. In effect, the psychotic 'hasn't acquired ... the Other', with them instead 'encounter[ing] the purely imaginary other', insofar as it is '[t]his other [that] negates him, literally kills him' (Lacan 1997, 209).

Importantly, this encounter with the Imaginary other should not reduce our understanding of psychosis to the Imaginary.[9] To do so would ignore both the Symbolic order and the Real, as well as later developments in Lacan's work (notably, the sinthome). Further still, the psychotic ought not to be conceived as nothing more than an '*I-cracy*': a masterful 'I' that fully knows the 'self' that it is identical to (Lacan 2007, 63).[10] As is evident in Miller's (2013) account of 'ordinary psychosis', there remains an 'emptiness' to the subject which characterizes psychosis. Accordingly, what has not occurred in psychosis is a Symbolic overwriting of the Imaginary (Fink 1999). If Symbolic mediation successfully occurs, then feelings of aggression and ambivalence are clearly curtailed by forms of Symbolic authority which provide at least some explanation to the subject's existence. Without these explanations—explanations that can be questioned by the subject—there is no dialectic to identity and psychosis can ensue, leaving the psychotic beholden to forms of 'imaginary compensation' (Lacan 1997, 193).

To this extent, the psychotic's relation to the Imaginary stems primarily from their position towards the Symbolic order and, specifically, to language and the signifier. This can be founded upon the contention that, at the level of the signifier, there is a failure on behalf of the psychotic to relate to the Other and the Symbolic order, leaving the psychotic lost *within* language. Importantly, this does not suggest a separation from language. Indeed, 'thrust into the foreground, that speaks all by itself, out loud, in its noise and furor' (Lacan 1997, 250), the psychotic remains tethered to language in such a way that language's very form—the signifier—takes on a certain 'reality'. It is on this basis that '[w]ords are taken as things, as real objects' by the psychotic (Fink 1997, 75). Thus, it is the signifiers themselves—what Lacan's algebraic forms refer to as 'S2'—which remain 'unbound' and independent to the psychotic (Fink 1997).[11] This is why, for Lacan, 'there must be disturbances of language' in examples of psychosis (1997, 92); disturbances that stem from the psychotic's relation to the object *a* (Vanheule 2011b).

Nothing but a skull: the non-mediation of the object *a*

To begin our discussion of the object *a*, we can first consider the important revisions that Lacan's theoretical developments would have on his well-known essay, 'The Mirror Stage as Formative of the *I* Function as Revealed in Psychoanalytic Experience' (2006a). Here, Lacan details how it is through the act of looking that the subject misrecognises the bodily wholeness that they see before them in the mirror image. This image is illusory, as the sense of wholeness that it achieves can only ever be conceived through the mirror's impression. Yet, as McGowan (2020) highlights, what this fails to consider is Lacan's (2004) later work on the gaze. Indeed, McGowan notes:

by the time he [Lacan] develops the concept of the gaze as a form of the objet a, this focus undergoes a profound transformation. Rather than facilitating an illusory ego identity in the mirror relation, the gaze is the deformation that places subjects in what they see. All the forms of the objet a play a similar disruptive role for the subject. When one encounters a form of the objet a or impossible object, one encounters a fundamental disruption in the field of experience.

(2020, 232)

Inscribed in the object, the gaze (as object *a*) does not belong to the subject—as depicted in the act of looking—but, instead, confirms the subject's lack of mastery, the very failure to see it all (Lacan 2004). What the gaze denotes, therefore, is an absence that cannot be seen: 'the object *a* is precisely that part of the loss that one cannot see in the mirror, the part of the subject that has no mirror reflection, the nonspecular' (Dolar 1991, 13).[12] Thus, one's Symbolic identity is predicated on 'an object that the subject separates itself from in order to constitute itself as a desiring subject'—the object *a* (McGowan 2007a, 6). It is the very loss of the object *a* which undermines the subject's Imaginary sense of mastery.

There is no better example of the effects of the object *a*, and its depiction in the gaze, than Lacan's (2004) reference to the Hans Holbein the Younger's painting, *The Ambassadors* (1533). In the painting, two men stand beside a collection of objects, including, amongst other things, two globes, an oriental carpet, and a quadrant. Amongst these objects there sits, at the bottom of the painting, an anamorphic object: an object that when looked at directly cannot be made sense of. The blurred impression suggests something, but the outline cannot be properly conceived. Yet, when one alters one's position, the blurred shape becomes visible: one sees a skull within the painting. Despite their accumulated wealth, Holbein's inclusion of the skull helps to convey the men's vanity and their eventual mortality; for Lacan, however, the skull is unique in its capacity to aver the gaze (the object *a*). What the anamorphic skull presents for the onlooker is the inclusion of their look in the painting itself. In so doing, any presumed distance between the subject and the painting is dissolved. One must, to see the skull, change their very position. In this way, the subject is implicated in the picture and, what is more, to see the skull, something must be lost. In other words, one's ability to 'see' the skull requires that one loses the clarity of the previous image: that of the wealthy men and their accumulated objects.

Importantly, the painting reveals that the act of 'seeing is not a neutral activity' (McGowan 2007a, 7). Rather, the lack of 'any safe distance' is demonstrative of the fact that 'the existence of the gaze as a disruption (or a stain) in the picture—an objective gaze—means that spectators … are in the picture in the form of this stain, implicated in the text itself' (McGowan 2007a, 7). This also reveals how the presence of the subject is dependent on the disruption, or more precisely the division, that the painting posits.[13] Importantly, for Lacan, one's position as a subject is predicated on this very division.

In the case of psychosis, the gaze, or object *a*, is neither absent nor lost. Essentially, when looking at Holbein's painting the psychotic sees nothing but the skull. In psychosis, the distortion of the object *a*—that is, 'the deformation that places subjects in what they see' (McGowan 2020, 232)— goes unacknowledged, so that the disruption of the gaze is 'domesticated' (especially in the case of delusions). The psychotic is not included in the image 'as what doesn't fit' (McGowan 2020, 232), and, as a result, they fail to recognise themselves in the distortion of the image. Ultimately, the image bears no relation to the psychotic: it fails to undergo a Symbolic mediation, and, thus, the image becomes a persecutory Other.

To further account for the effects of this failure, we can turn to Hamza's example of the double in the mirror. Hamza notes that '[w]hen we look in the mirror, we see ourselves *plus* something we cannot see without the reflective surface: we see the world *with us in it*' (2019, 50, italics in original). It is for this reason that when we view our reflection in the mirror, 'we see the world "without our absence"—that is, without that blind spot which marks our indelible immersion in it' (Hamza 2019, 50). Yet, what would happen if our image suddenly moved, beyond our own control? Indeed, Hamza asks, 'what if the reflected image were suddenly to start moving while I remained in the same position?' (2019, 51). In such a scenario, '[t]he anguishing effect of the double— of someone other than me who is nonetheless me—is not that he is a poor copy of me who fools other people into believing in his authenticity', rather:

> [t]he problem is that the double is effectively *more me than myself*: the blind spot from which I gaze at the mirror, this *absent* standpoint which at the same time marks my embedding in the world and divides me from it, is *absent* in the double: as I gaze at him, *I see myself fully embedded in the world*—more so than myself (insofar as I include this absent standpoint from which I see the double). My being in the world is marked by an alienation from this grasping at once my own being, as I am deprived from the capacity of seeing myself 'from the outside,' but the double is constituted through *the alienation of this alienation*, the embedding of my image in the image of the world in a fit more perfect than the one I experience within my own skin.
>
> (2019, 51, italics in original)

In Hamza's example, there is a clear sense of disruption that is felt on behalf of the onlooking subject: a disruption forged in the realization that their very being is founded on an alienation that the double does not achieve. What the psychotic misses—indeed, what does not occur in the psychotic's perspective—is the very division that is afforded by the onlooking subject and the moving double. While observing the double's movements, the psychotic accedes to the 'reality' of the double's being. As a result, the psychotic is, much like the double, alienated from their alienation: that is, they are deprived of the mediation that is afforded to the 'absent standpoint'. Accordingly, for both the double and the psychotic, there is no absence, indeed, no loss of the object *a*. In fact, 'for the mirror image to contain the object *a*, a wink or a nod is enough' (Dolar 1991, 13)—the gaze is present, the double is 'real'.

Drawing together Lacan's *objet a*, and the effects of its non-mediation in psychosis, we can begin to determine the psychotic's unique position. That is, if one's access to the Imaginary resides within the very loss of the object *a*, as well as the separation of the Imaginary from the Real, then, in the case of psychosis, no loss occurs. Consequently, '[i]n psychosis the object *a* is not separated from the subject, nor is it integrated in the ego or in the subject: as a mere element of strangeness, the object *a* is manifested in reality' (Vanheule 2011a, 152). With regard to the object *a*, 'normality' resides in the absence it evokes and the desire it establishes. Yet, what is 'normal' for psychosis is a reality where this object *a* is made present; a presence that nonetheless allows the psychotic to live with their 'madness'.

Evidently, the relative efficacy of such 'madness' can mean that the identification of psychosis can prove difficult. However, as previously noted, it is in examples of 'language disturbance' that psychosis can reside. Though, for Lacan, 'psychoanalysis has but one medium: the patient's speech' (2006c, 206), this focus on language poses a number of important significances for Lacanian analysis. Indeed, while it dislodges those conceptions that seek to personalize examples of psychosis as a private pathology, not unlike the biological reduction of psychotic symptoms, it also locates the subject within the structure of language and the position they procure therein. Following Lacan's well-known maxim: 'the unconscious is structured like a language' (2004, 20),[14] the unconscious is not beholden to the individual but can instead be viewed as part of a socially-shared signification that has important affects upon the subject and their relations. As a result, the subject can only 'ex-sist' by borrowing signifiers from the Other (Lacan 2006a, 6). In effect, 'the unconscious is the Other's discourse' (Lacan 2006d, 436), insofar as the subject is inherently related to the Other and the meaning it affords.

In the case of psychosis, it is not simply that the unconscious exists 'outside' the subject, but that 'the unconscious is present but not functioning' (Lacan 1997, 143). Here, Lacan reveals how '[t]he psychotic is a martyr of the unconscious, giving this term martyr its meaning, which is to be a witness' (1997, 132). The psychotic's position as a witness to unconscious formations takes hold, specifically as '[m]anifestations of the unconscious [that] are experienced as external realities'; that is, 'strange messages that cannot be framed in terms of one's own broader mental life' (Vanheule 2011a, 71). Conceived as 'strange messages that come from without' (Vanheule 2011a, 71), unconscious formations impede upon the psychotic, delivering unfathomable messages that can, on the one hand, belie understanding, or, on the other, expose the psychotic to unique revelations sent only to them. This suggests that in critically examining, as well as applying, Lacan's conception of psychosis, one should not necessarily pay too close attention to the psychotic's imagination, but, rather, to how Imaginary dynamics take shape within a Symbolic structure that reveals its own disturbances. To fully appreciate the influence of these disturbances, we can turn to the effects of alienation and its impact on the subject's racialization.

Non-castration and psychosis

In psychoanalysis, the subject is constitutively alienated in the signifier.[15] In elaborating on this point, Lacan would draw from structural linguistics in order to emphasize how the distinctions that Freud made between the subject and the object were dependent upon the subject's alienation in language (McGowan 2013). Here, the relation between the subject and the objects that it engages with is forever mediated through the use of language, so that whenever the subject interacts with a specific object—a 'book', for example—they are never accessing the object itself. Instead, '[t]he subject's alienation into language deprives it of immediate contact with the object world … mean[ing] that the indirectness or mediation introduced by language deprives the subject of a direct relation to the object world that it never had' (McGowan 2013, 27). The key to these remarks is the fact that the subject never had 'a direct relation to the object world' and that their experiences of the object, and the world around them, is grounded in an inherent sense of loss (or lack). It is this experience of loss which serves to constitute the subject through 'an initial act of sacrifice' (McGowan 2013, 26). By sacrificing one's immediate access to the object through language, the distinction between subject and object is established. Without the subject experiencing this loss there would be no desire to engage with other objects or the various other subjects that they encounter.

On this basis, any human identity is predicated on the necessity of alienation: a prerequisite which fundamentally distinguishes between the chaos of the body and the procurement of an identity that is drawn from the outside world. This does not mean that we should dismiss our psychic alienation as presenting an inherently negative account of the subject; instead, what it does suggest is that it is only by reconciling oneself with alienation—the inherent sense of lack—that the subject's relation to the world and its sense of identity can be forged (Žižek 2022).

Furthermore, this does not mean that the subject simply 'accepts' their alienation (though it is constitutive). On the contrary, whether one subscribes to a particular identity, or chooses to resist or redefine the identity they have been prescribed, we are always encountering an inherent alienation: we are always engaging with identity 'as ontologically foreign' (Verhaeghe 2019, 370). In sum, despite the alienation that language establishes, its significance for the subject is required. McGowan asserts:

[t]hough language derails the subject's efforts at articulating itself, language is 'divine' because this derailment makes evident and enables the subject to grasp its lack of self-identity, which is what others who lack this derailing cannot do. The subject's alienation in language is the site of its freedom through self-division.

(2014, 9–10)

It is, therefore, through language that the subject's relation to the world is never 'whole', but instead, 'cut up' into parts, with each part differentiated by the Symbolic label it is prescribed. Whether one is referring to the necessary 'cut' or 'separation' that ascribes the subject's 'self-division', what each term collaboratively establishes is the subject's inherent paradox. That is, for the presence of the subject to exist, a fundamental absence is required. This absence is grounded in the subject's 'castration', which is not a literal castration of a body part, but a 'Symbolic castration' founded upon the alienation that language establishes—or, as McNulty suggests, 'the loss of full being to language' (2014, 56). It is through the Symbolic order that our 'encounter' with castration is played out in 'how we attempt to repress it or manage its effects, and how we go about developing an ethics in response to it' (McNulty 2014, 56).

Undoubtedly, this locates the subject in a precarious position, forever located in the paradox of requiring language in order to symbolize that which language forever prevents them from accessing. In the case of psychosis, this paradox bears a particular significance in that one's castration is denied. In fact, whereas the threat of castration is either repressed, as in the case of neurosis, or disavowed, in examples of perversion,[16] for the psychotic, castration is outright ignored—indeed, castration does not exist.

This can have a significant effect on the psychotic's relation to language. For example, consider Freud's (2003) famous account of the *fort-da* game: while watching his 18-month grandson play with a cotton reel, Freud noted how the child's enjoyment stemmed primarily from throwing the reel ('*fort*', meaning 'gone'), which was subsequently retrieved and given back to them ('*da*', meaning 'there') by the child's parent. Though, for Freud, the game signified a fundamental relation between the child and mother, for Lacan (2004), the game proved significant in emphasizing the importance of the 'cut' and the effects of separation for the subject.[17] In throwing away the reel (absence), and then it being returned (presence), the reel served to signify the child as an object separated from the mOther. Consequently:

[b]y thus staging the Other separating from the object (reel-baby) and then coming back to it, the infant understands the comings and goings of the Other as manifestations of her desire, on which the infant draws in order to and correspondingly become a desiring subject.

(Razon et al. 2017, 3)

What is more, it is with regard to the reel's separation that the child can conceive of itself as an object separate to the Other: that is, as the object a.[18] It is here that we can begin to see how 'the *objet petit a* ... arises at the very place of castration' (Žižek 2008, 58). The presence of the *objet a* can only ever be accessed through the process of its very absenting—the 'cut' enacted between the *fort* and the *da*.

It is, however, without the cut—that is, without the *fort-da* distinction—that the subject is left without castration, and, thus, lacks the very creativity which underscores their relation to the Symbolic order. It is for this reason that the psychotic 'has rejected all means of access to castration' and thus 'all access to the register of the symbolic function' (Lacan 1997, 13). Without castration, the psychotic loses the very Symbolic support which can only ever be provided through the subject's 'sacrifice' to Symbolic castration. This draws attention to Lacan's unique reversal of Freud's castration complex, insofar as it is not the threat of castration that is significant for the subject, but the threat of *not* being castrated (Zupančič 2008).

Psychosis and the forced choice

For Lacan, there is always a 'treasure trove of signifiers' (2006f, 682) from which every speech act requires a selection. While the previous section highlights the effects of castration upon this selection, the subject is, nonetheless, forced to choose from these signifiers in order to communicate. It is through this 'forced choice' that the effects of alienation can be considered.

In his use of the example, 'your money or your life', Lacan (2004) demonstrates the importance of the forced choice and the irreducible loss that frames one's act of choosing. For example, when faced with the dilemma of choosing between one's money or one's life, we come to realise that it is not simply a case of choosing one and losing the other. Rather, whichever choice one makes, loss remains constitutive. If I choose my life, I have life but no money to live; if I choose money, then I have no life in which to spend it. The choice, therefore, is asymmetrical: I can only ever choose 'my life'—the (forced) choice is decided for me.[19]

We can take this example of the forced choice and apply it to the structure of the cogito.[20] Here, the division between thought and being can be expressed through the Cartesian 'I think' and 'I am', with 'the subject ... forced to choose between the two as part of its condition of entry into the field of the Symbolic order' (Flisfeder 2021, 172). Drawing upon Lacan and Žižek's discussion of this choice, Flisfeder highlights that the choice between thought and being 'becomes a foundational forced choice for the subject' (2021, 172).

Moreover, by sticking to Lacan's (2004) introduction of the forced choice, we can uncover the significance of this fundamental choice and its effects upon the subject.[21] This can be found in Lacan's account of alienation and separation. In what Lacan refers to as 'the *vel* of alienation' (2004, 211), the dilemma proposed between thought and being is accounted for. That is, while the subject is left choosing between thought devoid of being (and, therefore, thought itself) or a being without thought, there remains an inherent ambiguity to this choice; an inherent contradiction that is constitutive of the subject's alienation: indeed, as 'that by which man enters into the way of slavery' (Lacan 2004, 212).

Under the logic of psychosis, this choice takes on a unique significance. Indeed, while it is clear that '[w]ithout alienation, there is psychosis' (Fink 1999, 195), it is apparent that psychosis presents its own form of alienation. This is not the alienation which Felix Guattari sought to treat—whereby the act of treating psychosis was predicated upon the inherent socializing of the treatment itself (Thornton 2018)—but a total alienation or, rather, an 'inescapable alienation' (Hook 2022, 135) that prescribes the psychotic an 'all-encompassing subjectivity' (Žižek 2014, 72) or a 'psychotic suffocation' (Žižek 2022, 280).[22] In clinical treatment, there are variations as to the severity of alienation in psychosis, with discrepancies being drawn between such a total alienation and examples where the psychotic subject manages to 'escape' Symbolic alienation. It is in the case of the latter, however, that we see a return of the forced choice: even if the psychotic 'does not enter into the initial alienation in the chain of ideas from the parent', they are, nonetheless, always subject to the laws of the signifier, if only on the basis that, for them, '[w]ords seem to have no effect' (Leader 2012, 154). In either case, the psychotic suffers a form of alienation far removed from the constitutive alienation that is prescribed to the subject of the signifier.

In fact, Lacan goes so far as to suggest that psychotic alienation is an 'alienation [that] is radical' (1997, 205). This alienation is radical for Lacan because the psychotic holds no 'space' from which to delineate their relation to the signifier and, thus, their subjectivity. Without experiencing the constitutive effects of alienation there remains no creativity in the identifications that the psychotic adopts. As a result, the social identities which they ascribe to are fully performed. The radical nature of this alienation is prescribed through the all-encompassing social life narratives that the psychotic can adopt, and which are similar to the previously discussed 'as if behaviours'. Again, what we see here is the lack of any gap for which the psychotic can navigate their existence. More importantly, it is in masking this 'gap' that we can begin to explore the role of race in aiding psychotic alienation.

Race and psychotic alienation

In his account of Lacan's forced choice, George highlights how, in the case of slavery, it is the slave 'who is forced to attain subjectivity via the signifier of the Other' (2014, 364). Accordingly, in a replaying of the forced choice, the slave's 'subjugation [is] justified by his racial identity', so that 'the slave thus personifies and makes manifest the condition of alienation inherent to all subjectivity' (George 2014, 364). Echoing the forced choice, 'your freedom or your life' (Lacan 2004), the slave is forced to choose a life deprived of freedom. Consequently, it is in the forced choice that the slave's racial identity serves as the very crux of their subjugation.

However, what can be added to George's (2014) account is the extent to which this racial identity comprises the raced subject's alienation as well as the 'choice' it avers. Here, racial difference works to fix the subject to the 'naturalness' of *their* race, thus neutralizing the subject's constitutive alienation through a psychotic formation. In other words, what one's racialization induces is a psychotic alienation that ties one to the total alienation of *their* race. It is in this fight with the alienating effects of psychosis that the only 'true' escape from alienation—accepting one's constitutive alienation—is obscured through a psychotic 'existential self-destruction' (George 2016, 121).[23]

Indeed, what this self-destruction ultimately rests upon is an obfuscation of the 'gap' that constitutes the subject. This 'gap' is underscored by the fact that, for any subject, there remains a division between who they think they are (their own Imaginary constructions) and what they are assigned (social Symbolic roles, such as, 'father', 'wife', or 'king'). In effect, 'how I am socially recognized, my social or symbolic identity, ... is always qualified by a minimal gap' (Hook 2012, 127), which, in and of itself, serves to constitutes one's subjectivity as well as the various (mis)communications that frame and generate our social interactions.

This gap speaks to the way in which race works through its own forms of essentializing that reduces the subject to either biology or culture. What is important is that such forms of essentialization (inherently false) should not be reified as distinct categories separating, for example, White from Black. Ultimately, the forced choice is, for all subjects, a constitutive feature of being a subject. Essentially, what remains 'false' in the forced choice is not the 'force' it expels, but the 'choice' it provides. All subjects are 'forced' to choose the only available 'choice'. All subjects are, to this extent, subjected to the (forced) choice, so that when one is prescribed *their* race it is the very nature of the forced choice that is obscured and/or excluded in the essentialization of racial difference. It is in this way that race functions to mask the subject's constitutive alienation.

Racial prescription: alienation and desubjectivation

What remains essential to race is the way it seeks to mask and obscure the gap which the forced choice avails. In cases of neurosis, and, specifically, the hysteric, one's Symbolic role is always questioned. Indeed, as Hook asserts, 'Symbolic roles ... are not groundless; reasons can be given for them, it's just that ... the grounds for the grounds remain questionable' (2012, 127). What is important, however, is that '[a] gap of sorts must open, otherwise unbearable anxiety—or the prospect of psychosis—will result' (Hook 2022, 135).

The importance of this 'gap' can be seen in Descartes's well-known account of the subject, as 'I think, therefore, I am' (*cogito, ergo sum*). It is against Descartes that we can fully grasp the importance of the 'gap' for Lacan, as evident in his reply: 'I am not, where I am the plaything of my thought; I think about what I am where I do not think I am thinking' (2006d, 430). For Lacan, the subject does not 'appear' in either thought or being, rather, 'it is the very alterity of self-recognition that allows the subject to be. ... *[T]he self that is recognised must be other than the self that recognises itself in it*' (Murray 2016, 120, italics in original). Consequently, while 'Descartes worked to occlude the gap between the self that recognises and the self that is recognised' (Murray 2016, 120), we can trace a similar occlusion in the case of psychosis: one in which there is no 'gap' (or recognition of the 'gap'), but instead an over-proximity to the Other and a failure to acknowledge one's alienation.[24]

Considered through a Lacanian lens, we can determine how the Cartesian gesture posits its own recital of the forced choice. In Descartes's 'I think, therefore I am' (*cogito, ergo sum*), what is relegated to being is thought itself, or, rather, what is procured is a form of being from which thought is made unconscious so that 'the current notion of "thinking" relies on a tacit choice, a rejection of thought that relegates it to the unconscious' (Dolar 1998, 29). In fact, by reversing Descartes's *cogito, ergo sum*, Dolar notes that:

> it should be read as *sum, ergo cogito*, the choice of being to found thought, but this is what strikes with inanity the thought produced by this choice. The forced choice of *sum, ergo cogito* is the invisible truth of the Cartesian gesture.
>
> (1998, 29)

What this forced choice of *sum, ergo cogito* expounds is the sense in which being is 'nothing' but a gap (or contradiction) in being itself: in a deliberately contradictory form, being is a nothing that is something. We can rephrase this slightly so that being is a hole that is itself an object: a no-*thing* (Zupančič 2005). The paradoxes of the forced choice, therefore, can be seen in the constitution of being, whereby if 'one [were to] choose being, one would have to espouse the object, precisely the object that Lacan has labelled *objet a*, the object that detains being, but a being over which one cannot be master' (Dolar 1998, 19). Such espousal lays claim to a position of psychosis, from which the presence of the *objet a* posits its own 'desubjectivation' (Dolar 1998).

Read in this light, what choice does the psychotic make? Subject to its own 'desubjectivation', is it possible for the psychotic to choose? What occurs in such a dilemma is a choice that one never had the choice in choosing, or, as Braunstein asserts, '[t]he lesson of psychosis ... is that there is no choice; psychosis is not a choice' (2015, 85)—in other words, there is no reconciliation with the forced choice and the freedom therein. Importantly, this does not suggest that the psychotic is 'free' *not* to choose, but what the psychotic takes seriously is the choice itself (Žižek 2000). In psychosis, what is chosen is the very fact that the choice is made for them, so that, through the imposition of *the* choice, the psychotic's responsibility (in choosing) is obscured.

It is this 'choice' that race assuages, indeed, 'an apparatus of being', which, as George explains, serves 'as a tool for masking the central lack of subjectivity' (2014, 360). In effect, race masks through its very naturalness, absolving the subject from the act of choosing. One does not necessarily 'choose' their race but is instead prescribed *their* race. This racial prescription is confirmed by an assumed set of racial markers that function to delineate, as well as assign, the subject *their* race. Here, '[t]he biological fact of phenotypic variations functions in racial discourse as race's alibi, masking the inherent arbitrariness of racial distinction by internalizing and eternalizing difference as an embodied permanency' (George 2016, 40). By 'masquerading as an inherent component of nature indicative of visible, natural variations in groups of humans' (George 2016, 40), race remains an endowed prescription that 'naturally' determines one's racial being. It is when one chooses to refuse this prescription that trouble ensues. We are reminded here of the case of Rachel Anne Dolezal (Nkechi Amare Diallo), a former education director in the U.S., who identified as Black and claimed Black ancestry, despite being born to White parents. Whether or not one believed that Dolezal had committed herself to a life of racial appropriation, what seemed to underscore the frustrations and anger directed towards Dolezal was the very fact that she had the gall to 'choose'. Subsequently, when set against an investment in the phenotypic categories that race presents, race is 'not at all malleable' (Seshadri-Crooks 2000, 4). In fact, '[w]e cannot change it because race is supposedly inscribed on one's body' (Seshadri-Crooks 2000, 4).

Accordingly, if, following George, 'race functions to occlude the space of this gap and thereby compounds the alienation in the Symbolic that is experienced by the subject' (2014, 360), then we can begin to determine how race's occlusion of the forced choice avers a unique form of psychotic alienation. This can be conceived as signalling the psychotic's alienation *from* the Symbolic as opposed to their alienation *in* the Symbolic, so that, in effect, race refuses to maintain, or even uphold, the very gap which structures the subject's creative relation to the signifier and the process of signification.

This is not to suggest that race bears no relation to the Symbolic. Instead, when confined to one's 'being'—to the 'apparatus of being' that race provides (George 2014, 360)—a scaffold is erected from which some form of being is achieved for the subject. This being, however, is complicated by the fact that its articulation can only ever be conceived and expressed through the Symbolic. By providing a position in relation to being, the racialization of the subject follows a psychotic formation, through which the subject's being, as well as that of the other, becomes marked by the rigidity of the signifier. This functions to fix the subject's being to a prescribed racial classification.

Notes

1. In 1931, Aimée (Marguerite Pantaine) stabbed the French actress, Huguette Duflos, while suffering from psychosis. The title of Lacan's doctoral thesis is *De la psychose paranoïaque dans ses rapports avec la personnalité* (On paranoic psychosis as it relates to the personality) and was published in 1932.
2. Importantly, all three are 'different logics by means of which sense is made of the world, and nothing more' (Vanheule 2011a, 137).
3. These four eras map Lacan's theoretical trajectory. Here Lacan's account of psychosis follows: 1) the Imaginary; 2) the signifier; 3) the *objet a*; and 4) the Borromean knot, or the Real. See Vanheule (2011a) for further discussion of these eras.
4. Lacan's account of Joyce proves significant, if only for the fact that it effectively details how interpretations of Joyce's enigmatic prose, which was, at times, deliberately fragmentary, allowed him the possibility of living with psychosis—or at least preventing its more debilitating effects.
5. If we consider that 'normal' is often based upon a subject's ability not to confuse fantasy and reality then, as McGowan notes, '[s]uch normality, however, is impossible a priori: no one experiences reality without some fantasmatic investment. Which is to say that what we fantasize that we will see informs what we do see' (2007b, 16).
6. Echoing this, Žižek adds, 'we do not all have to be mad in reality, but madness is the reality of our psychic lives, a point to which our psychic lives necessarily refer in order to assert themselves as "normal"' (2022, 339).
7. Specifically, in considering the actions of the English serial killer, Harold Shipman, Leader asks '[w]ere the murders a sign of his madness or, in fact, a desperate attempt to cope with situations that had blocked his everyday, normal madness from functioning?' (2012, 275).
8. Unlike Svolos, I am hesitant to link the effects of ordinary psychosis to a decline in the Name-of-the-Father, specifically, its importance in examples of psychotic foreclosure, and the subsequent social and political repercussions that this establishes (Chapter 7 will introduce the significance of the Name-of-the-Father in psychosis) (Svolos and Rouselle 2022). Svolos notes that 'it would be fair to say we have moved away from universalism and a domination of the name-of-the-father in social and political formations' (Svolos and Rouselle 2022). While there is ample evidence to suggest that we are experiencing a general decline in the Name-of-the-Father as a form of authority, it is always in relation to this decline that the foreclosure of the Name-of-the-Father maintains its significance as something 'lost' or foreclosed. Instead, the decline of the Name-of-the-Father is a decline in its Symbolic efficiency (a position that rests upon the importance of the Name-of-the-Father in Symbolic interpretation). Even in cases where the subject's Symbolic mediation is disrupted or dislocated, there is always a Symbolic mediation of the Imaginary, which is tied to the Real.
9. This follows Svolos's allusion to the predominance of identity politics in contemporary politics and the prevalence of the Imaginary in bypassing Symbolic mediation (Svolos and Rouselle 2022). For Svolos, '[t]he imaginary is no longer subservient to the symbolic but has developed an autonomy of its own' (Svolos and Rouselle 2022). It is the 'autonomy' of the Imaginary as separated from Symbolic mediation, which, I believe, overplays the relevance of the Imaginary in Lacanian psychoanalysis and, specifically, psychosis. (To clarify, Svolos does not refer to a 'break' between the personal and social/political, but to a relationship where they are 'uncoupled' [Svolos and Rouselle 2022].)
10. McGowan offers further clarification when he notes that, '[t]he imaginary is simply a perspective within the symbolic, a way of seeing that fails to grasp its own symbolic determination' (2004, 19).

11 It was in his failure to relate to the signifier that Judge Schreber was subject to what he referred to as 'nerve-language': 'divine rays' that invaded his body, while also influencing and manipulating his behaviour (Schreber 2000).
12 It is on this basis that 'objective reality' is constituted for the subject. As Dolar notes, '[i]t is this loss of the object *a* that opens "objective" reality, the possibility of subject-object relations, but since its loss is the condition of any knowledge of "objective" reality, it cannot itself become an object of knowledge' (1991, 13).
13 This sense of being a 'stain' or a 'spot' in the image is accounted for when McGowan notes, 'you think that you are looking at the painting from a safe distance, but the painting sees you—takes into account your presence as a spectator' (2007a, 7). This is itself a reinterpretation of Lacan's (2004) story of his trip with the fishermen. While travelling on a fishing boat, Lacan spots a sardine can bobbing on the water's surface. Upon seeing the can, one of the fishermen says to Lacan, '[y]ou see that can? Do you see it? Well it doesn't see you!' Here, Lacan's presence on the fishing boat underscores the fact that he remains 'out of place' (he sees the can, but the can does not 'see' him). He is the 'stain' in the scenario.
14 In Lacan (2004), this line reappears on pp. 149 and 203.
15 This stands in contrast to a Marxist analysis, where alienation refers to the process of commodity fetishism and the capitalist mode of production.
16 Here, the neurotic employs a number of 'defences' that allow them to manage their castration. Repression enables the neurotic to obtain a limit to *jouissance*. As will be later discussed, the neurotic acknowledges the Name-of-the-Father, whereas, for the psychotic, the Name-of-the-Father is foreclosed. Thus, there is no limit to *jouissance* for the psychotic.
17 For this reason, castration presents a pivotal point in the subject's existence in the world, revealing how our Symbolic interactions and Symbolic supports provide various manifestations of dealing with the subject's inherent lack (the lack in the Real). These dealings are often encountered through the threat of castration. Again, not a literal threat, but a threat that is managed and transmitted through language, through the very 'cut' that *is* the subject: '[t]he subject is that cut itself, and what falls away through the action of cutting is the object' (Regnault 1995, 71). Following the curvature of a Mobius strip, '[i]t is interpretation that cuts the strip and produces both subject and object' (Regnault 1995, 71).
18 In a sense, it is through the absence of the object *a* that the subject can begin to relate to the presence of the Other, such as in the hysterical question: what object am I for the Other?
19 Importantly, the subject's indebtedness to the 'forced choice' should not be conceived as a 'false ideological choice'. This is apparent in Thakur, when he notes how 'citizens are given false choices in order to (mis)direct them from scrutinizing the real material conditions of social inequality. Following Hegel, Marx defined these forced choices as ideology' (2020, 178). Thakur adds that '[w]hat we need to do every time we are assaulted by such forced choices, … is to openly call their bluff' (2020, 178). By linking ideology with that of the forced choice, there is the latent suggestion that the act of critiquing ideology rests simply upon the realization that any ideology can be called out and overcome. What this ignores is the fact that such forms of critique are themselves reliant upon an ideological efficiency that presupposes its own critique.
20 As Dolar explains, 'the scene of the Lacanian cogito' occurs when 'one is pushed against the wall, the gun pointing at one's head, with an unfathomable voice crying out in the dark: "Your thought or your being! Make up your mind!"' (1998, 18).
21 Lacan's account of the division between thought and being, and its depiction in the forced choice, changes over the course of his seminars, with Flisfeder (2021) emphasizing that, for Žižek, the distinction between thought and being 'should be

read according to the two opposed logics of the masculine and the feminine in the sexual relationship' (Flisfeder 2021, 172).
22 In examples of non-psychosis, it is because 'the Other is lacking … that there is a remainder, an inertia that cannot be integrated into the Other' (Žižek 2014, 72). This remainder is the ambiguous *objet a*, which simultaneously posits both the lack in the Other as well as the excess that has no place in the Other. Importantly, 'the subject can avoid total alienation insofar as he posits himself as correlative to this remainder $ ◊ a' (Žižek 2014, 72). Such avoidance, however, does not take place in psychosis.
23 George (2016) considers the effects of this self-destruction in relation to Lacan's (1977) account of Hamlet, where he notes that '[Hamlet] escapes alienation from the Symbolic only by sacrificing the life he leads in it. Hamlet thus represents the dangerous path the subject embraces in his or her pursuits of freedom from alienation, displaying the psychic perils that … confront … African Americans in their battles against an alienating and oppressive social structure' (George 2016, 121).
24 We can appreciate the effects of the 'gap' in the formal structure of film, most notably, in examples where a 'cut' is used. In his analysis of the film, *Us* (Peele 2019), McGowan highlights how the cut between, what is believed to be, two disparate scenes in the film's prelude can 'also creat[e] a gap in our knowledge as spectators' (2019, 65). He adds: '[t]he gap in our knowledge that the cut enacts constitutes the narrative structure of the film. We cannot overcome this gap, not even through the flashback that fills in what the cut has elided. This gap in our knowledge produces the structure of the film, just like the lack in subjectivity constitutes the subject' (McGowan 2019, 65).

References

Benvenuto, Sergio. 2020. *Conversations with Lacan: Seven Lectures for Understanding Lacan*. London, UK: Routledge.
Braunstein, Nestor. 2015. "'You cannot choose to go crazy'." In *Lacan on Madness: Madness, yes you can't*, edited by Patricia Gherovici and Manya Steinkoler (85–98). Hove, UK: Routledge.
Burnham, Clint. 2018. *Does the Internet Have an Unconscious? Slavoj Žižek and Digital Culture*. New York, NY: Bloomsbury.
Deutsch, Hélène. 1942. "Some forms of emotional disturbance and their relationship to schizophrenia." *The Psychoanalytic Quarterly* 11: 301–321.
Dolar, Mladen. 1991. "'I shall be with you on your wedding-night': Lacan and the Uncanny." *October* 58: 5–23.
Dolar, Mladen. 1998. "Cogito as the subject of the unconscious." In *Cogito and the Unconscious, Sic 2*, edited by Slavoj Žižek (11–40). Durham, NC: Duke University Press.
Fink, Bruce. 1997. *The Lacanian Subject: Between Language and Jouissance*. Princeton, NJ: Princeton University Press.
Fink, Bruce. 1999. *A Clinical Introduction to Lacanian Psychoanalysis: Theory and Technique*. Cambridge, MA: Harvard University Press.
Flisfeder, Matthew. 2021. *Algorithmic Desire: Toward a New Structuralist Theory of Social Media*. Evanston, IL: Northwestern University Press.
Freud, Sigmund. 1981. *The Case of Schreber, Papers on Technique, and Other Works. The Standard Edition of the Complete Psychological Works of Sigmund Freud, Volume XII, 1911–1913*. London, UK: The Hogarth Press.

Freud, Sigmund. 2003. *Beyond the Pleasure Principle and Other Writings*, translated by John Reddick. London, UK: Penguin.

George, Sheldon. 2014. "From alienation to cynicism: race and the Lacanian unconscious." *Psychoanalysis, Culture & Society* 19, no. 4: 360–378.

George, Sheldon. 2016. *Trauma and Race: A Lacanian Study of African American Racial Identity.* Waco, TX: Baylor University Press.

Hamza, Agon. 2019. "Žižek and the dialectical materialist theory of belief." In *Slavoj Žižek and Christianity*, edited by Sotiris Mitralexis and Dionysios Skliris (46–66). Abingdon, UK: Routledge.

Hook, Derek. 2012. "Towards a Lacanian group psychology: the prisoner's dilemma and the trans-subjective." *Journal for the Theory of Social Behaviour* 43, no. 2: 115–132.

Hook, Derek. 2022. "The object of apartheid desire: a Lacanian approach to racism and ideology." In *Lacan and Race: Racism, Identity, and Psychoanalytic Theory*, edited by Sheldon George and Derek Hook (121–145). Abingdon, UK: Routledge.

Kunkle, Sheila. 2008. "Embracing the paradox: Žižek's illogical logic." *International Journal of Žižek Studies* 2, no. 4: 1–21.

Lacan, Jacques. 1977. "Desire and the interpretation of desire in *Hamlet*." *Yale French Studies, Special Issue Literature and Psychoanalysis: The Question of Reading Otherwise* 55/56: 11–52.

Lacan, Jacques. 1997. *The Seminar of Jacques Lacan, Book III, 1955–56: The Psychoses*, edited by Jacques-Alain Miller. London, UK: Routledge.

Lacan, Jacques. 2006a. "The mirror stage as formative of the *I* function as revealed in psychoanalytic experience." In *Écrits. The First Complete Edition in English*, translated by Bruce Fink, in collaboration with Heloise Fink and Russell Grigg (75–81). London, UK: W. W. Norton & Company.

Lacan, Jacques. 2006b. "Aggressiveness in psychoanalysis." In *Écrits. The First Complete Edition in English*, translated by Bruce Fink, in collaboration with Heloise Fink and Russell Grigg (82–101). London, UK: W. W. Norton & Company.

Lacan, Jacques. 2006c. "The function and field of speech and language in psychoanalysis." In *Écrits. The First Complete Edition in English*, translated by Bruce Fink, in collaboration with Heloise Fink and Russell Grigg (197–268). London, UK: W. W. Norton & Company.

Lacan, Jacques. 2006d. "The instance of the letter in the unconscious, or reason since Freud." In *Écrits. The First Complete Edition in English*, translated by Bruce Fink, in collaboration with Heloise Fink and Russell Grigg (412–444). London, UK: W. W. Norton & Company.

Lacan, Jacques. 2006e. "On a question preliminary to any possible treatment of psychosis." In *Écrits. The First Complete Edition in English*, translated by Bruce Fink, in collaboration with Heloise Fink and Russell Grigg (445–488). London, UK: W. W. Norton & Company.

Lacan, Jacques. 2006f. "The subversion of the subject and the dialectic of desire in the Freudian unconscious." In *Écrits. The First Complete Edition in English*, translated by Bruce Fink, in collaboration with Heloise Fink and Russell Grigg (671–702). London, UK: W. W. Norton & Company.

Lacan, Jacques. 2007. *The Seminar of Jacques Lacan, Book XVII: The Other Side of Psychoanalysis*, edited by Jacques-Alain Miller, translated by Russell Grigg. New York, NY: W. W. Norton & Company.

Lacan, Jacques. 2014. *The Seminar of Jacques Lacan, Book X: Anxiety*, edited by Jacques-Alain Miller, translated by A. R. Price. Cambridge, UK: Polity.
Lacan, Jacques. 2018. *The Seminar of Jacques Lacan, Book XXIII: The Sinthome*, edited by Jacques-Alain Miller. Cambridge, UK: Polity.
Leader, Darian. 2012. *What is Madness?* London, UK: Penguin.
McGowan, Todd. 2004. *The End of Dissatisfaction? Jacques Lacan and the Emerging Society of Enjoyment*. Albany, NY: State University of New York Press.
McGowan, Todd. 2007a. *The Real Gaze: Film Theory after Lacan*. Albany, NY: State University of New York Press.
McGowan, Todd. 2007b. *The Impossible David Lynch*. New York, NY: Columbia University Press.
McGowan, Todd. 2013. *Enjoying What We Don't Have: The Political Project of Psychoanalysis*. Lincoln, NE: University of Nebraska Press.
McGowan, Todd. 2014. "The insubstantiality of substance, or, why we should read Hegel's *Philosophy of Nature*." *International Journal of Žižek Studies* 8, no. 1: 1–19.
McGowan, Todd. 2019. "Two forms of fetishism: from the commodity to revolution in US." *Galactica Media: Journal of Media Studies* 1: 63–87.
McGowan, Todd. 2020. "The object of cinema." *Crisis & Critique* 7, no. 2: 229–243.
McNulty, Tracy. 2014. *Wrestling with the Angel: Experiments in Symbolic Life*. New York, NY: Columbia University Press.
Miller, Jacques-Alain. 2013. "Ordinary psychosis revisited." *Psychoanalytical Notebooks*, 26: 33–50.
Mills, Jon. 2019. "Lacan on paranoic knowledge." In *Lacan on Psychosis: From Theory to Praxis*, edited by Jon Mills and David L. Downing (10–46). London, UK: Routledge.
Murray, Martin. 2016. *Jacques Lacan: A Critical Introduction*. London, UK: Pluto Press.
Ragland, Ellie. 1995. *Essays on the Pleasures of Death: From Freud to Lacan*. New York, NY: Routledge
Razon, Laure, Olivier Putois and Alan Vanier. 2017. "The Lacanian concept of cut in light of Lacan's interactions with Maud Mannoni." *Frontiers in Psychology* 8: 1–10.
Regnault, François. 1995. "The Name-of-the-Father." In *Reading Seminar XI: Lacan's Four Fundamental Concepts of Psychoanalysis*, edited by Richard Feldstein, Bruce Fink, and Maire Jaanus (65–76). Albany, NY: State University of New York Press.
Schreber, Daniel Paul. 2000. *Memoirs of My Nervous Illness*, translated and edited by Ida Macalpine and Richard A. Hunter. New York, NY: New York Review of Books.
Seshadri-Crooks, Kalpana. 2000. *Desiring Whiteness: A Lacanian Analysis of Race*. London, UK: Routledge.
Svolos, Thomas, and Duane Rouselle. 2022. "Psychoanalysis and politics: Duane Rouselle interviews Thomas Svolos." *European Journal of Psychoanalysis*. https://www.journal-psychoanalysis.eu/articles/psychoanalysis-and-politics-duane-rouselle-interviews-thomas-svolos/.
Thakur, Gautam Basu. 2020. *Postcolonial Lack: Identity, Culture, Surplus*. Albany, NY: State University of New York Press.
Thornton, Edward. 2018. "Two's a crowd." *Aeon*, March 1. https://aeon.co/essays/a-creative-multiplicity-the-philosophy-of-deleuze-and-guattari.
Vanheule, Stijn. 2011a. *The Subject of Psychosis: A Lacanian Perspective*. Basingstoke, UK: Palgrave Macmillan.

Vanheule, Stijn. 2011b. "A Lacanian perspective on psychotic hallucinations." *Theory & Psychology* 21, no. 1: 86–106.
Vanheule, Stijn. 2019. "On ordinary psychosis." In *Lacan on Psychosis: From Theory to Praxis*, edited by Jon Mills and David L. Downing (77–102). London, UK: Routledge.
Vanheule, Stijn. 2020. "On a question prior to any possible treatment to psychosis." In *Reading Lacan's Ecrits: From Écrits: From 'The Freudian Thing' to 'Remarks on Daniel Lagache*, edited by Derek Hook, Calum Neill and Stijn Vanheule (163–205). London, UK: Routledge.
Verhaeghe, Paul. 2019. "Lacan's answer to alienation: separation." *Crisis & Critique* 6, no. 1: 365–388.
Žižek, Slavoj. 2000. *The Ticklish Subject: The Absent Centre of Political Ontology*. London, UK: Verso.
Žižek, Slavoj. 2008. *The Plague of Fantasies*. London, UK: Verso.
Žižek, Slavoj. 2014. *The Most Sublime Hysteric: Hegel with Lacan*. Cambridge, UK: Polity.
Žižek, Slavoj. 2022. *Surplus Enjoyment*. London, UK: Bloomsbury.
Zupančič, Alenka. 2005. "Reversals of nothing: the case of the sneezing corpse." *Filozofski vestnik* 26, no. 2: 173–186.
Zupančič, Alenka. 2008. *Why Psychoanalysis? Three Interventions*. Aarhus, DK: Aarhus University Press.

Chapter 5

The object *a* of race

According to Zupančič, it is a fear of *not* being castrated that underscores Lacan's account of anxiety:

> [t]his is why anxiety is usually not related to symbolic prohibitions but rather to them being lifted. It is the loss of this support that results in the apparition of those ghastly objects through which the lack in the real is present in the symbolic as an absolute 'too-muchness', ghastly objects which dislodge the object of desire and make appear, in its place, the cause of desire.
>
> (2008, 52–53)

Consequently, '[w]e experience anxiety when the absence that castration produces—the lost object, or *objet petit a*—ceases to be an absence' (McGowan 2013, 113). Or, as Seshadri-Crooks explains, '[i]t is as if the jigsaw puzzle were complete, but there were still a piece left over for which there is no place' (2000, 45). It is in this sense that castration plays a reassuring role for the subject, establishing the Symbolic distance that allows the subject the space to 'creatively' engage with the world around them as well as the other subjects they encounter. By denying the cut of castration, and the absence of the object *a* ('fort'), the psychotic does not achieve separation from the Other, and, as a result, is left without desire. Thus, it is in the presence of the object *a* that the subject is met with an anxiety that seeks its very translation through examples of racialization.

Racial anxiety, racial visibility, and the lack of a lack

In psychosis, the object *a* bears no virtual significance; it is, instead, a tangible object, appearing, as Lacan recites, in the 'pocket' of the psychotic (Vanheule 2011b, 99). This endows the object *a* with a presence, a real and imposing presence that further confirms the lack of separation between the psychotic and their object *a*. As a result, 'in psychosis the object *a* is not an external element that fuels desire in the subject, but a strange internal element the

DOI: 10.4324/9781003414209-8

subject has to manage' (Vanheule 2011a, 137). In the psychosis of race, it is this 'strange internal element' that finds its expression and management in acts of racialization.

Indeed, while 'the idea of the non-extracted object a suggests that *being* also poses a problem' (Vanheule 2011a, 138, italics in original), we can begin to see how such problems emerge from the fact that the object *a* remains a unique object, an object that 'has no substantial consistency of its own' (Žižek 2012, 175). It remains an impossible object, not just in the sense that it does not exist as a literal object, but that, for the non-psychotic, the object *a* remains separated.[1] In effect, the importance of the object *a* is that it stands as a place holder for the void or gap in reality, which, as nothing more than a cover for this gap, works to maintain reality for the subject. That there is a cover for this void/gap, does not reveal the void, but the fact of the cover itself. It is in this sense that the psychotic is left with the anxiety of facing the lack of a lack. Zupančič comments on the effects of this encounter:

> [t]he constitutive lack which, precisely as a lack, supports our symbolic universe and its differentiations, comes to be lacking. What emerges in its place is an 'impossible', surplus object that has no place in given reality and blatantly contradicts its laws.
>
> (2005, 181)

It is this 'surplus' which is experienced in the visibility of race. For Sheshadri-Crooks, '[r]acial identity seeks or locates its consistency on a different level—not meaning, but visibility—in order to retain paradoxically a semblance of lack or something extra-symbolic' (2000, 26). The paradoxes at play here—'a semblance of [one's constitutive] lack' and the 'some*thing* extra-symbolic'—remain fundamental to the psychotic position and the difficulties it establishes.

We can conceive of these paradoxes as born from the lack of a lack: a lack which is in and of itself lacking. To fully appreciate this uniqueness, it is important to remember that the most consistent characterization of the object *a* is the fact that it remains a 'positivization of a lack' (Žižek 2012, 175). Connections can be drawn here between this 'positivization of a lack' and Lacan's account of anxiety, whereby the 'sudden emergence of lack in a positive form is the source of anxiety' (2014, 61). It is in taking this positive form that examples of race are made visible: that the 'natural' presence of perceived racial differences become fixed to racial distinctions which elicit the 'chaos' and anxiety that the presence of such difference invites. Moreover, it is in encountering the lack of a lack, that 'the raced subject experiences anxiety' (Sheshadri-Crook 2000, 45). Seshadri-Crook notes:

> [t]here is a lack of a lack as it appears in that place that should have remained empty. It is a false door opening not onto a nowhere, but to an all-too-concrete wall. This anxiety then produces the uncanny object of

race, the arbitrary marks of the body, namely hair, skin, and bone. These marks then are properly the desiderata of race; they serve the function of the *objet a*.

(2000, 38)

Accordingly, inasmuch as 'it is a phobic object which ultimately sustains the body image' it is 'the racial body [that] is produced in just such a process' (Sheshadri-Crook 2000, 37). When considered through the structure of psychosis, it is this 'phobic object' which is derived from the *presence* of the lost object: the object *a*.

This function is brought to bear through acts of racism, where 'the presence of *objet a* as an unbearable torment' is experienced (Salecl 2002, 108). It also underscores those arguments that seek to associate certain bodily features as biologically determining one's particular race. For example, insofar as 'the human body [is] represented as the fundamental repository of the order of racial truth' (Gilroy 2000, 77), it is possible for Gilroy to affirm that:

[h]owever dissimilar individual bodies are, the compelling idea of common, racially indicative bodily characteristics offers a welcome short-cut into the favored forms of solidarity and connection, even if they are effectively denied by divergent patterns in life chances and everyday experience.

(2000, 25)

If the body is defined by forms of racial characterization, then what compels such characterizations to maintain their legitimacy can be found in the fact that 'race asserts its existential veracity through appeal to the eyes, through assertion of a natural and visible difference, marked in skin color' (George 2016, 39). Such appeal is made apparent in the positioning that race bestows, as noted in Fanon's (2008) epidermalization of inferiority. Here, the effects of a 'racial epidermal schema' work to prescribe a racial embodiment grounded in inferiority and racial stereotype (Fanon 2008, 84). As a result, one's racial classification becomes beholden to a tautology whereby race is clearly and visibly determined by the presence of one's racial visibility.

It is therefore in accordance with the object *a* that George (2016; 2022) conceives of the subject's racialization. Through the object *a* of race, a prescribed 'racial essence distinct to each racial group', which 'provides structure and coherence to fantasies of difference', the subject's racial 'essence' is determined and fixed (George 2016, 5, see also George 2022). Although this prescribed essence remains illusory, it nonetheless provides the basis upon which the subject's racialization—the path of racially marking and signifying the subject (such as attributing certain racial criteria to one's location in a particular racial group)—is formed.

Indeed, the presence of the object *a*, conceived from this point onwards as the object *a* of race, does not suggest a simple psychologizing of race, from which racism is nothing more than a projection of the psychotic's anxiety onto the other. Rather, as Seshadri-Crooks (2000) highlights, it is the *presence* of the object *a* of race, marked by one's skin colour and supposed racial attributes, that results in racial anxiety. Indeed, such racial fixity, and the subsequent anxiety it establishes, underpins the failure of psychosis to effectively mediate the subject's relation to the object *a*. Here, the positivization of lack takes on an added significance. In psychosis, the effects of this positivization can be deduced by the fact that while the psychotic remains tied to a level of Symbolic fixity, they fail to achieve the mediation that is required in navigating such fixity. The psychotic is placed amid the suffocating presence of the object *a*—a positivization of one's very lack—and the failure to manage or mediate this presence. The object *a* is, in effect, too much for the psychotic.

With regards to race, it is in the fixity of one's racial prescription—a prescription that seems to be 'naturally' endowed—that the mediation required to navigate such a prescription can result in examples of racial anxiety, paranoia, and tension, from which no distance to the object *a* or the Other is achieved. In fact, '[t]he psychotic's problem … is not that he dwells in a truncated symbolic order (Other), but … that he dwells in a "complete" Other, an Other which lacks the inscription of its lack' (Žižek 2012, 863). What is more, the lack of any inscribed lack does not present a sense of constitutive 'fullness', but an empty fullness: indeed, a confrontation with '[t]he void [that] is *not nothing*' (Ragland 1995b, 199, italics in original).

Accordingly, whereas '[t]he subject's attempts to name her lack are transient at best, giving her access to no permanent meaning, no solid identity, no unitary narrative of self-actualization', and while '[a]ny fleeting state of fullness or positivity that the subject may be able to attain must always in the end dissolve back into negativity; any endeavor to erase lack only gives rise to new instances of lack' (Ruti 2008, 491), in psychosis, it is the presence of the object *a*—the lack of a lack—that arrests any instance of the 'new'. Instead, what plagues the psychotic's relation to the manifested object *a* is that 'the subject cannot rely on it' (Vanheule 2020, 187). Such unreliability can again be traced to Lacan's account of anxiety, which he defines as 'not without object'. Lacan adds:

> [t]his relation of being *not without having* doesn't mean that one knows which object is involved. When I say, *He's not without resources, He's not without cunning*, it means, at least for me, that his resources are obscure, his cunning isn't run of the mill.
>
> (2014, 89, italics in original)

What is expressed in these remarks is the inherent opacity of the object *a*. Paradoxically, while the object *a* is present in psychosis, it remains unknown and obscure.

The hole becomes an object

It is important not to understate the paradoxical nature of the object *a*; an object which remains, even in cases of psychosis, an object that can never be fully accessed. That is, its presence can only ever be achieved through a decidedly paradoxical and uncanny form, which is brought to bear in psychosis. To help account for this presence, we can consider how it is in accordance with the object *a*'s uncanny form that the lack of a lack resides. For instance, consider the following example from Zupančič:

> [t]ake the image of someone's eyes being plucked out (and appearing autonomously), an image that seems to haunt the human imaginary from a very early stage, and which is often associated with the uncanny. When analyzing the uncanny aspect of this image, one usually points out two things: 1) instead of the eyes, two empty holes yawn in the person's face. 2) Eyes themselves, once detached from the body, appear as ghastly, impossible objects. In relation to the first point, one has the tendency to assume that the holes are terrifying because of the lack they imply, i.e. because they are holes, empty corridors leading to uncertain depths. Yet is it not rather the opposite that is really ghastly? Namely, that instead of the eyes, which—on the imaginary level—always suggest an *in(de)finite depth*, an opening into a possibly inscrutable, bottomless dimension of subjectivity (eyes being considered as 'openings into a person's soul'), the holes instead of the eyes are *all too shallow*, all too finite, their bottom all too visible and close. So that, once again, what is horrifying is not simply the appearance (or disclosure) of a lack, but rather that the 'lack comes to lack', that this lack itself is removed, that it loses its support. One could say: the moment when the lack loses its symbolic or/and imaginary support, it becomes 'a mere hole', which is to say—an object. It is a nothing that, literally, remains (there) to be seen.
>
> (2005, 182, italics in original)

Do we not see something similar in the final scene of the 2001 horror film, *Jeepers Creepers* (Victor Salva)? As we are shown the hanging body of the film's protagonist, the camera slowly moves towards their face, upon which we see nothing but empty eye sockets; just holes where the eyes once were. What is even more disconcerting is that there is no back of the skull. Due to its removal, we see straight through the empty sockets to the space outside (this is emphasized as the camera slowly moves towards the empty sockets). While for Zupančič (2005), the holes, where the eyes once were, remain 'all too shallow', in *Jeepers Creepers*, the holes are all there is—both the eyes, the skull, and the brain have been removed so that the holes take on an ever-greater presence. It is in both accounts, however, that we get a sense of the object *a* in psychosis: it is not the lack of eyes that causes anxiety but the fact that the 'lack comes to lack'… 'the hole' becomes an 'object'.

In effect, while the object *a* bears no substance—a 'hole' made 'object'—it is in examples of anxiety that 'lack [... emerges] in a positive form' (Lacan 2014, 61). We can further elaborate upon the positive form of this lack by following the Lacanian contention that 'the constitution of reality presupposes an element "falling out" (of it), supporting—through its very lack—the consistency of given reality' (Zupančič 2008, 50). In other words, '[t]here is a constitutive lack, which is of a different order than any lack that we encounter in our reality' (Zupančič 2008, 50). It is along these lines that Zupančič 'distinguish[es] between two kinds of negativity: the fundamental negativity of a constitutive lack (which is never visible as such, but through which everything else becomes visible), and an asserted or "posited" negativity, lack, absence, etc.' (2008, 50). Importantly, it is in accordance with the constitutive lack that the Symbolic can mediate 'something' from 'nothing'.

However, in psychosis, it is the mediation of the constitutive lack that is disrupted insofar as this disruption fundamentally obscures the lack inherent to both the subject and the Symbolic order, as well as the space required to manage one's relation to the Symbolic order. Here, the 'asserted or "posited" negativity, lack, absence' is Real, since what is asserted or posited is a 'something' that can be stolen. Yet, what this 'something' *is* remains arbitrary: what is 'stolen' by the other is, in most cases, almost anything, conceived as either 'our jobs', 'our women', or 'our rights'. Equally, it is these same 'somethings' which must be protected, an encapsulation that often gets translated into 'our democracy' or 'our freedom'. Ultimately, what is ignored in what must be protected is the formal 'nothing' that undergirds the very existence of *that* which requires protection.

Therefore, while the object *a* is itself 'a "something that stands for nothing"' (Žižek 2008, 105), what is obscured in psychosis *is* the 'fundamental negativity of a constitutive lack' (Zupančič 2005, 181); or, in other words, the 'negative magnitude' that inheres to the object *a* (Žižek 2008). Žižek notes:

> [t]he basic premise of the Lacanian ontology is that if our experience of reality is to maintain its consistency, the positive field of reality has to be 'sutured' with a supplement which the subject (mis)perceives as a positive entity, but is effectively a 'negative magnitude'.
>
> (2008, 105)

For the non-psychotic, it is the object *a*'s 'negative magnitude' that is (mis) perceived as giving structure to 'positive' reality. It is this 'negative magnitude' that is lost amidst the presence of the object *a*:

> [w]hen, in psychotic experience, *objet petit a* is actually included in reality, this means that it no longer functions as a 'negative magnitude', but simply as another positive object: as for positive facts (objects of experience), there is nothing to distinguish a psychotic position from the

positions of a 'normal' subject; what a psychotic lacks is merely the dimension of 'negative' magnitude underpinning the presence of 'ordinary' objects.

(Žižek 2008, 105)

Consequently, when confronted with their object *a*—the visible presence and obvious experience of one's racial difference—the psychosis of race lacks the 'negative magnitude' underpinning 'ordinary' reality. In the psychosis of race, the object *a* is present as 'a quasi-object in the guise of which the lack assumes positive existence (appears as an object)' (Žižek 2017, 221). This 'positive existence' can be found in how the subject 'sees' the object (be it any racial feature) that visibly prescribes one *their race*.

We can elaborate on the effects of this 'quasi-object' by considering that if the object *a* of race 'has no substantial being of its own, [then it] is nothing but the positivization of a lack' (Žižek 2012, 175). Importantly, this is 'not a lacking object, but an object which positivizes a lack (negativity), whose positivity is nothing but a positivized negativity' (Žižek 2012, 175). Ultimately, as 'a strange internal element the subject has to manage' (Vanheule 2011a, 137), the object *a* constitutes a 'positivized negativity' that is materialized in the process of racialization and, thus, attributed to and possessed by the subject.

Therefore, when conceived as a positivized negativity, what the psychosis of race fails to grasp is the constitutive lack that the object *a* embodies. Indeed, without the 'negative magnitude' (Žižek 2008, 105)—without the inherent lack that constitutes both the subject and the Symbolic order—the psychotic is left with the lack of a lack (a positivized negativity). It is this lack of a lack, encapsulated in the very presence of the object *a*, which helps to signify in psychosis 'a structural incapacity/impasse that has been converted into an attribution of *the other's* inherent blameworthiness' (Hook 2022, 44, italics in original). By attributing an 'inherent blameworthiness' to the other, the capacity to produce meaning is forged through the use of certain racial stereotypes that seek to provide meaning where the lack of a lack is confronted (Seshadri-Crooks 2000).[2]

A troubling lack or a form of nothing

While for the non-psychotic there remains 'a search for the Lacanian *object a*, the fantasy object within the Symbolic, … that promises the subject completion' (George 2014, 361), in examples of psychosis, this object *a* is no longer searched for, but is instead 'obtained'. It is through the presence of the object *a* that 'an illusory relation to being' is upheld (George 2014, 361); one in which various forms of racism can take shape. Consider, for example, the case of fascism: 'what fascism obfuscates (forecloses even) is not the Symbolic as such but the gap that separates the Symbolic from the Real' (Žižek 2016, 180).[3] What is prescribed through this obfuscation is the demarcation of the other's racial difference; an act of racism whereby the Real finds its return in anxious and paranoid reactions to racial difference.

To help clarify this we can consider how in his account of psychosis Lacan makes it clear that 'what is refused in the symbolic order re-emerges in the real' (1997, 13); later adding, what is 'nonsymbolized reappears in the real' (1997, 86). In examples of racism, what returns in the Real are the various forms of social oppression that remain tethered to the signifier and to a Symbolic structure that racially prescribes and determines one's sense of being. Ruti notes:

> [s]uch signifiers immobilize the subject into debilitating nodes of meaning, marking it with—and making it the unwilling bearer of—the oppressor's aggression. They turn the deprivileged subject into an object of use for the oppressor (so that the subject becomes an instrument of the oppressor's sadistic jouissance).
>
> (2012, 80)

This debilitation not only refers to the alienating effects of the Symbolic structure—and those subject to structural forms of racism—but also to the racist fantasies, delusions, and paranoias that serve to uphold and maintain examples of racism. What returns in these latter examples are forms of racist aggression that should not simply be read as eruptions of violence (though racism can be found in acts of violence), but also as a return of the Real through acts of racial prescription that posit 'debilitating nodes of meaning' for the racialized.

It is here that the object *a* of race offers a certain consistency to the subject. Paradoxically, this consistency is best understood through the inconsistencies it evokes: an illusory guarantee to being that maintains a troubling lack or form of nothing; an indication of the Real that returns to racially mark and position the subject. In the U.S., the troubling significance of this process is outlined by George, who notes how:

> [t]he concept of race came to center African American identity because it not only augmented the signifier's essential function of striking being from the subject, actively restricting the slave's access to fantasies of self, but also presented itself as an object of contention that promised to re-establish the illusory existence of this being.
>
> (2016, 32)

It is this 'illusory existence' that affords *some* protection and consistency. In fact, while 'race is often exceedingly empowering for African Americans ... offer[ing] subjects a sense of direction, belonging, and self-worth' (George 2016, 32), such empowerment is not unlike the 'consistency' that can be obtained in certain psychotic formations (such as that discussed in the aforementioned 'ordinary psychosis' and 'as if' behaviours). Furthermore, what underscores this empowerment is how 'an external unit of information is adopted uncritically because of its reputed value in revealing a truth about the subject's being' (Vanheule 2011a, 26). In the context of one's racialization, this 'truth' is prescribed through a visible externality: 'an external unit of information', such as skin colour, that serves to prescribe one's racial difference. While Vanheule links this 'external unit of information' with Lacan's mirror stage and clinical paranoia, we can focus on how it is in accordance with this external unit that 'the subject believes that his own being is identified by what is revealed' (2011a, 26), insofar as what is revealed is the subject's racial being as an uninterrogated ground to reality.

This lack of interrogation finds its correlation in the ongoing connections between race and genetics. For Sheshadri-Crooks, 'the issue remains that destiny is not uncorrelated to genetics' inasmuch that 'no amount of argumentation disarticulating the two will do away with the fact that because *something* is inherited as "race," your life is predetermined for you' (2000, 16, italics in original). This predetermination is echoed in Gilroy's reference to 'the consolidation of a genomic raciology that promotes forms of resignation in which we are encouraged to do nothing while we wait for those decisive natural differences to announce their presence' (2000, 108). In both accounts, the 'existential condition' that race prescribes is echoed by the fact that we are 'born into a pre-existing symbolic constellation in which we must recognize the significance of our being' (Zupančič 2000, 176). It is in accordance with this recognition that the psychosis of race provides its own contradictions: delimiting one's being to a racial classification that unequally inhibits and restricts the subject just as much as it assumes to define and establish the subject's relation to the vagaries of this very being.

In psychosis, therefore, the object *a*'s '*lack of reality is part of its being*' (Tupinambá 2021, 128, italics in original). It is 'the form which attaches an otherness to its consistency, an otherness-to-reality' (Tupinambá 2021, 128).[4] This otherness is linked to the inherent (in)consistency of the object *a*, in that while the subject is prescribed a certain racial identity in the Symbolic— Black, White, etc.—they remain colours that are primarily prescribed and never embodied. As George asks: 'for who has ever seen a person who is *literally* white or black?' (2022, 249, italics in original). Instead, 'subjects become mottled, spotted, stained with a coloration that allows them to mimic a preexisting, racial Symbolic reality' (George 2022, 249).

We can now begin to determine how it is in accordance with the non-separation of the object *a* in psychosis that the object *a* of race is prescribed to the subject: a prescription that is confirmed and made visible in the bodily features that supposedly define one's race. The object *a* is what endows one with a racial inscription that is confirmed by the visibility of phenotypic variations that propose a certain permanence to one's racial being. It is 'the object *a* that is given body by … the racial or sexual other' (George 2016, 143, n.2), and, thus, is inherent to the process of racialization. This racial essentialization is indicative of the various visible differences that frame the human population, and which are considered to 'naturally' differentiate human groups.

For this reason, the object *a* refers to a host of uncanny attributes that underpin the subject's racialization—such as taste, clothes, food, and language—as well as the bodily marks that are used to assign otherness. Such denotations allow for differences to be conceived and fantasized. This is apparent in the racist's fantasmatic constructions of the other (who may steal one's object *a*); in the racial attributions that frame and position the victim of racism (as openly flaunting or enjoying their object *a*); and in the very way that racism delimits a hierarchization of race where one race is viewed above all others, as seen in examples of fascism (we must protect our object *a*). More importantly, there is the banality of these 'racial' features: indeed, a 'semiotic flexibility of race [that] plays differently across different bodies' (Winnubst 2004, 47, n.28). For no reason other than the visibility of difference itself, certain features are selected and delineated according to a racial logic based on nothing more than its own perpetuation. This results in forms of racial anxiety that expose the subject to the trauma of the other—*their very presence*.

'Us' and 'them'

In psychosis, the trauma of the other's presence stems from its inability to properly account for the other's difference (Ragland 1995a). Here, difference is inferred in the presence of an otherness that the psychotic struggles to separate from, and, thus, struggles to navigate. In fact, while the psychotic seeks to manage what they conceive as the intrusive presence of the other—their very otherness—it is in the trauma of confronting the object *a* that the subject's relation to difference is foreclosed.

This can be seen 'when we recognize the underlying similarity between one's parent and one's sexual partner' (McGowan 2007, 180). The exposed similarity is only ever negated when the object-cause of desire, that which the subject finds attractive about their sexual partner, 'remains under the guise of difference' (McGowan 2007, 180).[5] Without desire, difference is expunged, so what returns in psychosis is the trauma of the object *a*—its very presence.

What is more, if the function of the object *a* is to maintain its difference through a myriad of impossible objects that can never be accessed but which, nevertheless, work to orientate our desire, then, in psychosis, it is the presence of the object *a* of race that results in the renunciation of this *inherent difference* (the 'gap' which constitutes both the subject and the other; or the 'difference' that would make a difference [see Zupančič in Hamza and Ruda 2019]). In effect, it is only in the object *a*'s *absence* that the subject's desire, and, more importantly, the difference that sustains desire, is upheld. When this does not occur, when the traumatic presence of the object *a* is confronted, the foreclosing of difference '*returns in the Real*' (Žižek 2008, 211, italics in original). As noted, this return establishes itself 'in the guise of racism, which grounds political differences in the (biological or social) Real of the race' (Žižek 2008, 211). The effect of grounding political differences in the Real is that it reduces, essentializes, and, thus, fixes both the subject and the other to the particularity of one's biology or culture: a unique form of (non-)differentiation that erects and even forces 'difference' through the multiplicity of sameness (Black 2021).

Confined to the object *a*, we can begin to determine how examples of racial difference follow a rigid essentialization that functions to segregate between 'us' and 'them'. This act of segregation—an act that both locates one to a specific racial category, while at the same time differentiating oneself from other racial categories—can be identified in delusional forms of thinking which suggest their own psychotic formation. This is highlighted by Leader, who notes how, in psychosis, 'the world is divided up according to simple binary oppositions and two-place value judgements: pure and impure, good and bad, black and white, guilty and innocent, and so on' (2012, 326). In fact, when reduced to 'friend' and 'enemy', Davids outlines the following:

> [o]ne is not described as racist—it is always an *accusation*, for which one is condemned. Anything said in one's defence only makes it worse, and the only thing to do is to own up and atone. However, deep down one hates being treated in this way and, deep down, will surely have revenge—even if it cannot be today. Alternatively, one is cast as a virtuous victim of racism, survivor and saviour; by virtue of having experienced it one becomes the authority on racism. This, I think, is a way of allowing the victim to have revenge, to *do* something to us. In addition, the atmosphere turns easily hostile and suspicious, it is impossible to think, and political correctness becomes the order of the day. We feel divided into friends and enemies.
>
> (2011, 48–49)

What is evident in Davids's account is how the distinction between friend and enemy, racist and racist victim, follows the same formal structure. Moreover, it is in accordance with a psychotic position that this similarity is played out in forms of delusional thinking and examples of paranoia that remain fixed to the categorization of different racial groups.

Fixing race

Under the logic of psychosis, we can re-approach Seshadri-Crooks claim that '[t]he shared insecurity of claiming absolute humanness, which is what race as a system manages, induces the social and legal validation of race as a discourse of *neutral differences*' (2000, 7, italics in original). It is through the discourse of 'neutral differences' that the presence of the object *a* of race is averred. The certainty of this presence can be identified in other examples, such as genetic arguments, whereupon Leader (2012) explains how common misunderstandings regarding 'genes' often follow a psychotic form:

> [d]espite the admonishment of many researchers, the popular view of a gene remains that of a 'unit character', a single element that would be responsible for specific physiological or behavioural traits. Eugenics theorists in the early twentieth century argued that specific genes would cause nomadism, crime, unemployment, indolence and dissolute lifestyle, and these were linked in turn to the 'bad blood' of Jews, blacks and the mentally unwell. ... By the 1920s, it was known that different genes could affect the same characteristic, just as a single gene could affect different characteristics. Despite these facts, the unit character theory still pervades contemporary understanding of genetic causality, and in the early 1990s biologists suggested finding another term, as 'gene' had become so prone to misinterpretation. Genes were seen as isolated causal agents rather than as parts of complex networks of biological interactions that usually depended to a large extent on what was going on in the surrounding world. Many biologists recognized that the old nature/nurture opposition could no longer be maintained in the way that it once had been. Indeed, the effort to make a gene responsible, splitting it away from everything else that might concern a human life, has a certain psychotic quality to it, as if one entity could be deemed the culprit, just as in paranoia one unique agency is designated as the cause of one's problems.
>
> (2012, 139)

As can be seen in Leader's example, any determinate 'fixing' bears a psychotic quality that serves to engender polarized forms of thinking. In assigning a specific cause to a particular 'problem', genetic causes are subsequently used to propagate a sense of 'scientific neutrality', which works to affirm the impartiality of racial differences, most notable perhaps, when one hears the response... 'it's genetic'.

What underscores this argument, however, is the psychosis that it inevitably relies upon. Indeed, we see this echoed in the logic of slavery and the operations of the slave trade. In the process of auctioning slaves, Johnson details how slaves 'were ... transformed into exemplars of the category to which they had been assigned; but once the categories of comparison had been established and embodied, the slaves were supposed to once again become visible as individuals' (1999, 119). Consequently, while each slave was *categorized* in accordance with other slaves, according to some assumed classification of significance, once categorized, the slave was then perceived through *their* individuality. Ultimately, in the act of assigning slaves to a category, which functioned to endow them a comparable price, it was then the visibility of the slave's individuality, their own unique properties, which assured the slave's value. Here, a psychotic form of ordering, classifying, and fixing racial categories according to a presumed racial essence, beholden to each yet every subject, is brought to light in the auctioning of slaves. It is this same contradiction that 'confront[s] the symbolic constitution of race and of racial looking *as* the investment we make in difference for sameness' (Seshadri-Crooks 2000, 159, italics in original).

On this basis, we can locate examples of racism as beholden to the psychotic's failure to fully grasp the '*neither one, nor the other*' (Lacan 2004, 211, italics in original); a distinction that recalls the structure of the forced choice. Indeed, while, in the structure of psychosis, the subject remains beholden to the 'forced choice'—for them there is no choosing, except that which they were prescribed—they are, in this way, alienated from their own alienation to the signifier (or the Symbolic order/Law). As a result, the psychosis of race is fixed to an imaginary form of freedom bestowed through one's racialization. Ultimately, there is no 'freedom' in being assigned *a* 'race', for such an assignment fails to appreciate the subject's self-division, and, by extension, there is no self-identity in one's racial classification, outside of the very inconsistencies that this classification relies upon.

Notes

1 Žižek frequently likens this relationship to the Mobius band, whereby at any point on the band there are two-sides that maintain an obverse separation. In psychosis, the two-sides of this band are flattened.
2 As Seshadri-Crooks highlights, '[t]his is the very definition of the stereotype as a form of discourse that attempts to produce meaning where none is possible' (2000, 143, parenthesis removed).
3 Žižek elaborates here by explaining that it is the Jew who serves as the 'contingent external intruder' (2016, 180). Fascism externalizes '[t]he Jew as the enemy [that] allows the anti-Semitic subject to avoid the choice between working class and capital: by blaming the Jew whose plotting foments class warfare, he can advocate the vision of a harmonious society in which work and capital collaborate' (Žižek 2016, 180).
4 Tupinambá helpfully draws upon Saul Kripke's account of unicorns as comprising such an 'impossible object' (2021, 128). Here he adds, '[c]onsider a thing whose *lack of reality is part of its being*—something which, if we were to find an example of it in reality, this real version would *not* be what it is because it is part of the being of this thing to be unreal, and so the real version would *lack its lack of reality*. … [I]t is not the case that we cannot think what a unicorn is—it is not impossible to think an impossible object—but, were we to find such an animal in the world, it would *not* be a unicorn, because among the properties which define the unicorn—looking like a horse, having a horn on its head, and so on—there is also the property of *being mythical*. … Due to this "unreal" condition, we cannot posses a unicorn, nor directly play with one. We might, however, enjoy the unicorn: that is what bedtime stories are for' (Tupinambá 2021, 128, italics in original).
5 Indeed, this 'guise [is] perpetuated by changing objects of desire' (McGowan 2007, 180).

References

Black, Jack. 2021. *Race, Racism and Political Correctness in Comedy – A Psychoanalytic Exploration*. Abingdon, UK: Routledge.
Davids, Fakhry M. 2011. *Internal Racism: A Psychoanalytic Approach to Race and Difference*. New York, NY: Palgrave Macmillan.
Fanon, Frantz. 2008. *Black Skin, White Masks*. New York, NY: Grove Press.

George, Sheldon. 2014. "From alienation to cynicism: race and the Lacanian unconscious." *Psychoanalysis, Culture & Society* 19, no. 4: 360–378.
George, Sheldon. 2016. *Trauma and Race: A Lacanian Study of African American Racial Identity*. Waco, TX: Baylor University Press.
George, Sheldon. 2022. "The Lacanian subject of race: sexuation, the drive, and racial subjectivity." In *Lacan and Race: Racism, Identity, and Psychoanalytic Theory*, edited by Sheldon George and Derek Hook (241–262). Abingdon, UK: Routledge.
Gilroy, Paul. 2000. *Against Race: Imagining Political Culture Beyond the Color Line*. Cambridge, MA: The Belknap Press of Harvard University Press.
Hamza, Agon, and Frank Ruda. 2019. "Interview with Alenka Zupančič: philosophy or psychoanalysis? Yes, please!" *Crisis & Critique* 6, no. 1: 435–453.
Hook, Derek. 2022. "The object of apartheid desire: a Lacanian approach to racism and ideology." In *Lacan and Race: Racism, Identity, and Psychoanalytic Theory*, edited by Sheldon George and Derek Hook (121–145). Abingdon, UK: Routledge.
Johnson, Walter. 1999. *Soul by Soul: Life Inside the Antebellum Slave Market*. Cambridge, MA: Harvard University Press.
Lacan, Jacques. 1997. *The Seminar of Jacques Lacan, Book III, 1955–56: The Psychoses*, edited by Jacques-Alain Miller. London, UK: Routledge.
Lacan, Jacques. 2014. *The Seminar of Jacques Lacan, Book X: Anxiety*, edited by Jacques-Alain Miller, translated by A. R. Price. Cambridge, UK: Polity.
Lacan, Jacques. 2004. *The Four Fundamental Concepts of Psycho-Analysis*, edited by Jacques-Alain Miller. London, UK: Karnac.
Leader, Darian. 2012. *What is Madness?* London, UK: Penguin.
McGowan, Todd. 2007. *The Real Gaze: Film Theory after Lacan*. Albany, NY: State University of New York Press.
McGowan, Todd. 2013. *Enjoying What We Don't Have: The Political Project of Psychoanalysis*. Lincoln, NE: University of Nebraska Press.
Ragland, Ellie. 1995a. *Essays on the Pleasures of Death: From Freud to Lacan*. New York, NY: Routledge.
Ragland, Ellie. 1995b. "The relation between the voice and the gaze." In *Reading Seminar XI: Lacan's Four Fundamental Concepts of Psychoanalysis*, edited by Richard Feldstein, Bruce Fink, and Maire Jaanus (187–204). Albany, NY: State University of New York Press.
Ruti, Mari. 2008. "The fall of fantasies: a Lacanian reading of lack." *Journal of the American Psychoanalytic Association* 56, no. 1: 483–508.
Ruti, Mari. 2012. *The Singularity of Being: Lacan and the Immortal Within*. New York, NY: Fordham University Press.
Salecl, Renata. 2002. *The Spoils of Freedom: Psychoanalysis and Feminism after the Fall of Socialism*. London, UK: Routledge.
Salva, Victor, director. 2001. *Jeepers Creepers*. American Zoetrope; Cinerenta-Cinebeta; Cinerenta; Medienbeteiligungs KG.
Seshadri-Crooks, Kalpana. 2000. *Desiring Whiteness: A Lacanian Analysis of Race*. London, UK: Routledge.
Tupinambá, Gabriel. 2021. *The Desire of Psychoanalysis: Exercises in Lacanian Thinking*. Evanston, IL: Northwestern University Press.
Vanheule, Stijn. 2011a. *The Subject of Psychosis: A Lacanian Perspective*. Basingstoke, UK: Palgrave Macmillan.

Vanheule, Stijn. 2011b. "A Lacanian perspective on psychotic hallucinations." *Theory & Psychology* 21, no. 1: 86–106.

7Vanheule, Stijn. 2020. "On a question prior to any possible treatment to psychosis." In *Reading Lacan's Ecrits: From Écrits: From 'The Freudian Thing' to 'Remarks on Daniel Lagache'*, edited by Derek Hook, Calum Neill, and Stijn Vanheule (163–205). London, UK: Routledge.

Winnubst, Shannon. 2004. "Is the mirror racist? Interrogating the space of whiteness." *Philosophy & Social Criticism* 30, no. 1: 25–50.

Žižek, Slavoj. 2008. *The Plague of Fantasies*. London, UK: Verso.

Žižek, Slavoj. 2012. *Less Than Nothing*. London, UK: Verso.

Žižek, Slavoj. 2016. *Disparities*. London, UK: Bloomsbury.

Žižek, Slavoj. 2017. *Incontinence of the Void: Economico-Philosophical Spandrels*. Cambridge, MA: The MIT Press.

Zupančič, Alenka. 2000. *Ethics of the Real: Kant, Lacan*. London, UK: Verso.

Zupančič, Alenka. 2005. "Reversals of nothing: the case of the sneezing corpse." *Filozofski vestnik* 26, no. 2: 173–186.

Zupančič, Alenka. 2008. *Why Psychoanalysis? Three Interventions*. Aarhus, DK: Aarhus University Press.

Chapter 6

Psychosis and lack
A nothing made something

Symbolically castrated, it is lack that constitutes the Lacanian subject. It is through this lack, or at least the sense that one seeks a recuperation to one's lack, that a lost enjoyment is pursued. We seek this enjoyment in desire: be it the desire for a new job, a new house, or some other perceived satisfaction, which, even if achieved, fails to quell the desire it provokes. What proves antagonizing for the subject is that we are often met with the other's enjoyment. The impression here is that it is the other who achieves full enjoyment and is, therefore, non-lacking.

As evident in cases of jealousy and aggression, this enjoying other is an obfuscation of the fact that the subject, the other, and the big Other are constituted through lack. Based on the inherent inconsistency of the Symbolic order, the subject is left in a position of interpreting, deciphering, and reading what the other subject desires, as well as seeking to make sense of what their gestures, suggestions, and actions mean. Thus, it is interpretation that produces the subject and the Other (the subject and the object) (Regnault 1995).

Previous chapters have sought to highlight how this lack is constituted for the subject through their location in language (Symbolic castration) and in the forced choice (alienation) which the subject is faced with when seeking to make sense of their being through Symbolic meaning (whether this be language, cultural institutions, or social etiquettes). This leaves the subject in a unique position: a position of 'non-meaning', whereby any 'meaning' is always a 'forced choice' that ultimately requires the subject to submit to a Symbolic order of meaning, which they are obliged to both use and decode. This produces a 'gap' in being for the subject.

In examples of racial psychosis, this process is complicated. Insofar as all subjects are marked by lack, the psychotic's lack, much like their alienation, remains unique. While occupying a position of externality to the signifier, it can be assumed that the psychotic achieves no lack. Through the failure to achieve Symbolic castration, the psychotic is not plagued by lack. However, as the following sections will detail, this is not necessarily the case. Arguably, it cannot be said that the psychotic does not lack, if only on the grounds that to conceive of a non-lacking subject would confound the possibility of referring to a 'subject' as such.¹ Rather, there are ways of registering lack and it is the registering of a 'psychotic lack' that can be considered in accordance with race.

More precisely, we can consider how in psychosis lack falls upon the signifier, which fails to effectively articulate the subject. In contrast to the subject's constitutive lack, there is, in psychosis, 'a lack, at the level of the signifier' (Lacan 1997, 201). There is, in other words 'a deficiency, … a hole in the symbolic' (Lacan 1997, 156), so that '[i]n psychosis, the subject lacks a symbolic compass at the level of the Other, due to which subjectivity remains undefined in its confrontation with the questions of existence' (Vanheule 2011, 71). This lack of a symbolic compass is reflected in the psychotic's relation to the 'forced choice', which grounds them in a level of non-meaning from which their relation to the signifier and meaning is truncated—indeed, there is a fracture that marks their relation to the signifier, or as Vanheule asserts, 'the Symbolic loses its internal organization, which obliterates the structure in language' (2011, 114). The obliteration of this structure means that there is, for the psychotic subject, 'disorder at the level of the Other' (Vanheule 2011, 114). In studies on psychosis, this disorder is often managed or tested through examples of delusion (Vanheule 2011). The premise of this book is that race plays a fundamental role in relating to this disorder. Race provides an answer, albeit false, to the failure of Symbolic mediation that underpins psychosis.

Following George, what race elicits is its own form of mediation, so that, essentially, '[r]ace … attempts to mediate our relation to … lack' (2022, 244; see also George 2016). Such mediation, however, is not a form of assimilation, but a fashioning of the racial signifier: a signifier that does not simply mediate the relation to lack, but also obscures the very 'gap' that endows the subject's investment in the Symbolic order. Whereas creative capacity is founded in the constitutive lack (the gap/hole) that resists symbolization and establishes the (non-psychotic) subject as a subject of signification, without the mediation of the Symbolic order there is no negotiation for the subject to desire an identity. In its place, race functions as a form of mediation that serves to comprise the subject's being: desire is foreclosed and the gap in being is resolved... one *is* one's race.

Lack and loss

It is here that we can begin to consider how lack takes on a certain form in the psychosis of race. What occurs in psychosis is a relation to lack that appears as a form of 'loss'. This sense of loss differs to the loss that is perceived as part of the non-psychotic's Symbolic castration, 'a loss which is in itself liberating, giving, "productive," opening up the space for things to appear in their (meaningful) being' (Žižek 2012, 861). Instead, for the psychotic, 'loss can only be purely *privative*, a question of something being taken from them' (Žižek 2012, 861, italics in original). Thus, the mediation that race affords effectively transposes the subject's constitutive lack into a private sense of loss: indeed, as a *something* that can be lost.

In examples of racist fantasy, it becomes apparent how such fantasies work off the assumption that something has been stolen (and lost) from the subject, or that the subject's loss is outdone by the other's gain. Here, it is often the other who is conceived to be enjoying at the expense of the subject (McGowan 2022a; 2022b). This suggests that racist fantasies do not simply work from a position of domination, but that fantasies of the other can also perpetuate a sense of loss on behalf of the fantasizing subject. Racist fantasies that posit the other as superior, or with some advantage relevant to the subject, are sustained by the concern that it is the other's superiority, their non-castration, which permits them a level of enjoyment that cannot be matched. In so doing, '[t]he racial other, not the very structure of subjectivity, [becomes …] the bar preventing the subject from enjoying the way it imagines it might' (McGowan 2022a, 24).

Consequently, it is the psychotic's failure to conceive of lack as inherent to the structure of subjectivity that allows it 'to render loss empirical rather than ontological' (McGowan 2013, 47). When loss is empirically conceived, it can be perceived as avoidable. Such avoidance structures the psychosis of race through examples of racism that demand the removal or suppression of the other so as to avoid the sense of loss that their presence permits.

In fact, when conceived through the psychosis of race, the psychotic's private sense of loss can serve to inhibit those seeking to transform or resist examples of racist subordination. Here, George highlights how:

> in trying to transmit to the broader American culture not just the often ignored social realities of their lives but also a message so frequently grounded in racial fantasy, African Americans bind themselves to an Imaginary truth driven as much by a recognition of social loss as by a desire to mask the personal lack these losses recall. This conflation of lack and social loss restricts the models through which agency for African Americans is imagined.
>
> (2016, 71)

It is the 'conflation of lack and social loss' that posits a psychotic significance. In effect, the agency afforded to the creativity that lack sustains is excluded, so that any space for liberation is foreclosed (Žižek 2012). Without 'the empty space which "triggers" the process of symbolization' (Žižek 1999, 28), the psychotic does not obtain the distance that is required in symbolization. Instead, when tied to loss, one's racial identity effects a relation to being, one in which the liberatory potential of the signifier is ultimately negated. As a result, in the psychosis of race, race provides a compensatory identification for one's loss; yet, as a form of identification, it remains inherently lacking. Though it provides a certain continuity of being for the subject, it is fundamentally empty due to the foreclosure of any Symbolic support.

An empty set, the presence of a void, and the sunken place... nothing as something

What race provides for the subject is not unlike the empty set: 'a set which has no elements' but which nonetheless 'transforms nothingness into something by *marking* or *representing* it' (Fink 1997, 52, italics in original). If we consider a subject's name, for example, we can conceive how this 'name' bears no inherent relation to the subject it refers to. Nevertheless, overtime 'this signifier—more, perhaps, than any other—will go to the root of his or her being and become inextricably tied to his or her subjectivity' (Fink 1997, 53). In other words, one's name becomes inseparable from one's sense of self. However, in psychosis, there is no root to take hold. In psychosis, one's name, and, analogously, one's race, remains nothing more than a prescribed ascription; a sense of being which one is bestowed.

What can be stressed in this account is the sense of emptiness that abounds one's racialization. Certainly, while forms of racial solidarity can seek to curtail examples of 'emptiness', securing a footing in the Symbolic by identifying with other individuals who share the same 'race', these forms of identification remain 'empty', if only for the very reason that one's racial identification remains tied to the object *a*. In effect, when using 'race', and when promoting one's racial identity, one enacts a psychotic externalization that is ambivalently located between a racial Symbolic order, which defines and structures this very identification, and a psychotic sense of loss, which leaves the subject with nothing else but a detachment to the Symbolic order. Here, the subject's 'loss of reality' is ultimately a loss of one's constitutive alienation; lost, that is, to a racial prescription that serves as a form of depersonalization.

This sense of emptiness is often exhibited by proponents of racial realism, or the pseudoscientific belief that biology determines one's race (and, thus, one's racial inferiority or superiority). After founding the blog *The Emptiness*, American neo-Nazi Michael 'Enoch' Peinovich included the following mission statement: '[t]he purpose of this site is to deconstruct empty social constructs. It is also to show how people themselves become empty when they enslave themselves to these empty social constructs' (Southern Poverty Law Centre n.d.). Peinovich's racism is frequently underscored by a sense of paranoia that draws heavily from racial conspiracy theories (such as Holocaust denial and White genocide).[2] Accordingly, in both his podcast and written commentaries, it is the conviction that one must 'fight' the emptiness that the social construction of race promotes which helps to bestow, for Peinovich, the biological importance of race. In effect, despite his own racial convictions, Peinovich's racial outlook remains beset by the 'empty social constructs' that threaten *his* race. However, it is only by enacting one's racial personalization (a fixation on the object *a* of race) that the psychosis of race posits a depersonalizing void.

Indeed, for Lacan, '[t]here is nothing more dangerous than approaching a void' (1997, 201), and, to this effect, in psychosis this danger is fuelled by the fact that it is an encounter with 'nothing'. According to Kingsbury and Secor, usually 'we encounter the void as a missed encounter, that is, as a something that does not happen' (2021, 7). In examples of psychosis, however, it is a something that does indeed happen, so that what is encountered is a nothing *as* something. This nothing as something is enacted via the presence of the object *a* in psychosis: 'the presence of a hollow, a void' (Lacan 2004, 180). What encapsulates this 'something' grounded in 'nothing' is the object *a* of race, insofar as what constitutes race is essentially 'nothing'—an illusory classification that entraps the subject within a racial Symbolic order that they are a part of and determined by, but which they are also removed from.

In the psychosis of race, one is tied to this void (the object *a*), which ultimately serves as the very source of one's racial identity. While '[n]o set of qualitative descriptions can establish black or white identity across all possible worlds', this does not mean that 'black and white do not exist', an error that Seshadri-Crooks attributes to critical race theory (2000, 141). Rather, when tied to the object *a*— that is, to the void as such—the subject does not miss their encounter with nothing, but instead lives with a nothing that is something: a something that is both prescribed and assumed by the subject as granted by their race.

The presence of this nothing as something can be found in the use of the 'sunken place' in Jordan Peele's *Get Out* (2017). In the film, the lead character, Chris (Daniel Kaluuya), is put under a form of hypnosis by his partner's mother, Missy (Catherine Keener). This involves Chris being hypnotically transferred to a 'sunken place', a sort of no-place that is represented in the film as a form of drowning. In the hypnosis, Chris seems to 'sink' within a void of nothing from which he cannot escape. According to Brown, '[t]he Sunken Place … represents the necropolitics of contemporary black existence' (2020, 113), which is effectively rendered throughout the film, most notably, in its alternative ending. In the film's alternate conclusion, the final showdown with Chris's partner, Rose (Allison Williams), sees Chris arrested and imprisoned. In the film's final scene, '[t]he last thing the audience sees is Chris retreating, clad in an orange jumpsuit and framed by white prison bars as he descends deeper into the recesses of the prison—the Sunken Place' (Brown 2020, 118). While Brown considers whether the alternative ending may offer a more realistic conclusion to the film (in the chosen ending, Chris is not arrested), the depiction of Chris's 'descent' into the prison nonetheless captures the structural presence of the void as depicted in the multitude of sunken places that continually frame the lived experiences of Black racialization.

A something from nothing

Often, in examples of psychosis, there is the perception that '[e]verything means "something"' (Leader 2012, 171). Set against the complexity, or 'perplexity', of the world, '[c]ertain words or phrases may start to preoccupy the person, as if they had an inordinate weight even if their meaning is opaque'

(Leader 2012, 171). We can see here how this is echoed in the psychosis of race whereby the confrontation with the other's difference is perceived to mean 'something'. This something does not have to be well-defined but can, in its very opacity, work to contrive a something (that is different) from nothing (which is the same), thus establishing the regime of racial visibility (Seshadri-Crooks 2000).

One major consequence of this something from nothing is that it can leave the racialized subject devoid of any ontological basis from which their grounding in the world can be established. Indeed, Hudson notes:

> [t]orn between two impossibles—to be white and to be black—the first barred and second an impossibility in its own terms as there is no black 'being'—blackness produces no 'ontological resistance'—'turn white or disappear' sums up the ontological void of the black colonised subject. Made to want to be white, but incapable of this—he is black; and his blackness seen through his own 'white' eyes reduces him to 'nothing.' The colonial symbolic is so constructed as to give the black subject nothing to hold onto—no orthopaedic support for an identity—just a whiteness forever eluding him and a blackness that doesn't 'exist' in any case.
>
> (2013, 264–265 cited in Thakur 2020, xvii)

In this description, we read how the positivization of a lack—the reduction and perpetuation of 'nothing'—is racially prescribed to the colonized subject. This is echoed in Fanon's (2008) account of racial hailing. Reduced to 'an object among other objects', Fanon's being remains hollow: a lack that is unable 'to uncover the meaning of things' (2008, 89). It is this sense of an objectivized lack, a fixing to one's object a, that underscores much of Fanon's writing on the Black subject, who is both objectified and then negated by a racial Symbolic order.

As is the case in examples of psychosis, the psychotic may often feel as if their body is not their own. In fact, the '[l]oss of one's image has been a trope in conceptualizing the psychic violence done to black Americans, and more specifically black men, since the early twentieth century' (Wallerstein 2020, 267). This sense of 'invisibility is also a structural reality, most clearly represented in the mass incarceration and subsequent political and financial disenfranchisement of young black men' (Wallerstein 2020, 267). What is more, this invisibility is compounded by the fact that one's loss is delimited by a distinct racial classification. Despite the nonsense of such classifications, race becomes a positivized lack, indeed, a source of identity that confines as much as it defines.

We can observe the effects of this in George's (2016) critique of W.E.B. Du Bois, where, for George, Du Bois's account of racial being remains grounded in a fantasy of race. Indeed, throughout Du Bois's work there is a clear conflation between the fact that race does not exist and statements that conceive of race as providing an almost transcendental significance. This is evident when Du Bois notes that, '[t]he spirit that knows Beauty, that has music in its soul and the color of sunsets in its headkerchiefs; that can dance on a flaming world and make the world dance, too. Such is the soul of the Negro' (1969, 147). For Ibram X. Kendi, it is through propagating such a 'soul' that 'a split between an anti-racist and an assimilationist racist mind' can be found in Du Bois's work (Reynoso 2021, 65). Here, '[Kendi] poses that assimilationist racism rejects the essentialist argument of one race being inferior to others but accepts that cultural and societal factors have produced a superiority of certain racial groups over others' (Reynoso 2021, 65). Referring to this critique, Reynoso highlights how 'Kendi's scholarship implies a psychoanalytic point that anti-racism (like love) is not a pure state but remains in tension with what it opposes' (2021, 65).

In both George (2016) and Kendi's (2016) critique, examples of psychosis are uncovered which, fundamentally, point to the disorder and dislocation that the psychotic experiences when faced with the Symbolic order. Located outside of signification, yet indebted to its very logic, the racial signifier leaves the subject with nothing but their prescribed race: race presents a totality for the subject, obscuring their lack for an objectification *in* race that both limits their liberation, while, at the same time, serving as the very source of their illusory object (*their* object *a*). Again, it is here that the psychosis of race reveals its unique form of alienation. It is '[t]his paradoxical path toward freedom through alienation', which, as argued by George, presents 'an ambivalent relation to race for African Americans' (2014, 371). This ambivalence is reflected by the fact that to challenge 'racist implications' requires 'embracing the distinctions of self and other it promotes' (George 2014, 371). What remains key to George's account is that 'the distinctions of self and other' that race 'promotes' is just as apparent in examples of anti-racism that both require and rely upon the promotion and critique of these very racial distinctions.

Slavery and psychosis

These distinctions are further supported when one considers the forms of historicization that replicate the objectification of lack which characterized the slave. George notes:

> [r]acial identity itself, whether imposed by racism or willfully embraced by contemporary African Americans as the historical context for self-understanding and being, not only crystallizes for African Americans the indisputable link between slavery and the racism they continue to suffer but also may collapse their personal sense of being with the historical lack emerging from slavery. Racism is key to this conflation.
>
> (2016, 51)

Mirroring the slave, 'racism grounds the African American subject's psychic sense of lack not in the split self but in the racial past' (George 2016, 51).

What is prescribed by this past is a history of slavery which becomes the property (the object *a*) of Blacks, 'rather than a part of the ethical and intellectual heritage of the West as a whole' (Gilroy 1993, 49). In the history of slavery, for Whites and Blacks, lack becomes obscured through the availability of the object *a* of race, which consolidates the racial identifications underpinning slavery. That is, with no 'space' in which to navigate 'the historical lack emerging from slavery', the Black subject remains tied to the trauma of a past that cannot be traversed (George 2016, 51). This does not deny the history of slavery, but, rather, considers how this history serves as an appropriated symbol that racially locates and fixes examples of racialization in the past. It is through this past that race becomes a central point of identification.

For the slave, George (2016) refers to a 'para-being': a being that is based on the quantification of an assumed set of racial 'qualities' that frame the slave as an object whose very 'value' is to be accumulated and traded. Equally, for the slave owner, their being becomes predicated on the owning of slaves, which ultimately ensures and maintains their own 'market position'. In both instances, we see how it is the lack of a lack that coordinates the relation between slave and slave owner: for the slave, their lack is obscured by their assumed 'biological' and 'physical' qualities, which subsequently prescribes them an empirical value; for the slave owner, their lack is obscured through a sense of 'wholeness', which is founded upon the accumulation of slaves and the subsequent social, political, and economic benefits afforded by the system of slavery.

Certainly, the above formulation does not ignore the abject horror of reducing a human being to slavery; indeed, of reducing someone to the absolute lack of being that is averred when one is nothing but an object to be traded. Instead, what I draw attention to is how the structure of slavery worked to psychotically foreclose the subject's constitutive lack through reducing the slave to an empirically valued 'object'. Through the process of being bought and sold by White slave owners, the act of owning a slave could subsequently absolve (or obscure) the White slave owner of their own lack. Again, it is the way in which 'lack' becomes positivized in the structure of slavery, and in the relation between slave and slave owner, that a racial psychosis is found. In no uncertain terms, slavery is psychotic.

The certainty of psychosis

Due to the presence of the object *a* there is no mistrust awarded to the knowledge that one's racial belonging prescribes (there is no hysterical doubt in the case of psychosis): race provides a psychotic certainty. As Fink explains, '*[c]ertainty is characteristic of psychosis, where doubt is not*' (1999, 84, italics in original). This certainty means something to the psychotic, providing them a sense of meaning. Notably, for Schreber, his certainty was wedded to the fact that he stood at the start of a 'new race' (2000, 254). What the world lacked—indeed, what the Other lacked—could ultimately be restored through Schreber. It is this same certainty that underscores the psychosis of race, which, in its most fanatical examples, endows the subject, and their race, a unique role in logically restoring balance and equilibrium to the Other.

Moreover, it is in restoring balance and equilibrium that a surplus of enjoyment can be found in certain conspiracy theories that seek to overcome (or outright discount) any sense of doubt or scepticism. Referring to Zupančič's (2022) essay on conspiracy, Žižek describes how, in the case of COVID-19, 'COVID-sceptics like to claim that they just want a free debate, a readiness to listen to all sides and to make up their own mind, against the dogmatism of experts and science in the service of establishment' (2022, 306). Yet, while '[t]hey begin with scepticism, doubting all official theories, … they (almost magically) abolish this doubt by way of providing a unified total explanation—and this overcoming of doubt by a total explanation, a meaning of it all, provides an immense surplus-enjoyment' (Žižek 2022, 306).

The abolition of doubt, and the enjoyment therein, is enacted by both the Left and the Right. In the case of the far-Right racist, it is the lack of social order that seems to be the problem. A lack of order encapsulated by the denigration of shared cultural norms, unmanaged immigration, and the failure of law enforcement. While these problems prove symptomatic of society's decline, they also point to the culprits of this lack of order: 'the other'. For the Left, these same problems are perceived as the fault of the state to enact basic human rights, due to its neglect and/or corruption. As a result, it is the failures of the state that perpetuates forms of racial discrimination. In either case, despite their contrasting ideological positions, both the Left and the Right navigate their differences around the same underlying lack: the lack of an Other (the state) deemed capable of meeting the social failures that they perceive. It is this certainty of lack which gets played out in examples of racism as well as in the fetishization of one's racial agency.

In fact, George has noted how '[w]hatever credence they give to the existential value of race, African Americans frequently argue for race's value in a sort of poststructuralist approach to agency, whereby the subject must seek to appropriate and redefine the signifiers that define the subject' (2014, 361). It is through this poststructuralist approach to agency that a fetishizing of race takes shape through a persistent redefining of the signifiers that directly and indirectly structure the subject's racialization. Indeed, it is from the disorder of the Symbolic—its endless redefinition— that the subject's racial certainty holds value. In the surety that is afforded to one's race—and this includes the certainty of the racist, who places no higher value beyond their race, *and* the certainty of the non-racist, for whom one's racial dignity requires the reclamation of one's subordinated race—it is the subject's lack, and the inherent absence that structures the social order, which goes amiss. In psychosis, there is neither the recognition nor the appreciation that no political activity can assuage this lack. Instead, the psychosis of race obscures this very realization.

Racial designation

The effects of this obfuscation can be appreciated in accordance with the fact that, for Lacan, 'when we come into language, we must repress the way in which the meaning making system in fact is not closed and is impossible to finish' (Neroni 2022, 54). What becomes repressed is the 'missing signified': that which would endow the subject with complete knowledge. It is the lack endowed by this missing signifier which creates the subject's constitutive lack, the part of the subject that can never be known. In psychosis, there is no recognition of the non-existence of this 'missing signifier'. There is no 'gap' in examples of psychosis.

Nonetheless, as the above has sought to argue, this does not mean that the psychotic is devoid of lack. According to McGowan:

> [r]ather than respecting the gap in signification as the placeholder for the missing signifier, we should recognize that nothing exists in the gap and that nothing really is, for us, something. The gap marks the point at which senselessness itself is included in the world of signification. Nothing or senselessness is not a specter that haunts the system but the very basis of the symbolic system.
>
> (2013, 275)

There is an important distinction to be made in McGowan's remarks. That is, while it is politically important to recognize the inherent inescapability of the gap—the nothing that is something—in psychosis, problems occur when this nothing is *made* something; indeed, when this nothing becomes an 'object'. In the psychosis of race, there is no need to recognize that nothing is something, if only because this something visibly exists—in fact, it is confirmed in the visibility of racial difference. It is in this way that Seshadri-Crooks (2000) seeks to expose how the designations of Black, White, etc., work like nouns that ascribe one's racial identity. These nouns function as 'rigid designators—they are signifiers that have no signified. They establish a reference, but deliver no connotations or meaning whatsoever' (Seshadri-Crooks 2000, 141). In the psychosis of race, the 'naming' of one's race is rigidly defined in accordance with the foreclosure of the missing signifier: 'signifiers become *objects* in communication, rather than its vehicle' (Ragland 1995, 77). Here, the very 'nothing' that comprises the Symbolic order takes on a certain rigidity: a 'something' that is flatly recognized and non-dialectically attributed (i.e., it is not substituted for something else within the Symbolic order). Fixed to their being, the psychotic is left in a paradoxical non-meaning or non-sense.

It is here that we can begin to outline the contradiction that underpins the object *a* of race. While not ignoring the fact that the object *a* remains a 'nothing' which cannot be reduced to a specific, empirical object, in the case of psychosis, it is in the materialization of the object *a* that the visibility of racial difference is taken literally (serving as the basis for hierarchal forms of racial differentiation and belonging). In psychosis, therefore, both the Real and the Symbolic's failure to prescribe the Real become conflated. Race fixes an impossible possession that remains bound to the Real and the Symbolic: it endows the subject with *their* race, while also presenting the subject with the inherent nothingness of *their* racial prescription. Indeed, race can never say it all, but when it is assumed that it does—as evident when one is prescribed a racial/ethnic classification—one confronts the lack of a lack... the lack of one's constitutive lack.

This lack of a lack can be found in McGowan's account of Nazi anti-Semitism and the contradiction that even though the Jew was ascribed 'a particular race' (2020, 167), for the Nazi anti-Semite, 'this race has no proper identity' (2020, 168). It is for this reason that in his account of the racist fantasy, McGowan prefers his use of the 'racial other' over the 'racialized other'. In contrast to the 'racialized other', McGowan notes that 'there are versions of the racist fantasy in which the racial other is specifically deprived of being a race at all' (2022b, 196, n.2). Such thoughts were echoed by Nazi leaders, such as Joseph Goebbels, who noted that, '[t]he Jew is a nonrace among the races of the earth' (cited in Koschorke 2017, 148). In fact, while referring to a speech made by the Nazi leader, Jules Streciher, McGowan emphasizes how in Streciher's Nazi fantasy, 'there is no such thing as Jewish blood' (McGowan 2022b, 196, n.2). In Streciher's words: '[w]e know that the Jew received his blood from all the races of the world. Negro blood, Mongolian blood, Nordic blood, Indian blood—the blood of all races flows in this bastard race' (Bytwerk 2008, 88, cited in McGowan 2022b, 196, n.2).

What remains apparent from Streciher's speech, however, is that essentially Jewish blood could be *any blood*—a melange that worked to prescribe, fix, and determine the Jew's 'bad' blood. Though it can be asserted that 'Nazis do not hate Jews because of their Jewish identity but because Jews *lack* any particular identity' (McGowan 2020, 168, italics added), what seems to characterize this lack is that, in the case of Nazi anti-Semitism, such a 'lack comes to lack' (Zupančič 2005, 181). In other words, what comes to pass in fascist ideology is the existence of a Jewish 'particularity' that is paradoxically founded upon its own 'non-particularity'. Here, the lack of racial particularity is bound to a process of racialization whereby what ends-up constituting the Jewish race is the presence of all races, or, as Streciher details, all types of blood. Accordingly, while the Jew lacks any particular identity, it is this 'lack' that characterizes, and, thus, to a certain extent, 'positivizes' the Jew their own unique particularity (a nothing as something). In effect, the Jew occupies the object *a* (Žižek 2008): a nothing from which the 'bastard race' is made something.

Similarly, whereas in other cases someone can be (and will be) designated either 'White' or 'Black'—and, at a certain point, there will be 'a necessary truth to that designation'—the crux of the racial designation is that it fails to 'mean' anything beyond the prescribed designation (Seshadri-Crooks 2000, 141).[3] While this something is designated to the object *a* of race, it is the inherent 'senselessness' of the designation (its non-meaning) that plainly marks and haunts the subject's reality; providing them a racial 'certainty', as well as a position within the racial Symbolic order that is just as fraught as it is certain (here, the senselessness of race relies upon its own non-sense, see Chapter 2).

For example, in discussing the fetishization of skin colour, Gherovici turns to Morrison's *God Help the Child* (2016a), where Morrison 'show[s] that racism not only objectifies its victims, who are stripped of their humanity, and even of their souls, but that racism also dehumanizes the racists themselves' (Gherovici 2022, 186). In this sense, Gherovici highlights how Morrisons's narrative cleverly illustrates that for those who choose racism, ultimately, they 'would be nothing without it' (Morrison 2016, 143, cited in Gherovici 2022, 186). More to the point, Morrison's remarks should be taken literally: what is emphasized in this example is the very 'nothing' that it reveals—a nothing that is correlative to the subject's position in psychosis. With there being 'no such thing as race' (Morrison 2016, 143, cited in Gherovici 2022, 186), we are left with the psychotic's 'nothing': a nothing made something, or, in Morrison's example, with a racism that constitutes and orchestrates this very 'nothing'.

Notes

1 Here, Ruti highlights how 'Lacan invites us to acknowledge that regardless of all the busy and clamorous activity that we habitually undertake in order to suppress or ignore our lack, deep down we know that there will always be moments when it breaks out into the open with the piercing clarity and sadness of a foghorn' (2009, 102).
2 In the White genocide conspiracy, denials of the holocaust are bolstered by the belief that there exists a 'Jewish elite' determined to undermine the 'White race' through immigration, LGBTQ+ rights, and feminism (Lawrence et al. 2021).
3 In fact, Seshadri-Crooks asks: '[w]hat would be the cluster of concepts that could establish such an identity?' (2000, 141).

References

Brown, Kimberly N. 2020. '"STAY WOKE': post-Black filmaking and the afterlife of slavery in Jordan Peele's *Get Out*." In *Slavery and the Post-Black Imagination*, edited by Bertram D. Ashe and Ilka Saal (106–123). Seattle, WA: University of Washington Press.

Du Bois, W.E.B. 1969. *Dusk of Dawn: An Essay Toward an Autobiography of a Race Concept*. New York, NY: Schocken Books.

Fanon, Frantz. 2008. *Black Skin, White Masks*. New York, NY: Grove Press.

Fink, Bruce. 1997. *The Lacanian Subject: Between Language and Jouissance*. Princeton, NJ: Princeton University Press.

Fink, Bruce. 1999. *A Clinical Introduction to Lacanian Psychoanalysis: Theory and Technique*. Cambridge, MA: Harvard University Press.

George, Sheldon. 2014. "From alienation to cynicism: race and the Lacanian unconscious." *Psychoanalysis, Culture & Society* 19, no. 4: 360–378.

George, Sheldon. 2016. *Trauma and Race: A Lacanian Study of African American Racial Identity*. Waco, TX: Baylor University Press.

George, Sheldon. 2022. "The Lacanian subject of race: sexuation, the drive, and racial subjectivity." In *Lacan and Race: Racism, Identity, and Psychoanalytic Theory*, edited by Sheldon George and Derek Hook (241–262). Abingdon, UK: Routledge.

Gherovici, Patricia. 2022. "The lost souls of the barrio: Lacanian psychoanalysis in the Ghetto." In *Lacan and Race Racism, Identity, and Psychoanalytic Theory*, edited by Sheldon George and Derek Hook (183–204). Abingdon, UK: Routledge.

Gilroy, Paul. 1993. *The Black Atlantic: Modernity and Double Consciousness*. London, UK: Verso.

Kendi, Ibram X. 2016. *Stamped from the Beginning: The Definitive History of Racist Ideas in America*. New York, NY: Nation Books.

Kingsbury, Paul, and Anna J. Secor. 2021. "Introduction: into the void." In *A Place More Void*, edited by Paul Kingsbury and Anna J. Secor (1–28). Lincoln, NE: University of Nebraska Press.

Koschorke, Albrecht. 2017. "Ideology in execution: on Hitler's *Mein Kampf*." In *Tyrants Writing Poetry*, edited by Albrecht Koschorke and KonstantinKaminskij (131–146). Budapest, HU: Central European University Press.

Lacan, Jacques. 1997. *The Seminar of Jacques Lacan, Book III, 1955–56: The Psychoses*, edited by Jacques-Alain Miller. London, UK: Routledge.

Lacan, Jacques. 2004. *The Four Fundamental Concepts of Psycho-Analysis*, edited by Jacques-Alain Miller. London, UK: Karnac.

Lawrence, David, Limor Simhony-Philpott, and Danny Stone. 2021. *Antisemitism and Misogyny: Overlap and Interplay*. London, UK: Hope Not Hate.

Leader, Darian. 2012. *What is Madness?*London, UK: Penguin.

McGowan, Todd. 2013. *Enjoying What We Don't Have: The Political Project of Psychoanalysis*. Lincoln, NE: University of Nebraska Press.

McGowan, Todd. 2020. *Universality and Identity Politics*. New York, NY: Columbia University Press.

McGowan, Todd. 2022a. "The bedlam of the lynch mob: racism and enjoying through the other." In *Lacan and Race Racism, Identity, and Psychoanalytic Theory*, edited by Sheldon George and Derek Hook (19–34). Abingdon, UK: Routledge.

McGowan, Todd. 2022b. *The Racist Fantasy: Unconscious Roots of Hatred*. New York, NY: Bloomsbury.

Neroni, Hilary. 2022. "Confederate signifiers in Vermont: fetish objects and racist enjoyment." In *Lacan and Race: Racism, Identity, and Psychoanalytic Theory*, edited by Sheldon George and Derek Hook (51–64). Abingdon, UK: Routledge.

Peele, Jordan, director. *Get Out*. Blumhouse Productions; QC Entertainment; Monkeypaw Productions.

Ragland, Ellie. 1995. *Essays on the Pleasures of Death: From Freud to Lacan*. New York, NY: Routledge.

Regnault, François. 1995. "The Name-of-the-Father." In *Reading Seminar XI: Lacan's Four Fundamental Concepts of Psychoanalysis*, edited by Richard Feldstein, Bruce Fink, and Maire Jaanus (65–76). Albany, NY: State University of New York Press.

Reynoso, Joseph S. 2021. "The racist within." *The Psychoanalytic Quarterly* 90, no. 1: 49–76.
Ruti, Mari. 2009. *A World of Fragile Things: Psychoanalysis and the Art of Living*. Albany, NY: State University of New York Press.
Schreber, Daniel Paul. 2000. *Memoirs of My Nervous Illness*, translated and edited by Ida Macalpine and Richard A. Hunter. New York, NY: New York Review of Books.
Seshadri-Crooks, Kalpana. 2000. *Desiring Whiteness: A Lacanian Analysis of Race*. London, UK: Routledge.
Southern Poverty Law Center (SPLC). n.d. "Michael 'Enoch' Peinovich." https://www.splcenter.org/fighting-hate/extremist-files/individual/michael-enoch-peinovich
Thakur, Gautam Basu. 2020. *Postcolonial Lack: Identity, Culture, Surplus*. Albany, NY: State University of New York Press.
Vanheule, Stijn. 2011. *The Subject of Psychosis: A Lacanian Perspective*. Basingstoke, UK: Palgrave Macmillan.
Wallerstein, Hannah. 2020. "Hunting the real: psychosis and race in the American hospital." *Psychoanalytic Perspectives* 17, no. 3: 257–271.
Žižek, Slavoj. 1999. "The undergrowth of enjoyment: how popular culture can serve as an introduction to Lacan." In *The Žižek Reader*, edited by Elizabeth Wright and Edmond Wright (11–36). Malden, MA: Blackwell Publishing.
Žižek, Slavoj. 2008. *The Plague of Fantasies*. London, UK: Verso.
Žižek, Slavoj. 2012. *Less Than Nothing*. London, UK: Verso.
Žižek, Slavoj. 2022. *Surplus Enjoyment*. London, UK: Bloomsbury.
Zupančič, Alenka. 2005. "Reversals of nothing: the case of the sneezing corpse." *Filozofski vestnik* 26, no. 2: 173–186.
Zupančič, Alenka. 2022. "A short essay on conspiracy theories." In *Objective Fictions: Philosophy, Psychoanalysis, Marxism*, edited by Adrian Johnston, Boštjan Nedoh, and Alenka Zupančič (232–249).

Chapter 7

Race and foreclosure

For Lacan, any human relation requires a founding gesture, indeed, 'a third party [who] has to intervene, one that is the image of something successful, the model of some harmony' (1997, 96). This intervention is the intervention of the Law or that of the father: '[n]ot the natural father, but what is called the father' (Lacan 1997, 96). Accordingly, the Name-of-the-Father (*nom du père*) functions as a metaphor that positions the subject as well as defining the rules and regulations that structure their social relations. Assuming the Name-of-the-Father does not simply prescribe one a Symbolic place (a family lineage, for example), it also induces a prohibition: that is, the 'No' of the Father.[1] While Lacan's account of the Name-of-the-Father took many forms and involved various developments over the course of his work, what remains essential to his use of the concept is the Symbolic function it affords. Indeed, the Name-of-the-Father 'provides the human being with an internalized compass of culturally and socially viable principles, and facilitates understanding of the *(m)other* as well as the behaviour of *significant others*' (Vanheule 2011, 61, italics in original). It is, therefore, the Name-of-the-Father (the paternal metaphor) that both structures and orientates the subject to the socio-Symbolic order, a function which is foreclosed in psychosis. Ultimately, what is refused by the psychotic is the act of symbolization itself.

Adapted from Freud's *Verwerfung*, meaning 'repudiation', Lacan's (1997) foreclosure stands in contrast to the Freudian *Verdrängung*, which means 'repression'. While acts of repression are commonly associated with examples of neurosis, foreclosure is unique to psychosis. Primarily, Lacan's account of foreclosure provides a metaphorical function. The term is usually applied in legal discourse, whereby 'it designates a situation in which a homeowner is unable to make interest payments on a mortgage, as a result of which the lender may seize and sell the property' (Vanheule 2011, 68). In fact, following Chapter 4's discussion of alienation and the subject's relation to the signifier, it is not difficult to conceive of our relation to language as echoing that of a mortgage. We do not 'own' the signifiers we use, but we do live with them. In this sense, language is like a mortgage that is never paid. We live in it and use it, but we never own it.[2] It is this relation with language that is foreclosed in psychosis.[3]

DOI: 10.4324/9781003414209-10

Foreclosure and the Name-of-the-Father

We can consider how in examples of psychosis it is the foreclosure of the Name-of-the-Father that explains the absence of a key signifier, the location of which helps to regulate the subject's relation to the social order, giving it a Symbolic structure. Here:

> [f]oreclosure involves the radical rejection of a particular element from the symbolic order (that is, from language), and not just any element: it involves the element that in some sense grounds or anchors the symbolic order as a whole. When this element is foreclosed, the entire symbolic order is affected.
>
> (Fink 1999, 79)

Importantly, examples of foreclosure do not expel the subject from language, for 'if a signifier is excluded, then one must already be in the signifying order' (Žižek 2012, 860); instead, foreclosure refers to 'the exclusion or suspension of the symbolic efficacy of a key Signifier within their symbolic universe' (Žižek 2012, 860). While the suspension of this Symbolic efficacy works to confound the psychotic's Symbolic disorder, the failure to internalize the Name-of-the-Father—and, thus, the paternal metaphor—results in the very failure of the signifier to offer any interpretation or answer to the question of meaning in psychosis.[4] There is an impediment to the signifier, which leaves a 'hole' in the Symbolic.

Accordingly, it is foreclosure that allows the psychotic to avoid castration as well as the Law (for it is the Father that guarantees the Law). In psychosis, there is no admittance of the Law: the Law is arrested, thus allowing the psychotic to inhabit their own private world (and the designations of their prescribed race). We can also conceive of foreclosure as denoting a lack of credibility towards the Name-of-the-Father. This emphasizes that the Name-of-the-Father is not lost in psychosis; rather its metaphorical function has failed or is not required. Following Benvenuto, '[w]e could say that in psychosis we have an unfather, just as we say undecided or unable' (2020, 134). Furthermore, without the Name-of-the-Father the psychotic is left facing the enigma of the Other Usually, the '"Father" is the *answer* to this enigma, the *symbolization* of this deadlock' (Žižek 2004, 90, italics in original), but, with its foreclosure, we can conceive how the psychosis of race maintains an unbearable anxiety towards the Other.

The absent phallus

With the foreclosure of the signifier and the Name-of-the-Father, the psychotic achieves no phallic meaning. Indeed, it is important not to conceive of the phallus as referring to the biological penis, but as a requirement in Symbolic identification that works alongside the incorporation of the Name-of-the-Father. Vanheule elaborates:

> Lacan's formula of the paternal metaphor indicates that at the level of the unconscious answers to questions of the existence of the subject cannot be found. It is precisely the incorporation of the Name-of-the-Father that provides a framework to address them. In other words, the Name-of-the-Father provides a symbolic structure whereby answers to these questions can be constructed. In principle, this is done via symbolic identification. People answer questions of their own existence by adopting phallic traits—characteristics they assume make them desirable to others.
>
> (2011, 65)

In sum, the primary function of the Name-of-the-Father is to offer interpretations of the (m)Other's desire, interpretations which themselves are coordinated around the phallus.[5] The key here is that these interpretations are often assumed, so that, as noted by Vanheule, it is an *assumption* that grounds the adoption of certain phallic traits that are believed to help answer the Other's desire. To this extent, the phallus is a signification of lack—it represents an impossibility that can never be fulfilled, but it is this impossibility which endows the subject with the capacity to use the signifier to garner meaning and attempt interpretation. This does not mean that with the imposition of the Name-of-the-Father we encounter a total meaning or thorough answers to our questions; instead, what the Name-of-the-Father allows, and what the phallus encapsulates, is a tolerable acceptance—a constitutive lack—that structures and coordinates the subject's fundamental uncertainties (Vanheule 2011).

Due to the foreclosure of the Name-of-the-Father and the absence of the phallus, we can consider the psychotic consequences that occur. In psychosis, it is not necessarily the case that there is *no* phallus—and, thus, no lack—but that what is foreclosed is the phallus's capacity to endow interpretation (or, in other words, to acknowledge the 'gap' that would provide the signifier its interpretative capacity). There is a lack of a lack and, therefore, an absence of interpretation. As noted in Chapter 6, the absence of this lack does not provide any Symbolic fulfilment. With the psychotic remaining detached from the lack that endows the subject's entry into the Symbolic order—the subject's constitutive lack—they are left with the disorder of the Symbolic. There is a disruption in Symbolic mediation, resulting in the psychotic occupying their own unique relation to the process of Symbolic mediation (and, thus, an alternative relation to the Symbolic and the Other).

Moreover, it is not simply the case that these relations reject the phallus, but that by defying castration the psychotic has *their* phallus. Here, 'the phallus is a fantasy object *a* that has achieved discursive dominance as the representative of being, presenting itself as the possession that signals a completion that defies castration' (George 2016, 25). This defiance is obtained through the possession of the object *a* of race, a 'completion' that achieves discursive dominance by representing the subject's being—*their* race.

However, it is essential to draw a distinction between the phallus's Symbolic function, as that which provides meaning and which offers an answer to the Other's desire, and its 'obtainment' in examples of psychosis. This 'obtainment' posits an ambiguity in the psychotic's relation to the phallus. Here, Vanheule notes how, in Lacan's account of Schreber, it is 'Schreber [who] aims to be the point around which God's desire, which is chaotic up until then, is organized' (2020, 193). This results in an ambiguous conflation, where, rather than being conceived as exclusive, both 'being' and 'having' overlap (Vanheule 2020). Indeed, '[h]e who wants to be the phallus cannot have it, yet, when the radical abscence [sic] of a phallus is at stake, "being" and "having" are intermingled' (Vanheule 2020, 193).

Consequently, in the psychosis of race, the foreclosure of the phallus results in an intermingling of the distinction between 'being' and 'having'. In the process of racialization, this distinction is conflated, to the extent that the subject's *being* is tied to the fact that they have *their* race. Put differently, while 'being' prescribes a certain lack (a want to be), in the psychosis of race this 'being' is combined with the act of 'having' so that the prescription of race constitutes the positivization of lack itself. It is this conflation between 'being' and 'having' which denotes a lack of a lack: a lack of the constitutive lack that would endow the phallus its interpretative capacity.[6] There is in fact no need to debate or interpret one's racial distinction, if only on the grounds that one's racial distinction is visibly prescribed. These prescriptions, however, remain ambiguous, and it is in this way that race *masquerades* as the phallus: an object *a* which is inherently, and, paradoxically, nothing.

Certainly, this path takes a diversion to that followed by Sheshadri-Crooks (2000) and George (2014). In correspondence with Seshadri-Crooks's account of Whiteness as a master-signifier, George contends that it is Whiteness, as phallus, which encourages a sense of wholeness. Accordingly, while 'whiteness can never reconstitute being' (George 2014, 269), for George, this means that 'whiteness functions only as the *object a* that merely *promises* wholeness by simultaneously masquerading as the phallus, the castrated object that manifests the illusory site of bliss in the Imaginary form of the subjective-self' (2014, 269, italics in original). Where I draw a distinction is in the 'promise' that Whiteness affords and the 'mastery' it entails (Seshadri-Crooks 2000).[7] Indeed, the power that is afforded to the phallus does not lie in the satisfaction of potentiality obtaining the phallus as 'the castrated object'. Power always fails to provide satisfaction; it is 'the master's secret envy of the slave' which undermines any satisfaction that could be afforded to the totality of power (McGowan 2003, 32).[8] Rather, in the psychosis of race, the psychotic has *their* object *a* and, consequently, it has obtained the phallus, but without any meaning or the capacity to interpret meaning. Therefore, while, in accordance with George (2014), Whiteness fails to offer a sense of wholeness to the subject's being, ultimately, it is the formal structure of race that endows a psychotic position where meaning and the 'promise' of wholeness is marked by an empty acceptance: a nothing or non-meaning that bears no further interpretation... *race is what it is*. Instead, with the object *a* and the phallus at hand, what the psychotic is left with is a total *jouissance*.

An unhoused and unbounded *jouissance*

With the imposition of the Name-of-the-Father comes the subject's eviction from *jouissance*. In so doing, the subject can distance themselves from the object and its traumatic *jouissance* (as well as the desire of the mOther). In psychosis, however, there is no distance. With 'the stem of the Name-of-the-Father ... missing, the branches break loose; there is no tree or root system to hold them', and, what is more, '[t]here is no limit to *jouissance*, no spigot able to bear the pouring speech that spills every which way without a container' (Braunstein 2015, 94–95). This failure to contain leads to an engulfing of *jouissance* that marks the disorientation of the psychotic structure: indeed, a disorientation predicated on the very fact that there remains no distance to the object *a* of race and its phallic representations; no distance to the presence of the Other and the *jouissance* it experiences; and, thus, no distance to the over-bearing proximity of the Real.

The existence of an unhoused and unbounded *jouissance* is founded upon the psychotic's relation to the Law and its recourse to prohibition. Here, 'the function of prohibition reveals that the law ... cannot provide a guarantee of its meaning' (Seshadri-Crooks 2000, 41). In effect, '[t]he law ... speaks with a forked tongue' insofar as '[b]y prohibiting *jouissance* it discloses the subject's potential for it' (Seshadri-Crooks 2000, 41). This is certainly the case for the non-psychotic; yet, in psychosis, there is no prohibition of *jouissance*. Rather, with the full potential of *jouissance*, the psychotic readily perceives the Law's 'forked tongue'.

It is in this regard that the Law loses its metaphorical function in psychosis. While the Name-of-the-Father ensures that any signification and/or interpretation should not be taken literally, that there is a 'space' through which meaning, interpretation, and being can be debated and contested, in psychosis, the process of signification can only ever be taken literally. As a result, the Law can overwhelm the psychotic in their private *jouissance*. Further still, while the Law remains, it cannot be trusted. Here, we return to the very political frustrations that are enacted by both the Left and the Right, as well as to the underlying structure that binds examples of racism and anti-racism. For both the racist and anti-racist subject, what remains lost is the structuring absence which founds the Law. Whether it is the failure of the Law to curtail the other's uninhibited *jouissance*, as in the case of the racist, or the failure of the state to adequately tackle racial discrimination and inequality, as argued by the anti-racist, what traverses both positions is the Law's obscenity.[9]

Name-of-the-Father, primordial signifier, and the lack of credibility

There is an underlying sense in this approach that the Symbolic function of the Name-of-the-Father emanates from its role as the primordial signifier, that which McGowan clarifies as 'not the first signifier that we utter but the one that acts as a ground for all other signifiers' (2019, 51). It is 'the signifier of law that non-psychotic subjects integrate into their subjectivity' (McGowan 2019, 51). For Lacan, it is clear that the meaning of the primordial signifier is that 'it quite precisely means nothing' (1997, 151); a 'nothing' which nonetheless provides and ultimately grounds a certain efficacy to the process of signification. Here, McGowan clarifies, '[a]s long as psychotics remain speaking subjects, they cannot function without the primordial signifier. This signifier remains operative after the psychotic act of its foreclosure. But it loses its efficacy for the subject' (2019, 51). This loss of efficacy is compounded by the fact that the psychotic fails to acknowledge that the primordial signifier is 'nothing'.

It is for this reason that we can begin to uncover how the primordial signifier and the Name-of-the-Father are not grounded in some ultimate truth or essential essence, but that their 'credibility is purely an effect of speech pragmatics: it is only to the extent that a person has faith in a Father figure or master figure that his rules and explanations function as a law whereby sense can be made of desire' (Vanheule 2011, 136). There can, therefore, be various *Names*-of-the-Father; the key is that their existence and their authority rests upon whether they are *perceived* to be credible.

Accordingly, what occurs in foreclosure is not simply a rejection of the Name-of-the-Father, but a rejection of its very credibility. Indeed, for the psychotic, this presents a paradoxical position. In rejecting the credibility of the Name-of-the-Father, and in failing to acknowledge the inherent absence of the primordial signifier, the psychotic nonetheless prescribes the Name-of-the-Father an *assumed* credibility (in order to discredit something, one must conceive of it as holding credibility, if only to then be discredited). To this extent, there remains a certain truth in the psychotic's position. While, together, the Name-of-the-father, the Law, and the primordial signifier all obtain their authority because of the indifference that they hold for the subject, for the psychotic, it is the veracity of their indifference towards human experience that causes such distress. Ultimately, the psychotic struggles to appreciate and accept the fundamental non-sensicality of the signifier—that any primordial signifier or Law is simply a 'symbolic entity' (McGowan 2019, 53).[10] Though the psychotic has no problem conceding to the nonsense of the signifier, ultimately, they fail to *accept* it.

We can now begin to see how the lack of Symbolic efficiency is, in psychosis, tantamount to the lack of credibility that it bestows upon the Name-of-the-Father as well as the process of signification that it upholds—a paradoxical position that maintains a disjointed relation to the Symbolic order and its conceived inefficacy. The effects of this are considered by Žižek, who asks:

> [s]o what happens to the functioning of the symbolic order when the symbolic Law loses its efficiency, when it no longer functions properly? What we get are subjects who are strangely derealized or, rather, depsychologized, as if we are dealing with robotic puppets obeying a strange blind mechanism.
>
> (2001, 76)

Key to Žižek's reply is the 'strange blind mechanism' which confronts this 'depsychologized' subject. Whereas the effects of this depsychologization can be read as a form of psychosis, what the subject is left to 'obey' is a 'blind mechanism' that works to both position and segregate the subject and its reality. In fact, while drawing upon Lacan, Khan makes a direct link between racism and the decline in Symbolic efficiency and Name-of-the-Father:

> [f]or Lacan, racism is tied to the problematic of segregation, which is intensified as a consequence of the decline of the Name-of-the-Father in an age when the discourses of science and capitalism are bringing about fundamental shifts. In 'Proposition of 9 October 1967,' Lacan situates the extension of segregation in the context of Nazi Germany and the concentration camp, indicating that science rearranges social groupings at the same time as it introduces a universalizing principle that, in turn, accentuates processes of segregation.
>
> (2018, 149–150)

There remains an underlying paradox in Khan's account which speaks to the foreclosure in psychosis. Indeed, by 'rearrang[ing] social groupings at the same time as it introduces a universalizing principle that, in turn, accentuates processes of segregation', we can observe how any act of segregation relies upon a form of psychosis that perceives segregation as a principal of universality. Here, the foreclosure of the Name-of-the-Father results not in the failure of signification *per se*, but in the perpetuation of a Symbolic inefficiency which leaves the subject lost amidst a variety of Symbolic differences that rigidly define one's racial segregation (as well as that of others).[11] These differences are brought to bear through the segregation they infer, wherein new and ongoing forms of seclusion, which both mark and delineate the subject's reality, are enacted. In effect, the decline in Symbolic efficiency speaks not to its eradication, but to an unending variety of differences that are unmoored due to the foreclosure of the Name-of-the-Father. The process of meaning making is, in examples of psychosis, exactly what is lost in the Symbolic's declining efficiency, resulting in the multiplicity of sameness or a universal segregation. In so doing, the structure of psychosis presents an entire field of meaning, which is not just foreclosed to the subject, but which also emphasizes and perpetuates their very externality.

The master-signifier's inherent absence

Subsequently, in contrast to Seshadri-Crooks, for whom 'the structure of racial difference is founded on a master signifier—Whiteness—that produces a logic of differential relations' (2000, 20), it is, instead, the foreclosure of this signifier which works to perpetuate an array of racial differences that fundamentally delineate the subject from any racial other. To elucidate this point, it is important to give further clarification to Seshadri-Crooks, where she explains:

> 'Whiteness' should be discerned as an unconscious signifier, one that generates a combinatory with its own set of inclusions and exclusions that determine the subject. To be a raced subject is to be subjected to the signifier Whiteness. The law of Whiteness establishes race as a 'neutral' description of human difference. Thus, as a mode of ordering the world, the signifier Whiteness installs a system of racial difference that is unconsciously assimilated by all raced subjects as a factor of language, and thus as 'natural.' In other words, Whiteness, as the inaugural term of difference, is the primary signifier of the symbolic order of race. In this sense, Whiteness is the transindividual aspect of the unconscious which subjects us all 'equally' to the logic of race.
>
> (2000, 24–25)

Clearly, in the psychosis of race, the subject is 'subjected' to the signifier, but not necessarily in the way that Seshadri-Crooks follows. In Seshadri-Crooks's account, it is 'Whiteness' that inaugurates racial differences in the 'symbolic order of race'. The concern here is that to level 'Whiteness' in the role of the master-signifier—as the inaugurator of racial difference—is, in the first instance, to begin with a conception of 'difference' that is *then* unconsciously assimilated. This passes too quickly over the inherent emptiness of the master-signifier and the fundamental non-sense that underpins the Symbolic order. Ultimately, it assumes that we begin with difference rather than the inherent gap, the constitutive lack, which grounds the master-signifier (as well as the subject and Symbolic order). Along these lines, one's subjection to race occurs not at the behest of the master-signifier, but at the very failure to engage with the inherent absence of this signifier. In so doing, racial difference is psychotically assimilated due to the signifier being taken at face value and by succumbing to a rigid segregation that functions on the assumption of 'real' racial differences that are visibly perceived.

This in no way ignores the extent to which race comes to be perceived 'as a "neutral" description of human difference' (Sheshadri-Crooks 2000, 25). What compels this neutrality, however, is the very failure to acknowledge race's inherent absence. Indeed, while Seshadri-Crooks's critique sheds light on the inherent ambiguity of the master-signifier, 'Whiteness', what such a critique falls foul of is erecting such signifiers in order to be critiqued. When the critique of a 'master-signifier' is required, one should stay clear of succumbing to the job of the master-signifier itself—that is, of 'filling it out'.

Acknowledged and unacknowledged racism: fundamentalism, multicultural diversity, and rational racism

As argued in Chapter 3, we can conceive how race remains a contradictory phenomenon that detrimentally maintains its authority through its perceived neutrality, while, at the same, time embedding itself with a variety of signifiers, each of which give meaning to its significance. It is in this sense that the psychosis of race takes race *literally*. On the one hand, race, for many, bestows no meaning and no significance, a position often reflected in those who seek to present their 'colour-blindness'. Equally, for others, race presents a surplus of meaning, which explains and delineates everything there is to know about human beings. For the racist, it is these prescribed differences that are supported by an assumed racial hierarchy.

Considering the psychotic's relation to the Symbolic as predicated on a chaos of meaning, and a lack of interpretation, such chaos remains underpinned by a fundamental emptiness. Consequently, when confronted with the object *a* of race, the subject is met with both the inherent nothingness of the object (an impossibility which can never be defined) and a subsequent surplus which seeks 'something' to this nothing. It is in this way that the differences which underscore our racial designations become subject to a melange of racially-appropriated definitions and explanations—each of which provide no answer or response to race's underlying absence, beyond its own non-meaning.

Thus, despite such chaos, what remains significant to the psychotic's relation to the signifier is that the process of establishing meaning, as part of a signifying chain, does not occur. Importantly, we do not lose the signifier of race in the psychosis of race; instead, when foreclosed from the process of signification, the signifier appears in the Real. This Real grants an excess, which, while working within the disorder of the Symbolic, finds itself manifested in examples of acknowledged and unacknowledged racism. Here, the psychosis of race can be observed in fundamentalism, multicultural diversity, and rational racism.

1   Fundamentalism

Directed at the Other's lack of authority, the foreclosure that fundamentalism enacts offers a return to traditional forms of authority, such as religious authoritarianism. Yet, in expelling the Other 'as the guarantee of the minimally tolerable co-existence of subjects', fundamentalism avers 'a really existing Other subject', for whom the fundamentalist seeks the reassertion of the Law and its prohibition (Wells 2014, 100). The effect of this 'really existing Other' is that it assumes an Other of the Other: an Other that exists beyond the Other's lack of authority (this will be returned to in Chapter 8). There is, therefore, a psychotic certainty that underpins the fundamentalist's conviction; a conviction which both masks and obscures the constitutive lack that grounds the Symbolic order. What this return establishes is a form of psychosis that aims to eradicate the proliferation of particular identities. Much like the psychotic, the fundamentalist fails to see the lack that is inherent to these identities, and, thus, by seeking their eradication, serves only to bolster their apparent significance. It is in this sense that the fundamentalist's actions end up supporting what it wishes to prevent: the proliferation of cultural identities under capitalism.

2 Multicultural diversity

One important characteristic underpinning the psychotic's relation to the Symbolic order is their sense of detachment, or, as noted previously, the psychotic's externalization to the process of signification. In fact, while the psychotic has no problem engaging with signifiers, such engagement is marked by their dislocation from the effects of the signifier. It is this same dislocation that underscores examples of multicultural diversity, where a need to 'respect' other cultures, without ever engaging with these very cultures, is upheld. McGowan notes:

> [o]ne must respect the difference of, say, the American Indian culture lost with white conquest—and even learn about it, perhaps adopt certain aspects of it for oneself—but one must not work for a full return of this culture. One must respect Islamic religious practices, but one must not attempt to impose them universally, which is precisely what the real believer would do.
>
> (2013, 273)

What occurs in such examples is a form of psychosis predicated on the detachment that underpins one's multicultural position. The multicultural subject can, for instance, respect the other's culture, but there is never the requirement, nor the desire, to practice or perform the necessary work of engaging with the reality of this culture: that is, with the tensions, antagonisms, and differences that frame the other's idiosyncrasies.

In other instances, exhibiting one's multicultural credentials can also be achieved through assertions of 'White privilege': a predominantly liberal notion which aims to ensure that one becomes aware of the social privileges provided to them by their race (such as, being White). In fact, one of the major benefits of White privilege is that the White subject doesn't need to be aware of it—it is invisible. For Peggy McIntosh, the effects of this 'invisibility' functions metaphorically like an 'invisible knapsack' (McIntosh 1989). Here, 'White privilege is like an invisible weightless knapsack of special provisions, maps, passports, codebooks, visas, clothes, tools and blank checks' (McIntosh 1989, 1). This knapsack is unknowingly carried by the White *individual*, for whom the benefits and unearned assets of being White are irrevocably prescribed and assumed. In order to identify such benefits, McIntosh listed 26 conditions where her Whiteness functioned to provide her a certain privilege.[12] The overall purpose of McIntosh's original article was to help encourage forms of self-reflexivity so that these privileges could be realized and, hopefully, used to 'reconstruct power systems' (McIntosh 1989, 3).[13]

Ignoring the concern that such endeavours remain predicated on the fact that becoming consciously aware of one's privilege can, in some form or another, help to tackle racism, of greater concern is the fact that by promoting the notion that race exists as a form of unearned privilege is to succumb to the racist conviction that racial differences can be hierarchically arranged according to some predetermined metric of privileged status (Black 2020). Inevitably, it assumes 'that if the unprivileged only had the same privileges, they would be happy too' (Zalloua 2020, 29). Instead, by identifying and declaring the very privileges that are deemed to be attributable to the particularity of the White race, assertions of White privilege fundamentally assert that it is a 'privilege' to be immune from racism.

Furthermore, while working as a form of racecraft (Fields and Fields 2012), examples of White privilege openly announce the position of the White racist as superior to the racial other. On the one hand, accounts of White privilege function to identify the very privileges attributed to the White race, whilst on the other hand, it assumes that these same privileges are inherently invisible, and, thus, unbeknown to the White subjects who bear them. Certainly, this is not to discount the fact that there are a vast number of situations where being White is preferable to being Black. Yet, what examples of White privilege tend to assert, and this speaks to the list that McIntosh's (1989) article provides, is the paranoia in finding, identifying, and admonishing one's 'privilege' (if this is ever possible). Far beyond McIntosh's original list of '26 conditions', new forms of privilege must indefinitely be uncovered and decried. In so doing, the very structures that maintain such privilege go unchallenged, with race itself being politically valued. In its politically correct mode, this paranoia finds its comparison in the determination to locate, identify, and abhor any action deemed to be 'politically incorrect' (Black 2021). Formally, the effects of this 'politically correct' paranoia echo examples of racist paranoia, which see nothing but the other's malpractice everywhere.

This can also be seen in evocations of 'White guilt' and associated forms of racial atonement, which ultimately rely upon the pathological perpetuation of a host of anti-racism initiatives, steered by forms of White confession that elicit a level of paranoia and personal distance. While examples of paranoia are directed towards one's actions and behaviours, including the comments and manners of those around them (the politically incorrect), a sense of personal distance is predicated on the fact that the out-spoken multiculturalist, fully equipped with the cultural knowledge that underpins their anti-racist strategies and diversity/equality initiatives, never encounters nor achieves the inclusion of those very groups they seek to involve. Much like the aforementioned critique of White privilege, the discrimination underpinning structural forms of racism goes unchallenged and is ultimately ignored amidst a pathological concern with one's own anti-racism. The detachment this enacts is dependent upon the fact that such actions are maintained by, but also reliant upon, the racism that they seek to attack. Here, one's multicultural position remains separate to the 'victim' of racism as well as the racist perpetuator: a position that ultimately requires 'the other's' racism and the racist victim in order to be sustained. In the end, such actions work to cement the psychotic's failure to recognize both their own and the Other's constitutive lack.

3   Rational racism

The third form of psychotic management is the existence of a 'rational racism'. This follows closely Lacan's (1997) adoption of Hélène Deutsch's (1942) 'as if mechanisms'. What characterizes the 'as if' identification is the fact that 'expressions of feeling are "in form only"' (Leader 2012, 198). By adopting certain identities, the psychotic can behave 'as if' they have identified a position within the Symbolic order. Instead, what undergirds such forms of identification is 'their lack of affectivity, their uncritical nature and their lack of subjective implication' (Vanheule 2011, 73). This lack of affect is useful for the psychotic as it allows them to adopt a position without ever having to question the relevance, significance, or legitimacy of this position.

We can observe a similar function in those examples where one seeks a rational explanation to one's racism or where one's racism takes on a decidedly innocuous form. In the case of the former, it is in accordance with the sense of externality that is prescribed by the 'as if' identification that the rational racist is able to present their racism through forms of explanation which reveal no sentimentality or awareness.[14] In such instances, examples of racism work alongside, as well as mask, 'rational propositions that hold up well under scrutiny for racism' (Hook 2004, 684). Hook elaborates on such propositions when he draws upon the following example:

> it is not because Mr. X is black that I do not want to work with, live alongside, talk to, engage with him, it is rather because of the issue of cultural differences, problems of language, disparate backgrounds, and so forth that would make communication and hence cooperation difficult between us.
>
> (2004, 684)

The effect of providing a rational explanation to one's racism works to psychotically divest the subject from engaging with the premises of their reason. They can blindly identify with the racist content, without ever engaging with the explanation it relies upon.

In other instances, such rationalization may be bolstered by a distinct lack of affect on behalf of the subject, such as when certain innocuous statements are used in an often vague and matter-of-fact manner. For example, while 'All Lives Matter', 'Blue Lives Matter', and 'It's OK to be white' may be cynically asserted, it is usually the explanations that follow such statements that suggest a level of 'rationalization'. The effect here is that one's very implication in the asserted statement is, on the face of it, innocently normalized. Though appearing harmless in their apparent obviousness, the insincerity that such statements rely upon is hidden under a logic that assumes their apparent universality.[15] Again, what is ignored in such pronouncements is any further questioning of the very position from which these phrases are made.

Analogous to examples of 'rational racism' is the reference to one's assumed 'colour blindness'. Again, this is uniquely explored in the film, *Get Out* (Peele 2017). The film's twist centres upon the fact that both the film's protagonist, Chris, and us, as the audience, come to realize that Chris has been brought to his girlfriend's house, not to meet her parents and family, but to be auctioned to a group of nominally White and middle-class individuals who seek to appropriate Chris's body. Against his will, Chris is to be bought and then subjected to the 'Coagula Procedure'.[16]

Before undergoing the procedure, Chris is afforded the opportunity to speak to Jim Hudson (Stephen Root), the man who has purchased Chris's 'body', and, specifically, Chris's 'gift', his eyes (Chris is a skilled photographer and it is this talent which Jim wishes to appropriate through the surgical procedure).[17] The film plays on the concern that for certain White liberals there exists an almost pathological obsession with ideas of Blackness which are attributed to the Black body. While other scenes within the film suggest an obsession with Blacknesss, Jim's appropriation of Chris's body follows his own rational justification.

Upon explaining his reason for purchasing Chris, Jim responds: 'I couldn't give a shit what colour you are. What I want is deeper. I want… your eye, man. I want those things you see through'.[18] In this way, Jim accedes to a position of colour blindness, explaining that his involvement in the procedure remains underpinned by his own rational justification: the appropriation of a certain essence which he *sees* in Chris (his eyes), but which, for Jim, bears no relation to Chris's 'race'. This sense of colour blindness is further emphasized by the fact that Jim is blind:

> [a]s a blind man, Jim literally cannot see race; this is reinforced by his claim that he does not 'give a shit' what color Chris is. Despite his color-blindness, however, Jim is more than happy to benefit from a racist system that profits

on the theft and exchange of black bodies. Through the literalization of metaphor, Peele thus satirizes white complicity with systems of racist oppression.

(Gillota 2021, 13)

Here we observe how the psychosis of race is played out in a 'rational' response that bears no consideration to the racist Symbolic order that helps to sustain such a response. By not 'giving a shit' about the colour of Chris's skin, Jim's colour-blindness follows a path of rational non-interrogation—Chris's 'race' is beside the point (it is what it is). By allowing Jim to rationalize his non-racism, the prejudice supporting Jim's actions can continue, without question. In so doing, Jim's ability to partake in the purchase of Chris reveals a certain level of psychotic dislocation.

This sense of dislocation can also be seen in examples where one claims a 'moral humility' in issues connected to race and racism (Hook 2011, 498). This occurs when one accentuates their very dissattachment to the problems of racism and to the experience of living through or being affected by examples of racism. Without experiencing examples of racial violence, one can absolve oneself of understanding the effects of racism. Accordingly, 'the danger of this approach is that it leads all too easily to a type of privilege all of its own, to a type of moral exceptionalism' (Hook 2011, 498); an exceptionalism that is itself predicated on the subject's exemption towards *its* racism.

Slavery and the delusional metaphor

There remains one major function of the Name-of-the-Father that has yet to be discussed—its 'metaphorical' importance. At the crux of Lacan's paternal metaphor is the function it plays in prohibiting the signifier's potentially unending metonymy. Through the father's name, the paternal metaphor enacts an interdiction that is absolute. Yet, as previously noted, such an act bears no essential justification, beyond the importance that is attributed to the position of enunciation. Accordingly, while the metaphor is grounded in an inherent absence, the significance of the paternal metaphor is that, metaphorically, it 'replaces what isn't there with a signifier that is' (McGowan 2019, 62).

Due to the foreclosure of the parental metaphor, '[t]he metaphorical use of language is not available to psychotics' (Fink 1999, 91). In effect, the psychotic lacks the creative distance that is afforded to the metaphorical act, and, as a result, hallucinations and delusions can occur. With the failure of the metaphor to anchor the process of signification, '[t]he delusion is an attempt at a metaphor to make sense of the chaos of dissociated signifiers' (Braunstein 2015, 92). Here, 'a delusion can be qualified as a way of articulating the subject with respect to questions of existence when a support in the Symbolic is lacking' (Vanheule 2011, 121). Vanheule elaborates:

> [i]n its elementary form, a delusion reflects the conclusion that one's thoughts and actions are actively manipulated by an external force. This attribution does not safeguard the subject against disintegration, which is why a delusion is not considered to be stabilizing. Stability can be obtained by creating a delusional metaphor and by embedding the subject in a social bond. A delusional metaphor stabilizes the delusion from within. Through a central signifier it names the motives of the mad Other, which produces order in the Symbolic, and designates an identity for the subject. Moreover, by embedding the subject in a social bond a delusion can be stabilized from without. Inherently a delusion is a private undertaking. Lacan stresses that if the delusional metaphor itself can be introduced in cultural contexts, or if bonds of friendships can be maintained next to the delusion, a structure for articulating the subject is provided.
>
> (2011, 121)

To this end, the delusional metaphor affords a restorative role in psychosis; an explanatory function that allows the psychotic to find some sort of position in the process of signification, as well as ensuring that they can make sense of their experiences.[19] In short, '[t]he delusional metaphor attempts to remedy the failure in the paternal metaphor, bestowing meaning on the lack in the Other' (Braunstein 2015, 95).

To help explain the effects of the delusional metaphor in the psychosis of race, we can return to George's criticisms of Du Bois, for whom 'slavery functions as a dominating master signifier that delineates the meaning of Du Bois's racial identity' (George 201649). George explains:

> [n]ot only does [… slavery] substitute itself for Du Bois' proper name as the signifier that will structure Symbolic representation of his (racial) being, but it also conflates this being with the injury, insult, and discrimination both he and the nonwhite world suffer today and have suffered in the past, thus bonding them in a common identity. This substitution of identity and conflation of feelings is explained by a Lacanian understanding of metaphor as that which brings to a halt the metonymical sliding of desire and meaning through manifestation of a more lasting substitution.
>
> (2016, 49)

Accordingly, '[i]n pinning his identity to slavery, Du Bois moves from the operations of metonymy to a metaphorical process whereby slavery is substituted as the dominating signifier for his (racial) identity' (George 2016, 49). This is not to suggest that slavery was, or is, a 'delusion', or that the history of slavery (and its ongoing impacts) should be ignored. Rather, what underscores George's critique is the very way in which slavery comes to anchor and fix Du Bois's racial identity. As noted, 'metaphor involves the substitution of the signifier for that which it names, the function of metaphor is to remanifest being, to give presence, through language, to absence' (George 2016, 49). Thus, what occurs in the case of Du Bois is a remanifestation of being that is tied to slavery's past. By fixing his racial identity to the history of slavery, Du Bois obscures his inherent lack via a metaphorical 'fixing' that both restores, as well as binds, his very being to the trauma of slavery.

Following the psychosis of race, we can consider how the foreclosure of the parental metaphor is reflected in the stabilization that slavery as metaphor achieves for Du Bois. As an anchor in the process of signification, slavery takes on a level of stabilization that is not unlike the delusional metaphor. It is here that:

> [s]lavery allows for the historicizing and, thus, depersonalizing of both being and lack for Du Bois. This historicizing becomes possible because the racism of slavery that attempted to elide the being of slaves by pinning subjective lack exclusively to them also produced slavery as a central historical representative of subjective lack for later generations of African Americans. Racial identity itself, whether imposed by racism or willfully embraced by contemporary African Americans as the historical context for self-understanding and being, not only crystallizes for African Americans the indisputable link between slavery and the racism they continue to suffer but also may collapse their personal sense of being with the historical lack emerging from slavery.
>
> (George 2016, 51)

In effect, what slavery provides for Du Bois is an explanatory function; a form of organization that fixes his (racial) being to his subject (racial) identity. Where the delusion resides within the metaphor of slavery is in the metaphorical substitution it enacts: a reparatory function that organizes the subject 'away from personal lack and toward an external bad encounter that presents itself as a fixing manifestation of loss for all members of the race' as well as 'defin[ing] all lack and all suffering as racial' (George 2016, 52). Whereas what is obfuscated in the psychotic's use of the delusional metaphor is lack itself, it is in the case of slavery that 'personal lack is conflated with the mirrored lack of the slave in an unsuturing that fragments these subjects across time to bind personal lack to the historical past' (George 2016, 64). Though, for George, 'racism grounds the African American subject's psychic sense of lack not in the split self but in the racial past' (2016, 51), what is ultimately maintained in this relation to the past is the lack of a lack, or, as previously noted, a positivization of lack that is manifested in 'the historical lack emerging from slavery'.

What the psychosis of race provides, therefore, is an appreciation of how the trauma of slavery comes to constitute a metaphorical function that further obscures the subject's inherent lack. Here slavery is inculcated into a process of racialization that psychotically ties the subject's lack to the lack in slavery, thus ensuring the subject's racialization within the racial Symbolic order. As metaphor, slavery 'replaces the absent paternal metaphor and provides an anchor in discourse, based on which the subject's identity ("who am I?") and the desire of the (m)Other ("what do you want from me?") can be signified' (Vanheule 2011, 115). As a form of racial being, slavery further compounds the psychosis of race by the relative 'stability' it affords. This stability works to ameliorate the foreclosure of the paternal metaphor by masking the inherent antagonism of the social order. What the psychosis of race avows, therefore, is the 'impossibility' of a compromise that further fixes the subject to their prescribed racial being. As nothing more than the object to the subject's racial being (its object *a* of race), the history of slavery, and the trauma therein, becomes the property of Blacks (Haider 2018). In the end, the delusion that abides goes no further than supplementing lack with a past that frames and inhibits the subject's constitutive lack.

Notes

1 It is in this sense that repression allows the neurotic to function. In neurosis, 'the Name-of-the-Father is synonymous with the operation of repression—the repression of the trauma and the lack of Sense introduced by the trauma' (Fimiani 2021, 58). In other words, it is in accordance with the Name-of-the-Father—the prohibitionary 'No', for example—that the neurotic is able to repress the effects of its castration in language.
2 For Lacan, the subject is the 'slave of a discourse' whereby their 'place is already inscribed at … birth' (2006, 414).
3 It is through foreclosure that the psychotic's unique relation to the forced choice can be found. As noted, rather than acknowledging the inherent limitations imposed by the forced choice, 'the psychotic subject acts as if he has a truly free choice "all the way along"' (Žižek 2000, 19). In fact, we can go further and suggest that, for the psychosis of race, there is no need for a choice to be made: the act of *choosing* is itself foreclosed (as discussed in Chapter 4, the choice is already chosen).
4 The Symbolic function of the paternal metaphor is a sacrifice, on behalf of the subject, of the satisfaction it receives towards being the object of the mOther. Here, the Name-of-the-Father presents a certain translation of the enigma of the mother's desire. Žižek explains that, '[i]n this precise sense, "father" is, according to Lacan's account of the paternal function, a translation or a symptom: a compromise solution that alleviates the unbearable anxiety of directly confronting the void of the other's desire' (2004, 90).
5 The Name-of-the-Father provides a 'social mediation' of desire, which is foreclosed in psychosis (Samuels 2001, 5).
6 While '[t]he phallus is always a fraud' (McGowan 2021), it is this very fraudulence which is foreclosed in the overlap between 'being' and 'having'.
7 References to the promise of mastery that Whiteness establishes are highlighted throughout *Desiring Whiteness*, but this is neatly summarized when Seshadri-Crooks notes: '[f]or the subject of race, Whiteness represents complete mastery, self-sufficiency, and the *jouissance* of Oneness' (2000, 7).
8 McGowan adds: '[i]n an experience of absolute mastery, the master imagines that the slave has access to a *jouissance* that power cannot provide' (2003, 32).
9 This is echoed in Lacan's account of Schreber, where 'Lacan notes that such a God differs radically from the Christian God, which prevailed in Schreber's cultural

context. The Christian God guarantees a law or a principle, for example in Christianity God is love. Schreber's God, by contrast, does not incarnate a law. He is an absolutely untrustworthy figure, which points to foreclosure: the law in [*sic*] not installed at the heart of the Other' (Vanheule 2020, 191).

10 McGowan (2019) makes this point in relation to Schreber's account of God. While noting that 'Schreber's diagnosis of God's failure is accurate', McGowan adds that '[t]he only error in the delusion's approach to God (and the primordial signifier) is that it doesn't recognize God as a symbolic entity. Here, God is not the nonsensical signifier of law but an agent that intervenes in the human world. Despite his power and authority, God, for Schreber, is just another other who wrongly imposes the law on a humanity that he doesn't understand. God is guilty because Schreber conceives him acting like a fellow being rather than like a signifier' (2019, 53).

11 This variety echoes the obfuscation of the 'gap' in psychosis and of the, previously mentioned, 'radical obliteration of Difference, of the antagonistic gap' (Žižek 2006, 314).

12 Upon re-reading the article, I was immediately reminded of the work of Jordan Peterson and his *12 Rules For Life: An Antidote to Chaos* (2018). The problem with Peterson's self-help efforts is that they never contain the chaos they seek to manage. Unsurprisingly, four years later, Peterson was able to release *Beyond Order: 12 More Rules For Life* (2022). At 24 rules, why stop there? I appreciate that comparing McIntosh with Peterson may seem unfair, but what underscores both their efforts is a clear sense of paranoia reflected in the determination, conviction, and certainty that befalls any attempt to fully ac*count* for oneself.

13 Here, examples of self-reflexivity can work to expel further forms of racism, as argued in 'On Reflexive Racism: Disavowal, Deferment and the Lacanian Subject' (Black 2020).

14 Indeed, in failing to achieve a level of Symbolic authenticity to the identity they adopt, the psychotic is marked by a certain hollowness that fundamentally obscures the subject's constitutive lack. In effect, lack works to mask the lack of being through a cocoon of emptiness that comprises the psychotic's identity. What remains unique to such forms of identification, however, is that they require the psychotic to blindly conform to, or, in some cases, over-identify with, such a shallow identity.

15 Such statements can be conceived as examples of false universality (Black 2021).

16 In the film, the Coagula Procedure involves transplanting the brain of one individual into the body of another.

17 For Chris and Jim, it is Jim's brain which is being transferred to Chris's body. As part of the transplant, Chris's consciousness is transferred to the 'Sunken Place' (see Chapter 6). With Chris existing in the 'Sunken Place', and, thus, maintaining a 'limited consciousness', his body is directed and controlled by Jim's consciousness. When watching the film, I am always reminded of the previously mentioned Grace Halsell, the U.S. journalist, who, in seeking to experience the effects of racial discrimination, sought to assume Blackness by undergoing a 'racial transformation' that involved taking medication that darkened her skin's pigmentation (see Introduction). Halsell later published her experiences in *Soul Sister* (1969).

18 In a previous scene, where Chris first meets Jim, unaware of Jim's desire to purchase Chris, we realize that Jim is a blind art gallery owner, who, before he went blind, struggled as a photogragher. Through descriptions provided by Jim's assistant, we realize Jim is a fan of Chris's photography.

19 There is a connection that can be made here between the delusional metaphor in psychosis and Samuels's (2001) reference to naturalized metaphors in the work of Toni Morrison. Here, Samuels notes how Morrison uses examples of naturalized metaphor to help emphasize their 'pernicious effect' (Samuels 2001, 173, fn.5).

Referring to Morrison's *The Bluest Eye* (2016), Samuels argues, 'even if we all know that there is very little connection between human actions and nature's reactions, we cannot stop using these metaphors because they are so central to the very way we think' (2001, 173–174, fn.5). Where I see a connection between the delusional and naturalized metaphor is in the extent to which both forms of metaphor rely upon a taken-for-granted, common sense. In the case of the delusional metaphor, it is the 'delusion' which is taken literally.

References

Benvenuto, Sergio. 2020. *Conversations with Lacan: Seven Lectures for Understanding Lacan.* London, UK: Routledge.

Black, Jack. 2020. "On reflexive racism: disavowal, deferment and the Lacanian subject." *Diacritics* 48, no. 4: 76–101.

Black, Jack. 2021. *Race, Racism and Political Correctness in Comedy – A Psychoanalytic Exploration.* Abingdon, UK: Routledge.

Braunstein, Nestor. 2015. "'You cannot choose to go crazy'." In *Lacan on Madness: Madness, yes you can't*, edited by Patricia Gherovici and Manya Steinkoler (85–98). Hove, UK: Routledge.

Deutsch, Hélène. 1942. "Some forms of emotional disturbance and their relationship to schizophrenia." *The Psychoanalytic Quarterly* 11: 301–321.

Fields, Karen E. and Barabara J.Fields. 2012. *Racecraft: The Soul of Inequality in American Life.* London, UK: Verso.

Fimiani, Bret. 2021. *Psychosis and Extreme States: An Ethic for Treatment.* Champagne, CH: Palgrave Macmillan.

Fink, Bruce. 1999. *A Clinical Introduction to Lacanian Psychoanalysis: Theory and Technique.* Cambridge, MA: Harvard University Press.

George, Sheldon. 2014. "From alienation to cynicism: race and the Lacanian unconscious." *Psychoanalysis, Culture & Society* 19, no. 4: 360–378.

George, Sheldon. 2016. *Trauma and Race: A Lacanian Study of African American Racial Identity.* Waco, TX: Baylor University Press.

Gillota, David. 2021. "'Man, I told you not to go in that house': the humor and horror of Jordan Peele's *Get Out*." *The Journal of Popular Culture* 54, no. 5: 1031–1050.

Halsell, Grace. 1969/1999. *Soul Sister.* Washington, DC: Crossroads International Publishing.

Hook, Derek. 2004. "Racism as abjection: a psychoanalytic conceptualisation for a post-apartheid South Africa." *South African Journal of Psychology* 34, no. 4: 672–703.

Hook, Derek. 2011. "White privilege, psychoanalytic ethics, and the limitations of political silence." *South African Journal of Philosophy* 30, no. 4: 494–501.

Khan, Azeen. 2018. "Lacan and race." In *After Lacan: Literature, Theory, and Psychoanalysis in the Twenty-First Century*, edited by Ankhi Mukherjee, 148–166. Cambridge, UK: Cambridge University Press.

Lacan, Jacques. 2006. "The instance of the letter in the unconscious, or reason since Freud." In *Écrits. The First Complete Edition in English*, translated by Bruce Fink, in collaboration with Heloise Fink and Russell Grigg (412–444). London, UK: W. W. Norton & Company.

Lacan, Jacques. 1997. *The Seminar of Jacques Lacan, Book III, 1955–56: The Psychoses*, edited by Jacques-Alain Miller. London, UK: Routledge.

Leader, Darian. 2012. *What is Madness?* London, UK: Penguin.
McGowan, Todd. 2003. "Looking for the gaze: Lacanian film theory and its vicissitudes." *Cinema Journal* 42, no. 3: 27–47.
McGowan, Todd. 2013. *Enjoying What We Don't Have: The Political Project of Psychoanalysis.* Lincoln, NE: University of Nebraska Press.
McGowan, Todd. 2019. "The psychosis of freedom: law in modernity." In *Lacan on Psychosis: From Theory to Praxis,* edited by Jon Mills and David L. Downing (47–76). Abingdon, UK: Routledge.
McGowan, Todd. 2021. "The distribution of enjoyment." *European Journal of Psychoanalysis* 8, no. 1.
McIntosh, Peggy. 1989. "White privilege: unpacking the invisible knapsack." *Peace and Freedom* July/August: 1–3.
Morrison, Toni. 2016. *The Bluest Eye.* London, UK: Vintage.
Peterson, Jordan B. 2018. *12 Rules For Life: An Antidote to Chaos.* London, UK: Penguin.
Peterson, Jordan B. 2022. *Beyond Order: 12 More Rules For Life.* London, UK: Penguin.
Samuels, Robert. 2001. *Writing Prejudices: The Psychoanalysis and Pedagogy of Discrimination from Shakespeare to Toni Morrison.* New York, NY: State University of New York Press.
Seshadri-Crooks, Kalpana. 2000. *Desiring Whiteness: A Lacanian Analysis of Race.* London, UK: Routledge.
Vanheule, Stijn. 2011. *The Subject of Psychosis: A Lacanian Perspective.* Basingstoke, UK: Palgrave Macmillan.
Vanheule, Stijn. 2020. "On a question prior to any possible treatment to psychosis." In *Reading Lacan's Ecrits: From Écrits: From 'The Freudian Thing' to 'Remarks on Daniel Lagache,* edited by Derek Hook, Calum Neill, and Stijn Vanheule (163–205). London, UK: Routledge.
Wells, Charles. 2014. *The Subject of Liberation: Žižek, Politics, Psychoanalysis.* London, UK: Bloomsbury.
Zalloua, Zahi. 2020. *Žižek on Race: Toward an Anti-Racist Future.* London, UK: Bloomsbury.
Žižek, Slavoj. 2000. *The Ticklish Subject: The Absent Centre of Political Ontology.* London, UK: Verso.
Žižek, Slavoj. 2001. *The Fragile Absolute Or, Why is the Christian Legacy Worth Fighting For?* London, UK: Verso.
Žižek, Slavoj. 2004. *Organs without Bodies: On Deleuze and Consequences.* London, UK: Routledge.
Žižek, Slavoj. 2006. *Interrogating the Real,* edited by Rex Butler and Scott Stephens. London, UK: Bloomsbury.
Žižek, Slavoj. 2012. *Less Than Nothing.* London, UK: Verso.

Chapter 8

Psychosis and the Other

It is now clear that for the psychosis of race, it is the subject's relation to the signifier which is complicated. Unable to identify with the Symbolic, race offers its own form of 'meaning', its own 'non-sense', which prescribes the subject's sense of being. Though removed from the Symbolic, in the structure of psychosis the subject remains subjected to the racist signifiers that comprise the Symbolic order. As previously noted, there are ways of managing this sense of dislocation, be it through fundamentalism; an adherence to celebrating the effects of cultural diversity; or in examples of rational racism. While these examples speak to the racism that occurs as part of the psychosis of race, it is through the effects of foreclosure that the psychotic's relation to the Other is assured.

This relation to the Other can be identified as emanating from the psychotic's complications with the signifier. Indeed, for Lacan, an act of communication between two subjects requires that 'the symbol [or language] introduces a third party, an element of mediation, which brings the two actors into each other's presence, leads them on to another plane, and changes them' (1991, 155). It is in this sense that '[t]he subject is born insofar as the signifier emerges in the field of the Other' (Lacan 2004, 199). Throughout Lacan's work there remains the underlying concern that language is for the subject an 'Other' that exists externally to the subject. This is not to ignore the fact that as human subjects we clearly use language, but that our use of language never coincides with what we mean to say or how we feel. Accordingly, 'by being born with the signifier, the subject is born divided' (Lacan 2004, 199), and it is this division that is enacted through its subjection to the signifier and to the process of signification.

In the case of psychosis, the relation to this signifier is disrupted, with the effects of such disruption resulting in a unique form of psychotic alienation (see Chapter 4). Here, the psychotic is not simply alienated from their own sense of being, due to the 'cut' of the signifier, but is, to a certain degree, doubly alienated. In short, they cannot attain the separation that one's alienation achieves when acquiring 'meaning' through interpretation. It is through interpretation 'that people believe in language and use it as a guarantee for articulating their own existence' (Vanheule 2011, 42), and what is more, it is this 'belief' that presumes the subject's relation to the Other. Significantly, it is this belief in the Other that is not assumed in psychosis. Due to the effects of foreclosure, the Other fails to offer any guarantee to the psychotic's existence and to their own investment in language and signification: there is, instead, a disruption or 'hole' in the Symbolic. As a result, 'in psychosis the Other ... is excluded' (Lacan 1997a, 162).

However, it is important to note that with the exclusion of the Other, the Other is not lost. Instead, what the Other's exclusion establishes is the inability to achieve a relative distance to the Other. This distance is paramount to achieving relationships with other subjects, as well as providing the subject the means to orientate themselves in a Symbolic order that requires one's capacity to develop meaning. Accordingly, while there is no distance to the Other in psychosis, through their proximity they are able to identify its absurdity. Here, we return once more to the paradox that underlies the psychotic structure. As McGowan states, 'the psychotic is never psychotic enough' (2013, 129), meaning that while they are able to acknowledge a sense of disbelief in the Other, which, for them, holds no value or credibility, they nonetheless concede its influence. It is in critiquing the Other's credibility that the psychotic inadvertently proposes that there is such an Other who could be conceived as credible.

On this basis, we can conceive of the psychotic's relation to the Other as resulting from the fact that they fail to acknowledge the Other's castration. Indeed, while they are nonetheless aware of the Other's imposture, such recognition occurs due to the proximity which they hold towards the Other. In part, this proximity is brought to bear through the Other's location in the Real. With regard to the Schreber case, Bowie highlights how 'the causes of his [Schreber's] delirium may be traced back to an initial mispositioning of Subject and Other: the Other should be intrinsic to the signifying chain but has been moved to a position outside it' (1991, 109). He adds:

> [t]he Other should be exercising its legislative authority silently and invisibly in human speech—twixt cup and lip, between one syllable and the next—but instead has relocated itself beyond speech, over and against the Subject, 'in the Real'. There, it becomes not a law-maker but a tyrant, not one who maintains the threat of judicial punishment but one who exercises and withholds punishment in accordance with its own unfathomable whim.
> (Bowie 1991, 109–110)

With 'the signifier ... "unleashed" or "unchained" in the Real, ... the Other is presented as obscene' (Vanheule 2020, 203); or, as Bowie declares, a 'tyrant' for whom any action beholds the capacities of their 'unfathomable whim' (1991, 110). It is amidst such an 'unfathomable whim' that the psychotic's failure to acknowledge the Other's inherent imposture—the fact that the Other exists only to the extent that we believe it to exist—is enacted. That is, it is not simply the case that the Other remains an unfathomable entity, due to its inherent lack/castration, but that the exercise of punishment is ultimately ordained by an Other for whom their very authority is based on the notion of a 'whim'. There is always, in the structure of psychosis, a lack of belief in this authority, however cruel and monstrous. I would add here that it is in direct relation to this 'unfathomable whim' that the psychotic's lack of belief, and, in addition, their lack of desire, is achieved. In fact, the two are aligned in psychosis.

Desire and psychosis

It is important to remember that while '[d]esire is the result of our insertion into language, ... it can't be named by that language' (McGowan 2007, 159). This is to say that it is through the metonymic functioning of the signifier that one's desire functions, with the underlying premise that desire, in order for it to remain desired, must constantly move from object to object, with its very unfathomability being encapsulated in the impossibility of the object *a* (the object-cause of desire). As a result, '[t]here is no properly human desire at all in psychosis. Where the structure of language is missing, desire too is missing' (Fink 1999, 101). What is more, desire occurs in direct relation to the prohibition endowed by authority. As Fink asserts, '[p]rohibition ... creates desire: it is only when something is refused me that I first see what I want, what I lack, what I cannot have' (1999, 92). Here, 'the signifier of the Other qua locus of the law' (Lacan 2006, 485) is brought to bear through the Name-of-the-Father. Yet, with the foreclosure of the Name-of-the-Father, any proper relation to desire is thus denied.

As a result, what the psychotic 'lacks is the effectuation of the "primordial metaphor" by means of which the symbolic Other (the structural Law epitomized by the Name-of-the-Father) supplants *jouissance*' (Žižek 1992, 229), which, as Chapter 7 detailed, results in an unhoused and unbound *jouissance*. In support of this claim, Žižek refers to the character Norman Bates from Alfred Hitchock's *Psycho* (1960). By considering Bates as a 'prisoner of the psychotic drive', Žižek highlights how '[t]he ultimate function of the Law is to confine desire—*not the subject's own, but the desire of his/her (M)Other*' (1992, 229, italics in original). As a psychotic, 'Bates is therefore a kind of anti-Oedipus *avant la lettre*: his desire is alienated in the maternal Other, at the mercy of its cruel caprice' (Žižek 1992, 229), a position which is echoed in the aforementioned 'total alienation'. What is significant to Žižek's interpretation, however, is how Bates's lack of desire and the foreclosure of the Law/Name-of-the-Father takes place at the mercy of a cruel maternal Other, or to an Other whose very punishment remains at the behest of its 'unfathomable whim' (Bowie 1991, 110). In either case, we see no separation on behalf of the psychotic from the Other. Instead, the psychotic's lack of desire confounds the lack of any distance towards the Other.

We can again go further here in linking this lack of desire with the psychosis of race, especially with regard to Žižek's account of Bates as a 'prisoner' of his psychosis (Žižek 1992, 229). In his analysis of Morrison's *Beloved* (2007), George highlights how the character Sethe goes through a similar imprisonment, one that can be conceived as encapsulating a level of psychosis that is achieved when Sethe 'embrac[es] Beloved as the object *a* that fills her lack', thus 'becom[ing] a *full*, desireless subject with nothing to inspire in her the effort to carry on into the future' (2016, 81, italics in original). Referring explicitly to Lacan's (1997b) account of the 'joiner', George asserts that it is from this position that 'the subject can achieve nothing but some form of psychosis or perversion' (Lacan 1997b, 301, cited in George 2016, 82). What characterizes 'this psychosis is [that it is] marked precisely by a fullness, in the presences of the Real, that eliminates the dimension of desire and all subjective aspirations' (George 2016, 82). Without any desire, the subject is effectively a prisoner towards the Other; a prisoner to a racial Symbolic order that both prescribes and entraps their racial being.

What we witness in this confinement is the effects of the psychotic's forced choice, or, rather, their exemption from acknowledging what such a 'choice' requires. With no distance towards the Other, the psychotic does not seek a path of ignorance, but a rejection of knowing one's desire. Confronted with the impenetrability of the Other's desire, the psychotic fails to receive any benefit from the distance enacted by the constitutive question, '*Che vuoi?*', or 'What does the Other want from me?' (Žižek 2008b). With no proper relation to their desire, the psychotic is left 'painfully exposed to the other's desire' (Mills 2019, 36), so that what becomes clear in psychosis is that there remains a desire not to know the Other's desire. It is the refusal of this desire that serves to compound the fact that the Other holds no relevance nor credibility in psychosis.

Foreclosure and the Other's diversification

Throughout his seminar on psychosis, Lacan emphasizes how what is 'non-symbolized reappears in the real' (1997a, 86). Certainly, this is not to suggest that the Real and the Symbolic are separated to begin with. As Žižek makes clear: 'the Real is not external to the Symbolic', rather:

> the line of separation between the Symbolic and the Real is not only a symbolic gesture *par excellence*, but the very founding gesture of the Symbolic and to step into the Real does not entail abandoning language, throwing oneself into the abyss of the chaotic Real, but, on the contrary, dropping the very allusion to some external point of reference which eludes the Symbolic.
>
> (Žižek 2003, 69–70)

It is this 'line of separation' that is encompassed by the fact that '[t]he symbolic ... must include the negation of what it is not' (Copjec 1994, 121). In other words, to forge a 'line of separation', the Symbolic must ascribe the existence of the Real via the act of its negation. It is in accordance with the foreclosure of psychosis, however, that this negation of the Real fails to occur. In psychosis, there is no line of separation, indeed, there is no self-division between the subject and the signifier.[1] Instead, it is the 'chaotic Real' that returns (Žižek 2003, 69). Indeed, what returns is 'the proliferation of different versions of *a big Other that actually exists, in the Real*, [and] not merely as a symbolic fiction' (Žižek 2000, 362, italics in original). Here, the lack of trust that is afforded to the Other is grounded in the psychotic's concern that there remains an Other of the Other, secretly pulling the strings.

It is not difficult to draw a line of connection between the existence of this Other of the Other and the Far-Right conspiracists who seek elaborate explanations for the failings of the social order (such as conspiratorial forms of anti-Semitism). In such cases, it is always a 'they' who manages to deceive and manipulate the social order (Žižek 1992). What I wish to draw attention to, however, is the Other's 'proliferation': that is, its 'diversification' ('different versions of a big Other') which occurs as an effect of foreclosure (Žižek 2000, 362).

As noted, foreclosure does not mean the eradication of the Other, nor does it suggest that the psychotic follows the Lacanian maxim: there is no big Other.[2] Instead, what seems to constitute the psychotic's exclusion of the Other is an intense proliferation of the Other's function. Accordingly, while Lacan highlights that, in psychosis, 'the Other with a big O, qua bearer of the signifier, is excluded', he clarifies this by adding that '[t]he Other is thereby all the more powerfully affirmed between it and the subject, at the level of the little other, of the imaginary' (1997a, 194). It is at this level that an aggressive rivalry can take hold for the subject.

The effects of this affirmation of the Other and its relation to the Imaginary are brought to bear when it is considered how the Other's 'exclusion' results in the anxiety of confronting a multiplicity of 'small others'. Žižek notes how:

> Lacan's standard notion of anxiety is that, as the only affect that does not lie, it bears witness to the proximity of the Real, to the inexistence of the big Other; such anxiety has to be confronted by courage, it should lead to an act proper which, as it were, cuts into the real of a situation. There is, however, another mode of anxiety which predominates today: the anxiety caused by the claustrophobia of the atonal world which lacks any structuring 'point,' the anxiety of the 'pathological Narcissus' frustrated by the fact that he is caught in the endless competitive mirroring of his fellow men (a-a'-a''-a''' ...), of the series of 'small others' none of which functions as the stand-in for the 'big Other.' The root of this claustrophobia is that the lack of embodied stand-ins for the big Other, instead of opening

up the social space, depriving it of any Master-figures, renders the invisible 'big Other,' the mechanism that regulates the interaction of 'small others,' all the more all-pervasive.

(2008a, 36)

If we locate these 'small others' as the masters behind the Other's curtain, then it is in accordance with the racist fantasy that the racial other is believed to exist beyond the Other's authority, freely obtaining an enjoyment that bears witness to their non-castration. Moreover, it is '[i]n this figure' of the non-castrated small other(s) that 'the Imaginary (semblance) and the Real (of paranoia) overlap, due to the suspension of proper symbolic efficiency' (Žižek 2008a, 87). In conjunction with this suspension of Symbolic efficiency, 'the racist fantasy intervenes to provide a solution' (McGowan 2022, 26)—a solution which seeks an attempt at meaning for the psychotic. Grounded in fantasy, this meaning is never resolved, yet it endows the psychotic a way of navigating the Other's proximity by transferring the anxiety of its over-bearing presence onto a multiplicity of racial others, or, as Wells asserts, 'to the proliferation of small big Others in the Real' (2014, 102). While failing to constitute the Other, these small big Others serve only to consolidate the Other's 'all-pervasive' presence (Žižek 2008a, 36).

We can conceive of this presence as fostering 'new forms of *racism*' (Žižek 2000, 199, italics in original) that take hold when the line of separation between the Real and the Symbolic—the line which locates and positions the subject within the Symbolic order—is foreclosed. Typically, it is this line of separation which posits the gap—i.e., the lack—that allows one to contest and politicize the established social order. There is, however, no politicization of this gap in psychosis; instead, the psychotic is confronted with the Real, and, specifically, 'a Real other' (Vanheule 2011, 77). Vanheule elaborates:

> an other is 'Real' to the extent that his/her actions cannot be framed by means of the Symbolic or the Imaginary: conventional ideas on exchange relationships and social positions in a group do not provide the symbolic framework whereby sense can be made of the other's actions. This leads to a clear sense that the other is unpredictable. If the other's actions cannot be framed by taking oneself as an imaginary reference point, the effect of [psychotic] estrangement is complete.
>
> (2011, 77)

Ultimately, what such estrangement provokes is an immersion into fantasy. With no Symbolic support to locate *jouissance*, the psychotic structure confronts a traumatic *jouissance* that finds itself engendered in what is perhaps the key site of racial visibility—one's bodily features. With no escape from the other's presence, racist fantasies become formulated upon an assumed set of bodily attributes that unnervingly reside within the other.

Belief in disbelief

In psychosis we trace a number of important characteristics. There is a decline in Symbolic efficiency, with the Symbolic function of the Name-of-the-Father rejected. This leaves a hole in the Symbolic in the place once occupied by the father, so that it is the failure of the paternal metaphor that undermines the credibility of the Name-of-the-Father. What this amounts to on behalf of the psychotic is a lack of belief in the Symbolic order and in the position of the Other itself. We can draw connections here between the function of the Name-of-the-Father and the significance of the Other, both of whom encapsulate for Lacan a position of authority, from which our relation to this authority rests primarily on our belief in it.[3]

Indeed, when partaking in society, it is our very actions and behaviours that are guaranteed by the Other (for example, when I meet someone and shake their hand, this greeting is guaranteed by the Other, for whom such a greeting is regarded as neither odd nor unfamiliar). For Vanheule (2011), Lacan's work takes a different approach in outlining the importance of this guarantee in psychosis. Here, 'the non-instalment of a belief in the Other as a guarantee' means that the psychotic relies on no assurances from the Other (Vanheule 2011, 136). In fact, '[m]arked by a fundamentally sceptical and distant attitude, the Other's rules and explanations are not taken as a benchmark for addressing questions of existence' (Vanheule 2011, 136).

It is important not to confuse this position towards the Other as denoting one of cynicism. While, on the face of it, the cynic may openly share their ambivalence towards the Other, they nonetheless remain invested *in* the Other. That is, their 'transgressions' remain dictated by the Other, especially when these transgressions remain tied to the Law's obscene underside. Here, the cynical position is one that remains dependent on their disavowal, best encapsulated in the line: 'I know very well, but nonetheless…'.[4] By claiming knowledge ('I know'), and then disavowing their knowledge ('nonetheless'), the cynic always requires this disavowal in order to posit their knowledge. By disavowing their relation to the Other, the cynic ultimately requires this Other in order to maintain their cynical position… there can be no cynic without the Other.

Alternatively, in the case of psychosis, there is no belief in the Other and its authority. They remain removed from the Other so that they bear no relation to the Law and its interpretation, occupying instead a position outside the Law. The psychotic 'knows' the Law and acts accordingly due to their certainty. For the psychotic, their lack of belief, and the knowledge they have acquired, is grounded in certainty: while they know the Other lacks authority, and, thus, does not warrant their belief, they instead divert their conviction upon an Other of the Other who confirms the certainty of their knowledge (any knowledge to the contrary is foreclosed). Whereas the cynic disavows their relation to the Other, the psychotic openly asserts their position to an Other of the Other (as seen in forms of paranoia and conspiracy).

It is in this way that we can begin to determine how belief plays a key role in determining the psychotic's relation to the Other. Indeed, while, in neurosis, 'the disorder in the midst of being is resolved by making use of the Name-of-the-Father: through belief in the lawfulness of the world, the fundamental experience of lack is managed', in the case of psychosis, this 'basic belief is missing' (Vanheule 2020, 200). As a result, '[i]n psychosis, individuals have to invent the dimension of the law that neurotics take for granted' (Vanheule 2020, 200). This invention can take various forms, yet what it relies upon is the conviction it entails. This conviction is underpinned by the psychotic's unique relation to belief. Though the psychotic holds no 'basic belief' in the Other's authority, they nonetheless occupy a position from which their knowledge of the Other is assured. In short, the psychotic always 'knows' and it is this knowledge which underscores their relationship to the Other.

Importantly, this knowledge elicits a certain form of disbelief. Here, Zupančič emphasizes how 'those who are obsessed with avoiding all deception, and naivety, are precisely those who ultimately blindly believe that the Other *knows* exactly what she is doing, that is, is perfectly consistent in her existence and actions' (2008, 85, italics in original). In effect, '[d]isbelief is belief in one's own autonomy as guaranteed by the consistency of the field of the Other' (Zupančič 2008, 85). That is, it is in accordance with their assured 'disbelief' that the psychotic remains the only 'true' believer.

Consequently, due to their lack of belief in the Other, the psychotic occupies a position that is able to discern the Other's controlling presence. McNulty highlights how:

> [p]ersecuted by voices that no one else hears, that undermine his ability to communicate with other people or even to accomplish the most basic tasks of everyday life, the psychotic is acutely and viscerally aware that human beings are controlled by an Other who takes possession of their bodies and minds, speaks through them, and dictates their behavior. When Dr. Schreber complains of the malicious and uncomprehending God who forcibly rapes him, alters his physiognomy, and forces him to blurt out nonsensical or humiliating phrases against his will, he gives vivid expression to a fundamental human experience that is in no way unique to psychosis.
>
> (2014, 70)

What is vividly expressed in psychosis, and what remains fundamental to human experience, is the fact that Schreber's malicious God is not necessarily wrong. In fact, the subject's relation to the Symbolic order is always marked by the intrusion of the signifier and the imposition of the Name-of-the-Father, and, what is more, these impediments upon the subject take place in psychosis with no consideration towards the subject. While the subject's relation to the signifier remains a fundamental aspect of our human experience, including our social relations and interpretations of reality, it is in the case of psychosis that the Symbolic authority of the Other is endowed with the agency to freely control, sanction, and manipulate the subject. It is in this sense that the psychotic's disbelief serves as a form of defence, which makes them fully aware of the injustices performed by the Other (or, in Schreber's case, by an unjust, malicious God). Ultimately, for the psychotic, their disbelief is directly subjectivized—there remains the belief in one's disbelief.

Indeed, this belief in disbelief can also be approached through Lacan's *les non-dupes errant* ('the non-duped err'). Coffman explains how:

> [i]f one understands the so-called normal subject as misrecognizing himself in the world of actuality by believing its apparent logic to be the true ground of reality, the psychotic's misrecognition is double because he misrecognizes the extent to which he depends upon the world in which the 'normal' subject more easily, perhaps more naively, believes. For Lacan, double misrecognition is precisely how 'the unduped err[s]': the psychotic misrecognizes the extent to which the law of his heart is conditioned, in inverse, by the very world whose apparent disorder provokes his revolt.
>
> (2006, 21)

It is this defence that the psychotic pursues. Their only protection from the Other is that they are not naïve enough to commit to the Other's guarantee. The psychotic is not duped by the Symbolic order, nor do they defer to the authority of the Other, instead, what the psychotic fails to follow is 'the central status of deception in relation to the symbolic order', so that, as Žižek notes, 'the only way not to be deceived is to maintain a distance from the symbolic order, i.e., to assume a *psychotic* position' (1991, 79, italics in original). In effect, it is not simply the case that the psychotic is not deceived by the Symbolic order, but also that their assumed psychotic position falls foul to a double deception: the fictional conviction that they have the knowledge *not* to be deceived. Therefore, what is ignored in the structure of psychosis is the fundamental deception that characterizes one's relation to the Symbolic order. Whereas examples of psychosis take up the position of the non-duped, it is this very belief in disbelief that exposes one's relation to the fictions that comprise the racial Symbolic order, as well as to one's location in the process of racialization. The significance of this belief is demonstrated in the 1992 Bernard Rose film, *Candyman*.

Candyman and the 'duped who do not err'

Candyman begins with the protagonist, Helen Lyle (Virginia Madsen), as she seeks to complete her doctoral thesis on urban legends and, specifically, the mythical figure, 'Candyman' (Tony Todd). Encouraged by the novelty of the Candyman myth, Helen believes that the topic and its gruesome legend will help guarantee her a successful academic career, post-PhD. The Candyman myth involves the story of an African American artist, Daniel Robitaille, who is murdered by a lynch mob in the 1800s. After falling in love with and impregnating a White woman, for whom he had been commissioned to paint, he is viciously attacked and murdered by a mob sent by the woman's father. The mob cut off his right hand and smother his body in honey, whereupon he is subsequently stung to death by a swarm of attracted bees. His corpse is then burnt in a pyre, with his ashes being scattered across the stretch of land, where, in the present day, the Cabrini-Green housing project has been built (fully demolished in 2011, Cabrini-Green Homes was a real public housing project located on the Near North Side of Chicago). Notably, the fear associated with Candyman is visually rendered via the fact that, in the place of his right hand, he now brandishes a large hook—the very instrument that he uses to murder his unfortunate victims.

In the film's present day, the urban legend has taken hold of the local Cabrini-Green housing project, with a slew of recent murders being attributed to Candyman, a now-mythical figure whose legend terrorizes the Cabrini-Green residents. Helen's interest in the legend is confirmed following the recent murder of a local Black woman. The death forms part of a string of violent murders that have taken place within the housing project. With the opportunity to collect data for her thesis, Helen and a fellow student, Bernadette (Kasi Lemmons), visit Cabrini-Green in order to speak to its residents regarding the murders and their apparent ties to Candyman. Filmed on location, the film makes deliberate allusions to the years of neglect and abandonment that affected the real Cabrini-Green, with the housing project becoming synonymous with social degradation and urban degeneration in the U.S. It is against this decline that Helen seeks to expose how the Candyman legend allows the Cabrini-Green residents to cope with the day-to-day hardships of living in the urban environment.

Through Helen, a White woman, the film deliberately draws upon a number of racial tensions and antagonisms that frame her interactions with the residents of Cabrini-Green as well as Candyman himself. While visiting the Cabrini-Green projects, she is attacked by a local gang-leader, who, it is believed, has been acting under the Candyman moniker, even brandishing a hook, which he uses to attack Helen. After the arrest of the gang-leader, Helen and the police conclude that the criminal has been appropriating the Candyman myth in order to terrorize the project's residents. In one notable scene, Helen explains to a young boy, who lives in Cabrini-Green, that the Candyman does not exist; nothing more than an urban legend used by the gang-leader to incite fear and intimidation. Briefel and Ngai note:

> [w]ith her assessment of the Cabrini-Green inhabitants' relation to the figure called Candyman, Helen implies that she understands the origins of their social reality better than they do. For her, they are naively

translating reality into fiction. Helen fails to consider the possibility that to position herself as an educator, she may actually *need* to believe that they believe in the legend. From the privileged standpoint of an outside authority, Helen constructs herself as a missionary of social truth, as if in expiation of white liberal guilt.

(1996, 79, italics in original)

As evident in Briefel and Ngai's account, what is unique to the Candyman story is the extent to which the film plays with one's relation to belief. In fact, Towlson highlights how criticisms of the film were, at the time of its release, expressed by *The Chicago Tribune*, which levelled concern at 'how the screenplay seemed to represent the black community in the Cabrini-Green apartment complex as susceptible to superstition and urban myth' (Towlson 2018, 41). Yet, what such simple assessments ignore is the significance of belief and how, more importantly, the function of belief prescribes a racial psychosis that both frames and positions the film's characters.

In the wake of her attack by the local gang-leader, Helen continues her studies, safe in the knowledge that the criminal 'Candyman' has been arrested (thanks to Helen's identification, the local gang-leader is charged for the recent 'Candyman' murders). On the way to her car, however, the real Candyman suddenly appears to Helen. Amidst his eerie presence (cast in shadow, wearing a long coat, and brandishing his bloody hook), Helen succumbs to a trance-like state, whereupon Candyman declares the following: 'You doubted me. ... You were not content with the stories, so I was obliged to come. ... I am the writing on the wall, the whisper in the classroom! Without these things I am nothing...'. As Candyman's words echo around Helen, he specifically draws upon the power of belief and its significance in maintaining the fear he conjures. In fact, '[h]is desire to appropriate Helen into the sign of his own history hinges upon belief, or more properly, upon its lack' (Wyrick 1998, 106–107)—specifically, Helen's lack of belief.

In this sense, what the film seems to suggest is that it is Helen's very disbelief that serves as a disruptive force to Candyman's position as a symbol of American racism; a history that the White-liberal establishment would like to see overcome, and, thus, ignored. Instead, one's capacity to believe the Candyman legend requires that one *believes* in the reality of racial discrimination that the legend evokes. This includes the systemic forms of racial inequality that continue to blight the Cabrini-Green housing project. In order to 'see' such inequality one is required to *believe* in the 'spectral reality' of a malevolent phantom.

This is continued when we consider the relationship between the 'real' Candyman (the phantom, Robitaille) and the 'fake' Candyman (the arrested criminal). In distinguishing between the two, it is Helen's conviction—one echoed by that of the police and the wider academic society—that Candyman exists only in the belief of his congregation; that is, in the fear and superstition of the Cabrini-Green residents. Here, however, Garrett notes:

[t]he ghostly Candyman, as opposed to the gang leader, embodies not society's perceptions of the housing projects, but the horrible history of racial violence that has soaked the pages of the history in the United States. Helen and the police were perfectly willing to accept the reality of the fake Candyman, but it isn't until the real Candyman stares her in the face that Helen admits that he exists and still has the power to hurt people in the modern world.

(2020, 94–95)

What is clear from the film's narrative is the sense in which it plays with the audience's expectations, providing what seems to be a legitimate explanation to the Cabrini-Green murders, a criminal pretending to be Candyman. This explanation is later disrupted when we realize that the Candyman phantom is real, and, what is more, he's more than capable of enacting the murderous revenge that his legend conjures. Consequently, for Balasopoulos, 'it is not the "fake" Candyman that mimics the "true" one, but the "true", supernatural Candyman whose representation both displaces and condenses the threat of the socially deviant, sexually aggressive, and criminal racial other that the "fake" one embodied' (1997, 36).

What the film develops, therefore, is a parallax position between the duped and non-duped. Indeed, if we remember that in order to inhabit 'truth' one is required to follow the many Symbolic fictions that structure reality, so that, ultimately, one is required to be 'duped', then, for the 'non-duped', it is their knowledge that allows them to 'see through' the various Symbolic fictions that structure their social reality. Though Helen assures herself with the knowledge that Candyman is nothing more than a fiction, what she ultimately ignores is the discriminatory practices and social inequalities of a racially-inscribed Symbolic order that works to frame her perception of the housing projects—a perception that is just as much embroiled within a racialized image of the Black residents as ill-informed, poorly educated, and subsequently partial to myth and urban legend over rational explanation. When there is belief in one's disbelief, the racial other(s) is always to blame. In fact, after the arrest of the criminal Candyman, the Cabrini-Green residents are left to themselves, with no further attention given to them by either Helen, the police, or the city services.[5] Subsequently, what Helen's belief in disbelief fails to believe is *the belief* that speaks the truth of historical racial violence; a violence which continues to be experienced by the Cabrini-Green residents.

As the non-duped, Helen occupies the structure of psychosis, so that what proves significant about the film is how it reflects the very ways in which psychosis underscores our racialization. In declaring the Other's non-credibility, in disbelieving the credibility of the real Candyman, and in occupying the position of the non-duped, Helen does not simply observe the non-existence of the Other, but also disregards and discounts the very illusions that aver the Real antagonisms and contradictions that underpin the racial Symbolic order. As Žižek notes, 'we can [not] simply suspend ... "illusion" and "see things as they really are"' (1991, 71). To 'see things as they really' is to foreclose on those 'everyday' illusions and fictions that underpin our reality, including those that comprise and sustain our racial figurations. Therefore, what the non-duped cannot appreciate is the fiction that contradicts what they know, and it is in acknowledging this fiction that the residents of Cabrini-Green occupy the position of 'the "duped who do not err"' (Balasopoulos 1997, 37).

Subsequently, while examples of psychosis suggest a preference for the psychotic to believe their knowledge and to see through Symbolic fictions and forms of belief, it is from the position of the duped that 'fantasy negatively acknowledges what it is designed to deny' (Zornado 2017, 165). That is, 'by giving the subject a tool by which the truth may be disavowed in favor of the fantasy, the truth is negatively acknowledged, but only indirectly, as if without making eye contact' (Zornado 2017, 165). The effects of this negative acknowledgement can be further considered in examples of racial paranoia.

Notes

1 Importantly, the signifier is not lost in foreclosure (much like the foreclosure of the Name-of-the-Father, the signifier does not simply vanish). Though the psychotic is left 'adrift in the universe of signification without the anchoring point that the primordial signifier would supply', it is '[t]he foreclosed signifier [that] leaves the symbolic order and returns in the real' (McGowan 2019, 51–52).
2 Importantly, this statement does not reduce the functioning of the Other. As Benvenuto makes clear, 'for Lacan, the Other does not exist, just like the line of the horizon does not exist as a line' (2020, 131, parenthesis removed). In fact, despite us acknowledging that there is no Other, Flisfeder highlights how our interactions on digital media platforms suggest that we still hold onto 'the desire to will back into existence some figure of Authority or prohibition [some Other] on which the subject is able to constitute his or her desire, a figure of prohibition that appears lacking in the context of postmodern consumer society but that makes all desire possible' (2015, 567).
3 Indeed, the Name-of-the-Father can be conceived as 'the signifier of the Other qua locus of the Law' (Lacan 2006, 485).
4 A reference to Octave Mannoni's account of fetishist disavowal, encapsulated in the line, 'I know well, but all the same...' (Mannoni 2003).
5 In fact, it is implied that the only reason the police investigated Helen's attack and arrested the gang-leader was because she was a White woman in a 'dangerous' housing project.

References

Balasopoulos, Antonis. 1997. "The demon of (racial) history: reading *Candyman*." *Gramma: Journal of Theory & Criticism* 5: 25–47.
Benvenuto, Sergio. 2020. *Conversations with Lacan: Seven Lectures for Understanding Lacan*. London, UK: Routledge.
Bowie, Malcolm. 1991. *Lacan*. Cambridge, MA: Harvard University Press.

Briefel, Aviva, and Sianne Ngai. 1996. "'How much did you pay for this place?' Fear, entitlement, and urban space in Bernard Rose's *Candyman*." *Camera Obscura* 13, no. 1: 69–91.

Coffman, Christine. 2006. *Insane Passions: Lesbianism and Psychosis in Literature and Film*. Middletown, CT: Wesleyan University Press.

Copjec, Joan. 1994. *Read My Desire: Lacan Against the Historicists*. Cambridge, MA: The MIT Press.

Fink, Bruce. 1999. *A Clinical Introduction to Lacanian Psychoanalysis: Theory and Technique*. Cambridge, MA: Harvard University Press.

Flisfeder, Matthew. 2015. "The entrepreneurial subject and the objectivization of the self in social media." *The South Atlantic Quarterly* 114, no. 3: 553–570.

Garrett, Jacob. 2020. "Taking a look in the mirror: the inversion of middle class fears of urban decay and the representation of racial violence in Bernard Rose's *Candyman*." *Digital Literature Review: Ghosts and Cultural Hauntings* 7: 87–100.

George, Sheldon. 2016. *Trauma and Race: A Lacanian Study of African American Racial Identity*. Waco, TX: Baylor University Press.

Lacan, Jacques. 1991. *The Seminar of Jacques Lacan, Book I, 1953–1954: Freud's Papers on Technique*, edited by Jacques-Alain Miller and translated by John Forrester. New York, NY: W. W. Norton & Company.

Lacan, Jacques. 1997a. *The Seminar of Jacques Lacan, Book III, 1955–56: The Psychoses*, edited by Jacques-Alain Miller. London, UK: Routledge.

Lacan, Jacques. 1997b. *The Seminar of Jacques Lacan, Book VII, 1959–1960: The Ethics of Psychoanalysis*, edited by Jacques-Alain Miller and translated by Dennis Porter. New York, NY: W. W. Norton & Company.

Lacan, Jacques. 2004. *The Four Fundamental Concepts of Psycho-Analysis*, edited by Jacques-Alain Miller. London, UK: Karnac.

Lacan, Jacques. 2006. "On a question preliminary to any possible treatment of psychosis." In *Écrits. The First Complete Edition in English*, translated by Bruce Fink, in collaboration with Heloise Fink and Russell Grigg (445–488). London, UK: W. W. Norton & Company.

Mannoni, Octave. 2003. "'I know very well, but all the same…'." In *Perversion and the Social Relation, Sic 4*, edited by Molly Anne Rothenberg, Dennis Foster, and Slavoj Žižek (68–92). Durham, NC: Duke University Press.

McGowan, Todd. 2013. *Enjoying What We Don't Have: The Political Project of Psychoanalysis*. Lincoln, NE: University of Nebraska Press.

McGowan, Todd. 2007. *The Impossible David Lynch*. New York, NY: Columbia University Press.

McGowan, Todd. 2019. "The psychosis of freedom: law in modernity." In *Lacan on Psychosis: From Theory to Praxis*, edited by Jon Mills and David L. Downing (47–76). Abingdon, UK: Routledge.

McGowan, Todd. 2022. "The bedlam of the lynch mob: racism and enjoying through the other." In *Lacan and Race Racism, Identity, and Psychoanalytic Theory*, edited by Sheldon George and Derek Hook (19–34). Abingdon, UK: Routledge.

McNulty, Tracy. 2014. *Wrestling with the Angel: Experiments in Symbolic Life*. New York, NY: Columbia University Press.

Mills, Jon. 2019. "Lacan on paranoic knowledge." In *Lacan on Psychosis: From Theory to Praxis*, edited by Jon Mills and David L. Downing (10–46). London, UK: Routledge.

Morrison, Toni. 2007. *Beloved*. London, UK: Vintage Books.
Rose, Bernard. 1992. *Candyman*. Propaganda Films; PolyGram Filmed Entertainment.
Towlson, Jon. 2018. *Candyman*. Leighton Buzzard, UK: Auteur.
Vanheule, Stijn. 2011. *The Subject of Psychosis: A Lacanian Perspective*. Basingstoke, UK: Palgrave Macmillan.
Vanheule, Stijn. 2020. "On a question prior to any possible treatment to psychosis." In *Reading Lacan's Ecrits: From Écrits: From 'The Freudian Thing' to 'Remarks on Daniel Lagache*, edited by Derek Hook, Calum Neill, and Stijn Vanheule (163–205). London, UK: Routledge.
Wells, Charles. 2014. *The Subject of Liberation: Žižek, Politics, Psychoanalysis*. London, UK: Bloomsbury.
Wyrick, Laura. 1998. "Summoning Candyman: the cultural production of history." *Arizona Quarterly: A Journal of American Literature, Culture, and Theory* 54, no. 3: 89–117.
Žižek, Slavoj. 1991. *Looking Awry: An Introduction to Jacques Lacan Through Popular Culture*. Cambridge, MA: The MIT Press.
Žižek, Slavoj. 1992. "In his bold gaze my ruin is writ large." In *Everything You Always Wanted to Know about Lacan (But Were Afraid to Ask Hitchcock)*, edited by Slavoj Žižek (211–272). London, UK: Verso.
Žižek, Slavoj. 2000. *The Ticklish Subject: The Absent Centre of Political Ontology*. London, UK: Verso.
Žižek, Slavoj. 2003. *The Puppet and the Dwarf: The Perverse Core of Christianity*. Cambridge, MA: The MIT Press.
Žižek, Slavoj. 2008a. *In Defence of Lost Causes*. London, UK: Verso.
Žižek, Slavoj. 2008b. *The Sublime Object of Ideology*. London, UK: Verso.
Zornado, Joseph. 2017. *Disney and the Dialectic of Desire: Fantasy as Social Practice*. Champagne, CH: Palgrave Macmillan.
Zupančič, Alenka. 2008. *The Odd One In: On Comedy*. Cambridge, MA: The MIT Press.

Chapter 9

Paranoia and the racist fantasy

In his Ethics seminar, Lacan highlights how 'the moving force of paranoia is essentially the rejection of a certain support in the symbolic order' (1997b, 54). Without this symbolic support, there is no opportunity to navigate the Real, and, thus, the effects of its return prove characteristic of the structure of psychosis. However, what I wish to emphasize in this return is the very way in which examples of racial paranoia emerge from the confrontation with the Other in psychosis.

To help with this, we can turn to Lacan's account of the neighbour, where, in the Ethics seminar, he emphasizes how 'the neighbor is a pre-symbolic object characterized primarily by affect, appearing in the symbolic register prior to any and all representation' (Tutt 2012, 3). As a 'pre-symbolic object', the neighbour constitutes Freud's notion of the 'das Ding', translated as 'the Thing'. Tutt explains, '[t]he Other takes on this "thing-like" character for Lacan because the confrontation with jouissance produces an excess that always resists symbolization in the register of the real' (2012, 3). Positioned within the Real, it is in confronting the enigma of the Other, or the neighbour as Thing, that the excesses of the Other's *jouissance* take on an added significance in examples of psychosis.

Indeed, there are two modes to psychosis: paranoia and schizophrenia. Both posit 'two ways of relating to a non-extracted object *a*, in which the categories of the Other and jouissance have a different status in relation to the subject' (Vanheule 2011, 138). In examples of schizophrenia, it is the Other who takes up a position *within* the psychotic. There is no separation between the psychotic and the Other, or, at least, the distinction is blurred in such a way that the 'schizophrenic may believe that their thoughts and even feelings are not their own but somehow put there from the outside, or are even the experiences of someone else' (Leader 2012, 78). In examples of paranoia, there is a clear divide between the psychotic and the Other, so that, in contrast to Schizophrenia, the Other acts upon the psychotic from *without* (Leader 2012). In paranoia the psychotic remains an innocent victim, beholden to the Other's persecutions. Notably, Lacan's (1997a) focus on paranoia suggests that it constitutes a key function in psychosis.

DOI: 10.4324/9781003414209-12

What helps to cement the psychotic's paranoia is the certainty it evokes. Here, Leader highlights how 'paranoia lies less in the idea itself than in the certainty and the rigidity with which it is held and broadcast, and the place it occupies in that person's life' (2012, 77). It is this same rigidity that is found in examples of racial paranoia which establish clear points of segregation between different racial groups. In the structure of psychosis, it is the racial other's excessive presence that holds a particular point of contention.

Equally, it is not the content of the paranoid delusion which proves significant. The fact that one's paranoia 'lies less in the idea' is certified by the fact that the racial other occupies a unique, yet misguided, function in the psychotic's dislocation. As a result, the formation of paranoia serves as 'an attempt at recovery' through which the psychotic seeks to repair its relation to the world and the symbolic order (Freud 1981, 71). It involves a certain logic in that the construction of the racial other forms part of a racist system of meaning that explains the disorder and dislocation of the symbolic order. It erects a belief system that identifies and locates the racial other as a 'problem' that must be fixed.

Ultimately, what paranoia provides 'is the misdirected attempt to reconstitute your universe so that you can function again' (Žižek 1999a). This is why it is not enough to simply 're-educate' the racist, informing them that their racial paranoia is wrong. In fact, upon meeting the paranoid delusions of the anti-Semite, Žižek highlights that:

> [i]t's not enough to say anti-Semitism is factually wrong, it's morally wrong; the true enigma is: why did the Nazis need the figure of the Jew for their ideology to function? Why is it that if you take away their figure of the Jew their whole edifice disintegrates?
>
> (1999a)

In answer to this disintegration, we can assert how, in the structure of psychosis, it is in the very certitude of their paranoid delusion that the inconsistencies of the symbolic order are avoided, or, at least, 'patched over'. This avoidance is 'resolved' in the case of psychosis via the dislocation that is achieved between themselves and the Other. Consequently, we can, in accordance with Chapter 8, trace two key characteristics in the structure of psychosis and its relation to the Other and the resort to paranoia. First, there is the dislocation towards the Other; and second, there is the Other's diversification. However, what remains key to both characteristics is that, despite the disbelief in the Other's authority, the Other's presence is not diminished.

Indeed, '[w]hen the paranoid subject clings to his distrust of the Other of the symbolic community, of "common opinion," he implies thereby the existence of an "Other of this Other," of a nondeceived agent who holds the reins' (Žižek 1991, 81). In the psychosis of race, it is this 'nondeceived agent' which finds itself being erected in a diverse array of racial others who subsequently are conceived and positioned as the 'hidden force behind the law that manipulates the law for its own private advantage' (McGowan 2019, 71). This diversification emphasizes how, in examples of racism, it is the racial other who abuses social welfare, who does not uphold 'our' values, and who seeks to undermine 'our' securities and freedoms (in short, there is a social order, and it is 'them' who abuse it). What can be recognized in these examples is the clear sense of racial paranoia that underpins such claims.

Paranoia, to the rescue

Racism relies on paranoid and dangerous misinterpretations, which seek to identify a 'someone'—be it some racial group or individual—who sits beyond the rule of Law. It is in this sense a form of defence that explains, as well as demonstrates, the psychotic's relation to the other(s), who seemingly persecute and impinge upon the psychotic. In a certain manner, '[p]aranoia comes to the rescue' in the psychosis of race (McGowan 2021, 172). It works by identifying an other, for whom the Other's lack of authority can be attributed to. This follows a path whereby the gap between the Real and the symbolic is foreclosed, with the racial other occupying a place of social meaning, a form of interpretation, which amidst the structure of psychosis, allows one to make sense of the disorder. The impact here is that this denotes a return of the Real via a process of racialization that deprives the subject and the other of their agency (McGowan 2013). That is, '[b]y eliminating the gap in social authority and filling in this gap with a real authority who effectively runs the show'—in this case, the racial other—'paranoia deprives subjects of the space in which they exist as subjects' (McGowan 2013, 48).

We can go further here and begin to conceive how examples of paranoia emanate from the non-separation of the object *a*. Specifically, 'palpable manifestations of the object *a* in the paranoid person's life repeatedly "demonstrate" that the Symbolic universe is driven by a mad and maddening force, of which one is the tangible object' (Vanheule 2011, 140). Indeed, if we consider that the object *a* occupies a tangible reality in the psychosis of race, delineating and determining one's racial characteristics, we can begin to see how the object *a* comes to be seen as *constituting* one's way of life. The object *a* does not just refer to one's visible differences and distinctions, but also encapsulates the subject's form of life, as well as that of the other, prescribed in the clothes, food, and customs which they perform, and which actualize their very difference. What is noticeable here is that '[p]eople living through paranoia describe the object *a* as a concrete actuality, and as the ultimate proof that a jouissance-seeking Other wrongfully makes use of them' (Vanhuele 2011, 139). There is a tautology which underscores such claims, especially when we consider that what is obscured in psychosis is the fact that one's object *a* becomes 'actual' at the moment it becomes visible for the Other to make use of. As a result:

> in paranoia the jouissance emanating from the Other is experienced as being directed towards an element in one's own *actual* being: the Other hunts for the essence of one's own being, which is why all intrusions have such a devastating effect.
>
> (Vanheule 2011, 139, italics in original)[1]

These intrusions work to situate the racial other as a threat to the subject and are supported by forms of racist hostility.

According to McGowan, '[t]he paranoid subject usually adopts one of two possible attitudes toward the other', both of which are marked by a psychotic sense of loss (2013, 44). For example:

> [a]ccording to the first, paranoia serves to explain the loss of the privileged object. If I take up a paranoid attitude toward the other, I see her/his enjoyment coming at the expense of mine. The other enjoys the lost object that is rightfully mine. The other, having stolen my enjoyment, bears responsibility for my existence as a subject of loss. ... According to the second attitude, however, paranoia represents an attempt to convince ourselves that we have not lost the privileged object. We are paranoid not that the other has stolen the privileged object but that it plans to do so. The imagined threat that the other poses reassures us that we have the ultimate enjoyment and that this is what the other targets. By imagining a threat, we fantasize the privileged object back into existence despite its status as constitutively lost.
>
> (McGowan 2013, 44)

This speaks to the effects of a racial psychosis that works to obscure the fact that whether one has access to the object *a*, which is soon to be stolen, or whether one's access to the object *a* has in fact already been stolen, in either case, both the subject and other's noncastration undergirds a paranoia that finds itself easily rendered in acts of racism and racial hatred.

Therefore, what we see across both cases is an economy of loss which is brought to bear through the presence of the object *a*. What is not recognized nor acknowledged in the psychotic structure is the object's 'status as constitutively lost'. Instead, the presence of the object *a* of race takes hold in the paradoxes it evokes: an object that is both imagined, yet also existing; an object whose very privilege can be lost, while also constituting loss itself.

Get Out and 'counter-hegemonic Black paranoia'

Indeed, it is not the intention here to discredit examples of racial paranoia, but rather to consider how, in the case of psychosis, examples of racial injustice demand a certain level of psychosis in order to be interpreted and processed. This is effectively demonstrated in the 2021 sequel, *Candyman* (DaCosta). In one small scene, we watch the character Brianna (Teyonah Parris) come across 'a long stairwell leading down to an eerie cellar' (Wallace 2021). Referring to the significance of the scene, Wallace notes:

> [w]e know that she [Brianna] must go down there. She knows that she must go down there. She considers the dark path before her for a moment before gently but decisively shutting the door. 'Nope,' she says. Watching a screener, I imagined audiences losing it at this particular moment. How many times have we watched horror films in which the protagonist makes the inexplicable choice to go further into danger just to find out what's down there? For Black viewers, this habit is racialized: This is white-people shit, the joke goes. They obviously don't have enough to be afraid of in real life, so they go around looking for dangerous situations, opening the door, releasing the curse, unsealing the tomb. There's a reason 'Fuck around and find out' and its cousin, 'Play stupid games, win stupid prizes,' are Black proverbs.
>
> (2021)

Though the scene bears a comic significance, this in no way detracts from the paranoia that is evoked—a paranoia grounded in the fact that, for Black audiences, there are particular spaces that remain off-limits. Commenting on both the scene and the horror genre, the film's director, Nia DaCosta, explains:

> Black people would never be in a horror movie because they would not go into the haunted house, or go camping in the haunted woods, or investigate the mysterious sound. 'Nope, not for me—goodbye!' But it was also acknowledging that Black people have an awareness of how scary the world is in a very specific way. We're told about that from a young age in order to aid our survival.
>
> (White 2021)

What underscores DaCosta's remarks is the 'truth' that is expelled in certain actions that require a failure to commit to the very fictions that characterize the horror genre. Ultimately, it is by acknowledging and subverting these fictions that the truth of one's racial paranoia conveys the very horror of racial awareness itself.

Again, this is effectively demonstrated in *Get Out* (Peele 2017) and, specifically, the character Rod, played by the comedian, Lil Rey Howery. It is '[t]hrough this character, [that] Peele establishes the black humorist as black truth-teller, recognizing realities that others cannot or will not see' (Gillota 2021, 15). This is performed in various scenes throughout the film where Chris explains to Rod the 'strange' behaviours of his girlfriend's family. It is Rod who seeks to warn Chris of the potential danger he is in, detailing several preposterous outcomes, which, if Chris stays, will in no doubt befall him. Yes, the Armitages's are strange, but it's not like they are going to hypnotize Chris in order to perform a medical operation that will transplant a White man's brain into Chris's body… that's paranoid. There is, however, a truth to Rod's paranoia. Gillota notes:

> [a]fter his first night there, Chris calls Rod and admits that Rose's mother (Catherine Keener) hypnotized him to help him quit smoking (this hypnosis actually lays the groundwork for dooming Chris to the 'sunken place'). Rod's response is a telling mix of humor and horror: 'Bro, how you not scared of this, man? Look, they could have made you do all types of stupid shit. Have you fuckin' barking like a dog, flying around like you a fuckin' pigeon, lookin' ridiculous … or, I don't know if you know this, but white people love making people sex slaves and shit.' This is funny because of the hyperbole, the profanity, and Howery's well-timed delivery. The content, however, is deadly serious. Rod's suggestion that the Armitages may have Chris acting like a dog or a pigeon points to an awareness of the long history of whites treating black people like animals. Similarly, Rod's discussion of 'sex slaves' points to both slavery and the long history of sexual exploitation of black people. The irony of all this is that Rod's hyperbolic description is pretty much right: there *is* danger in Chris's hypnosis, and white people *are* getting sexual gratification from the black bodies that they steal.
>
> (2021, 16, italics in original)

What both DaCosta's cellar scene and Rod's elaborate descriptions effectively convey is the sense in which a 'counter-hegemonic black paranoia' (Jarvis 2018, 102) is, as Gillota reveals, 'pretty much right' (2021, 16). That is, what such forms of psychosis require is that one adheres to a set of racial fictions that are then expounded and performed as part of race's very critique. As a result, it is in examples of paranoia that both *Candyman* and *Get Out* reveal how the disruption of the racial symbolic order forces one to undergo a psychotic dislocation that is always, as seen in the examples of both Brianna and Rod, very easily dismissed and most often ignored.

The emphasis here is on the fact that the only way to relate to one's very racialization, indeed, to even critique a racist objection, is to resort to the certainty of a psychotic position. In the case of the racist, it is clear that their racist convictions follow a path of psychotic certainty. Confined to their object *a*, the racist's experiences of the other only confirms their convictions: they do smell; their food is weird; they do seem to have an easier path to obtaining jobs and social support; and it is their frustrations which are taken seriously. Again, psychosis does not lie in the 'truth' of these sentiments, but with the sincerity in which they are given. The psychotic very much believes, without much questioning, that the evidence supports their convictions: the 'psychotic is convinced not of the "reality" of what he or she sees or hears, but of the fact that it means something, and that this meaning involves him or her' (Fink 1999, 84). Ultimately, 'the subject identifies with the object of jouissance of the Other: beyond any reason the paranoiac 'knows' that another person, or more abstractly a force, has "got it in for him"' (Vanheule 2011, 138).[2] As a consequence, '[t]he Symbolic is invaded by a maddening force of which the subject is the mere object, and does not function as a guarantee whereby subjective identity can be articulated' (Vanheule 2011, 138–139).

It has already been noted that the Other holds no guarantee in psychosis. What this amounts to however is an 'encounter ... with the signifier as such' (Lacan 1997a, 320). Without the function of the Other as an abstract mediation in the subject's interlocution, 'the psychotic is inhabited, possessed, by language' (Lacan 1997a, 250). What further complicates this possession is the fact that its very articulation bears no relation to the signifier. Confronted with the hole in signification, the position of the psychotic is one that lacks the very means to identify with their constitutive lack: instead, the 'I' remains a hole (Leader 2012). It is important to re-emphasize at this point that such a 'hole' does not stand for the subject's constitutive 'lack', but, rather, is transposed for an apparent racial designation: an 'empty' form that posits no immediate significance for the subject, beyond their very differentiation. Possessed by language, yet foreclosed from signification, what is returned in psychosis is the Real.

'A Rockefeller Republican in blackface'

It is now possible to conceive how acts of racism form part of an economy of loss that seeks to locate the enjoyment of the other as dependent on the Other's inability to curtail such enjoyment, or to the failures of a symbolic order that does not fairly endow the subject with similar forms of privileged enjoyment. Indeed, what we see in examples of racial paranoia is the clear sense that there resides an insidious presence located within the other; a demarcation that acts as a further source of racial division. This is apparent when one 'fails' to follow and live up to the experiences and frustrations of their 'race', such as when accusations are made towards certain Back individuals, for whom succeeding in White society requires an appropriation of, or a succumbing to, White interests. While enveloped in forms of racial anxiety, Gordon highlights how there are those 'who can move through the white world so long as they offer themselves as black bodies with white consciousnesses' (Gordan and Chevannes 2018). Such criticisms were frequently levelled at former U.S. President, Barak Obama. In one notable account, the American philosopher and political activist, Cornel West, described Obama as 'a Rockefeller Republican in blackface' (Democracy Now! 2012).[3] Again, this is not to suggest that West's criticisms were in anyway false; instead, in making the claim, West's remarks offer a considered appreciation of the position from which they are made.

The premise of this position can be identified in how the framing of Obama as an inherently White President, performing 'Blackface', undoubtedly relies upon a level of racial paranoia: most notably, the fear that *within* certain Black individuals, especially those in positions of power, a White man insidiously resides. This confirms how it is not the 'content' of one's racial paranoia which proves significant, but the position it reveals: in this case, a critical understanding of the explicit lack of progressive change in U.S. politics and society during Obama's presidency.[4] In so doing, West's remarks reveal a psychosis of race that both frames and positions subjects in the act of racialization. It is here that the perception of reality and, specifically, the truth of one's claims about reality, become disturbed. Indeed, the truth rests not in the legitimacy of the accusations, which are levelled at the racialized other, but in the position towards the other that such paranoia conveys.

For example, in the wake of the Hurricane Katrina disaster, which hit the city of New Orleans and surrounding areas in August 2005, there were, during the disaster's aftermath, numerous reports which emphasized an 'explosion of black violence, rape and looting' (Žižek 2005). While it was later proven that many of the reported incidents did not take place, the conviction of the accusation meant that it didn't really matter. Instead:

> [t]he reality of poor blacks, abandoned and left without means to survive, was thus transformed into the specter of blacks exploding violently, of tourists robbed and killed on streets that had slid into anarchy, of the Superdome ruled by gangs that were raping women and children.
> (Žižek 2005)

Ultimately, the Black subject was positioned as 'the subject supposed to loot and rape' (Žižek 2005). According to Žižek, the reports of Black violence were motivated not by facts, but by racial prejudice. Though acts of violence undoubtedly occurred, it was not the reality of these acts which proved important—and especially not the underlying conditions that led to looting: the need for food and water that was unsupplied by state or federal services— but the racial paranoia that they helped to perpetuate.[5] Moreover, this paranoia proves pathological, insofar as what was revealed in the reports was an inherent disturbance *in* the reporting of 'reality' itself. It was the perception of truth and its relation to reality which underwent a psychotic disturbance. What the reports presented was an example of what Žižek refers to as 'lying in the guise of truth: Even if what I am saying is factually true, the motives that make me say it are false' (2005). The psychosis of race works from this very asymmetry, wherein a clear sense of racial paranoia, which relies upon the disturbance between reality and truth, is forged. In the case of Hurricane Katrina, the reality of the violence was true, yet the racial paranoia that motivated the reports was falsely driven by a racial prejudice grounded in the 'static illusion that things are as they are' (Ragland 1995, 48). Accordingly, what occurs in such examples of racial paranoia is the obfuscation of what is true and false in the perception itself. In fact, in the structure of psychosis, such a distinction doesn't even matter. There is nothing but 'the satisfaction felt by those who would be able to say: "You see, Blacks really are like that, violent barbarians under the thin layer of civilization!"' (Žižek 2005).

It is the obverse of these remarks that bear witness to the paranoia that frames West's comments on Obama. Clearly, the representation of Obama performing 'Blackface' is false (nor was he a republican), but the perception that underlies West's motive reveals an inherent truth in his position: the unequivocal failure of a political individual elected largely on a 'change' that was never realized and enacting policies that would, as West alluded to, put Obama to the right of President Nixon (Cohen 2012). What is unique to West's remarks, however, is that one can only engage with this truth through the falsity of its claim; that is, through its inherent inconsistency. Essentially, it is not the reality of the claim which reveals the truth (Obama clearly isn't a republican), but the truth that can be found in the fiction it evokes: '…every truth has the structure of fiction' (Lacan 1997b, 12).[6]

Fantasy and psychosis

What seems to propel examples of paranoia is the logic of exclusion that it endorses. In its dislocation from the Other, paranoia finds itself being directed towards the exclusion of a number of 'problematic' others, all of which impinge upon the psychotic in some form or another. Such paranoid exclusions underscore the racist fantasy. Key here is that in the presence of the object *a* there must remain the fantasy that the object *a* is under threat or in some way undermined by the other. Paranoia speaks to the threats that the other imposes so that all fantasies are enacted through a negative mode. That is, while one can fantasize about an ideal perfection—the perfect house, the harmonious society—such perfections are always interrelated with the nightmare, insofar as 'when we fantasize about our ideal, we fantasize simultaneously about the threats that imperil that ideal' (McGowan 2007b, 93). As a consequence, the ideal fantasy 'is supported by a disturbing paranoiac fantasy which tells us why things went wrong' (Žižek 1999b, 210).

In the psychosis of race, this 'disturbing paranoiac fantasy' finds itself directed towards an other *beyond* the Other—the other who has illicitly obtained the enjoyment that is denied. Despite the Other's failures, in the structure of psychosis the other's enjoyment serves at the expense of the subject, resulting in examples of racism and forms of hate. Whether it be derogatory language or physical violence, examples of racism undoubtedly rely upon, as well as refer to, a certain conviction in the other's alterity. Specifically, what is hated in the other is their enjoyment; an enjoyment predicated upon the perceived access to the object *a* which they have obtained. When the psychosis of race serves to fix the subject to their object *a*, we are left with the 'hatred [that …] is addressed to being' (Lacan 1999, 99)—a hatred directed towards the other. It is on this basis that:

> [t]he inherent paranoia of fantasy represents one of its chief dangers for the subject; it is one of the most difficult obstacles for the subject to overcome, simply because the subject rarely experiences the other's lack or failure to enjoy, which would contradict it.
>
> (McGowan 2007a, 99–100)

In examples of psychosis, this contradiction is ultimately undermined by the very fact that the 'gap that forever separates the fantasmatic kernel of the subject's being from the more "superficial" modes of his or her symbolic and/or imaginary identifications' is obscured (Žižek 1999b, 209); or, as Lacan describes, 'patched over' (1997a, 45). It is 'a hole, a fault, a point of rupture, in the structure of the external world [that] finds itself patched over by psychotic fantasy' (Lacan 1997a, 45). This points to an important distinction in the psychotic's relation to fantasy.

Indeed, usually 'for a fantasy to be operative, it has to remain "implicit" i.e., a *distance* must be maintained between it and the explicit symbolic texture sustained by it' (Žižek 1999b, 204, italics added). It would seem that the lack of any 'distance' is what characterizes the 'psychotic fantasy', resulting in examples of paranoia whereby the distance between the fantasy and the symbolic order is obscured to such a degree that, in psychosis, one's fantasy and paranoia are considered 'real'. Moreover, it is the lack of any distance that assures the psychotic their certainty: indeed, 'the world ... is transformed into what we call a fantasmagoria, but which for him has the utmost certainty in his lived experience' (Lacan 1997a, 69). This certainty occludes 'the experience of the fact that the fantasy-object, by its fascinating presence, is merely filling out a lack, a void in the Other', insofar as '[t]here is nothing "behind" the fantasy; the fantasy is a construction whose function is to hide this void, this "nothing"' (Žižek 2008b, 148).

As discussed in Chapter 6, what the psychosis of race provides is the transference of this 'nothing' into 'something'; a 'something' which remains inherently ambivalent in the psychosis of race. Indeed, to identify a clearly delineated 'race' is impossible, with any single classification being subject to geographical variations from which 'the identity of a person as "black" or "white" is contingent upon a cluster of concepts that are themselves too protean to be able to uphold anything like a necessary truth' (Seshadri-Crooks 2000, 141). Equally, '[w]e can cite historical evidence to show that groups that were once considered white are no longer classified as such for this or that reason, etc.' (Seshadri-Crooks 2000, 141).[7] As science routinely pronounces, there is more that is shared between 'races', than there is that differentiates them. Such pronouncements, however, do not prevent the ambivalence that race creates. Here, the inherent nothing which constitutes one's being is carried through a multitude of fantasmatic substitutes that offer no security in the psychosis of race.

Instead, in psychosis, fantasy seems to propose a form of purgatory. That is, in foreclosing castration, there is no 'I' which is excluded in the psychotic's fantasy (Lacan 1997a), yet there is also no 'I' for the psychotic to refer to. Indeed, rather than 'finding' this 'I' in the metonymy of the signifier, for the psychotic, '[i]ts identity and its position in the world are not articulated' (Vanheule 2011, 127). Without the lack of an 'I', there is nothing but the lack of a lack. While fantasy stages the subject's lost sense of being—lost on entry to the symbolic order—*the reality of the fantasy* in psychosis leaves the psychotic in a position stranded between that of the symbolic 'I', which all non-psychotics defer to, and the impossible 'I', the elimination of the lack that also eliminates the subject; or the subject as 'nothing' (Soler 1995). In the psychosis of race, the lack of this very lack is both masked and, thus, obscured, in the racial designation that one is prescribed. The psychotic's failure to traverse the fantasy—that is, to acknowledge the lack that inheres to fantasy—is ignored for the reality of the fantasy itself.

Fantasy, *jouissance*, and the other

The reality of the psychotic fantasy is, by its very nature, not ascribed to the psychotic's imagination, but to the perception that the reality of the fantasy is revealed or communicated to the psychotic. Referring to the case of Schreber, Vanheule highlights how:

> [i]n the incubation period before the outbreak of his second illness period Schreber, in a state of daydreaming, had the fantasy that it would be beautiful to be a woman submitting to the act of copulation. This fantasy, which concerns his sexual position as a man or a woman, was not qualified as a product of his own imagination—the type of judgement that would give rise to repression—but as a strange communication that was revealed to him, and that could not be put aside.
>
> (2011, 71)

The sense in which such 'strange communication' resides from without is, in the psychosis of race, conveyed through the visibility that race confers. It is in this sense that one does not 'choose' one's race, but, instead, is prescribed their race as a demarcation that occurs from without. A demarcation matched by forms of racial paranoia. Certainly, while it is the subject who is raced, it is not the subject who commands such racialization. Instead, the racialized body is read as an act of communication that dictates one's race.

Accordingly, while 'fantasy lays bare the hidden kernel of the desiring subject to the subject itself, and this is one reason why we resist fully immersing ourselves in fantasy' (McGowan 2007b, 64), in examples of psychosis, there is no resistance. Where the presence of the object *a* is confirmed, there is nothing but the reality of the fantasy. In short, the fantasy speaks: '[i]t's a fantasm [*fantaisie*], but unlike the fantasm, or fantasy [*fantasme*], that we highlight in the phenomena of neurosis it's a fantasm that speaks, or more exactly, it's a spoken fantasm' (Lacan 1997a, 144). It is in such cases that the racist fantasy—that is, the proof that the racial other really is like their fantasy image—works to confirm the psychotic's certainty.

What such a fantasm denotes, however, is 'a structural flaw in the constitution of the fantasy' itself (Braunstein 2015, 91). This flaw is perceived at 'the interval in the matheme of the fantasy, where the lozenge ◇ makes fantasy possible' (Braunstein 2015, 91). As Braunstein adds, it is the failure of this 'interval' which means that '[t]he paths of desire and fantasy are defenses against jouissance, closed off for the psychotic' (2015, 91).[8] There is, therefore, no distance and no defence for psychosis in fantasy. Instead, with no protection through the distance that fantasy establishes, the psychotic 'subject is exposed to jouissance and finds himself besieged and torn apart by it' (Braunstein 2015, 92). It is with regard to *jouissance* that 'the certainty that some troubling substance of enjoyment has been illicitly procured by the other' (Hook 2022, 44) bears a psychotic significance that compounds 'the libidinous corporeality of being': that is, 'a state of being that is not (yet) determined by the signifier' (Vanheule 2011, 127).

This confrontation with an unsated *jouissance* presents itself in forms of racial paranoia, which is directed towards the racial other itself. It is the other's *jouissance*, their very idiosyncrasies, that impinges upon the subject (such as their clothes, food, and dialect). There is always 'something' about the other that confronts and torments in the psychotic structure, and which confirms their segregation. Here, '[r]acism is segregation that marks as different subjects and groups that have elaborated, constructed, and organized a mode of jouissance incommensurable with the jouissance of another group' (Khan 2018, 159).[9]

This helps to highlight how the ongoing impact of racial hatred does not reside entirely at the level of its construction—that is, in how certain groups are constructed along racist lines—but that the impact of racism bears a relation to the Real of *jouissance*. The effects of this are helpfully clarified by Zupančič:

> [a]lthough it can be factually true that Muslim culture has a different idea of manhood and womanhood than 'our' Christian culture, the moment we start imagining what 'these Muslim men would do to our women,' this is no longer about any factual difference; the structure of fantasy, of our fantasy, is already fully operative—which is to say that with these fantasies it is our own jouissance that we attempt to control, regulate, keep at bay.
>
> (2019, 97)

I would add that in the psychosis of race the subject's 'own jouissance' is indicted to a regulation that fundamentally fails to be controlled and kept at bay. In the structure of psychosis, the racist fantasy is not just fully operative, but determined, fixed, and brought to life: in sum, the racist fantasy is made real by its embodiment *in* the racial other itself. This once again speaks to the fact that, for the racist, it is not enough to prevent their racism with better knowledge. For the psychosis of race, such knowledge is already foreclosed.

Uncastrated *jouissance*

The significance of the racist fantasy rests not simply in its racist depiction, but also in the ways it both frames and positions the subject in a process of racialization. For example, in his analysis of how '[t]he unspoken pleasures of minstrelsy linger, … within the modern-day cartoons watched by children', George draws upon the examples of Mickey Mouse and Bugs Bunny to highlight how the popular cartoons work to 'identify the black body as childlike [and] unrestrained by the conventions of civilized society' (2022, 257). He adds:

> [s]uch cartoons present the image of a (black) body that exudes eruptive *jouissance*, one that rejects the partitioning of the body into partial drives through a nimble elasticity and boisterous exuberance—indeed, through a vibrant *animation*—that defies the true conditions of human subjectivity and embodiment. In keeping with the minstrel tradition, these cartoons aim at representing the bliss of an unrestrained corporality capable of accessing an impossible, absolute *other jouissance*.
>
> (George 2022, 257, italics in original)

This comic depiction of uncastrated '*other jouissance*' is echoed in film, most notably, in the Blaxploitation genre, and its use of racial stereotypes to depict and frame the Black body. Originally made for Black audiences, critical consideration of Blaxploitation cinema can be conceived as denoting a level of Black pride and power, with the depiction of Black individuals and communities transcending other genre conventions that tended to portray Black characters as either villains or victims. Emerging in the U.S. during the 1970s, the genre echoes Hoyt's (2016) reflections of growing-up in Boston (Massachusetts), during this time. He describes how:

> growing up in the 1960s and 1970s in an urban neighborhood … Blackness was in transformative ascendancy…, transmogrifying from a stigma to a source of pride, defiance, solidarity, and a complicated aesthetic that somehow held and conveyed all of these energies.
>
> (Hoyt 2016, 95)

This 'complicated aesthetic' would underpin films such as *Foxy Brown* (Jack Hill 1974), *Shaft* (Gordon Parks 1971), and *Cotton Comes to Harlem* (Ossie Davis 1970). Specifically, in accordance with the genre's recognition of, and appeals to, Black agency, such films rely upon a reclamation of racial identity that reveal their own psychotic structure.

For example, across its various subgenres, Blaxploitation cinema would frequently evoke a characteristic 'sticking it to The Man' (or, a 'sticking it to the Other') narrative, with its protagonists drawing from, as well as performing, a litany of racial stereotypes. As a result, the depiction of political and social antagonisms affecting Black communities was subsumed within narratives that portrayed the overcoming of such antagonisms at the behest of a single, Back character. Despite the genre's emphasis on the socio-economic inequalities in U.S. race relations, ultimately, the genre's Black characters were easily portrayed as bearers of a radical *jouissance*, endowed with the capacity to manipulate and resist the Other. Enveloped within this psychotic position, the Blaxploitation genre allows us to conceive how the psychosis of race proves appealing. In their refusal to sacrifice enjoyment, it is the psychotic who stands apart from the effects of castration.

This is further demonstrated in McGowan's (2004) reference to the fictional serial killer, Hannibal Lecter. Here, McGowan notes that it is the:

> refusal to sacrifice enjoyment [... which] makes a psychotic like Hannibal Lecter so attractive to those of us who have made the sacrifice. Lecter clearly enjoys, and even though we might shy away from the results of the way he enjoys, we are nonetheless drawn to him.
>
> (2004, 201, fn.12)

What is apparent, however, is that Lecter may not be the only psychotic. Indeed, what seems to underpin the Blaxploitation genre, as well as our interests in the heinous activities of Lecter, is a form of enjoyment that proves demonstrative of psychosis. That is, it is not simply the case that audiences enjoy the cannibal Lecter, or that they end-up rooting for the trained martial artist and private detective, John Shaft, but that to enjoy the very conception of an other who manages to stand apart from the Law is itself a form of psychosis. In psychosis, there is always the other for whom the Other's authority bears no impact upon; who, in existing outside the Law, manipulates the Other, undermines its credibility, and thus escapes its appeal. Consequently, what remains attractive in psychosis is the fantasy of an other whose very enjoyment sits outside society's symbolic restrictions. What underscores the racist fantasy is how this position is psychotically invested in the apparent unrestrained enjoyment that is attributed to the racial other.

The horror ignored: paranoia and social antagonism

What characterizes the subject's relation to *jouissance* and the other, as depicted in examples of racial paranoia and racist fantasy, are 'the *exaggerated attributions made of the enjoyments experienced by others*' (Hook 2022, 44, italics in original). For Hook:

> [t]his helps us explain how racism can be understood both as an experience of *jouissance* ('the thrill of hate') and as type of possession (in the form of our libidinal treasures or in the malignant, 'illegal' enjoyments of others). Upon reflection, it becomes apparent that these two aspects of enjoyment—'our' libidinal treasures and what fundamentally embodies 'their' otherness—are two sides of the same coin, two inflections of the same fantasy. There is, on the one hand, the narcissistic *jouissance* of the appealing fantasy object that (we believe) encapsulates what is most precious about us. And then there is the vexing feature of the other—typically something super-abundant and exaggerated—which positivizes my own lack in a threatening feature *possessed by them*.
>
> (2022, 44, italics in original)

The characteristics that Hook outlines closely follow that of the psychotic structure, with the other's enjoyment suggesting a point of imposition that directly impacts upon the subject. Furthermore, the 'positivization' of the lack, transposed upon the perceived threats of the racial other, reveals how the reification of lack becomes an object of possession for both the subject and the other, as well as a key attribute in acts of racialization. The *jouissance* at play here is one that denotes a lack which is, paradoxically, too full, or, rather, too close, in its presence. What can be added to Hook's account, therefore, is how this 'fantasy object'—an object of inherent lack—becomes rendered and fixed to the presence of the object *a* in psychosis. This includes the very ways in which one's race serves to embody and encapsulate what is different about the other and oneself. In so doing, the 'two aspects of enjoyment'—the subject and the other's enjoyment—become assumed within the presence of the object *a*.

This bears witness to the unique position that psychosis presents. Whereas 'the emergence of the [impossible] object creates a rift within the fantasy and exposes the desire of the subject' (McGowan 2007a, 241, n.24), it is with the foreclosure of the Name-of-the-Father, and the presence of the object *a*, that the failure to domesticate such desire leads to its return in the other and the *jouissance* they have obtained. Thus, what seems to structure the signifier's agency is the other's *jouissance*; indeed, that which delimits the symbolic order through a process of racialization that remains tied to the racist fantasy. What the racial fantasy elides is the experience of the racial other in its very radicality.

There is, therefore, a certain potential in the fantasy that is ultimately lost or obscured amidst the certainty that one's racism provides. Though what returns in psychosis is the Real other, what remains lost is the *Real* of this encounter. McGowan notes:

> [i]n the public world, subjects rarely encounter the real dimension of the other. ... In the public world, we experience the other playing a part, acting out a symbolic identity, but we don't experience what the other is when no one is looking. It is at this point that we can begin to recognize the radical potential of fantasy. Fantasy permits us the impossible view of the other; we fantasize the hidden other. Clearly, this view of the other is our fantasy, not the other in itself, but it nonetheless acknowledges the disruptive and threatening power of the other *for us*—the dimension of the other that doesn't fit within a prescribed symbolic identity.
>
> (2007a, 196)

Amidst the disorder of the symbolic, it is the reality of the fantasy that prevents the psychotic from achieving such an 'impossible view'. In psychosis, the racial other is nothing but a 'disruptive and threatening power' which imposes on the psychotic's reality. What is more, whereas the goal of fantasy is to 'construc[t] a narrative that explains the loss of the [impossible] object and/or points toward its recovery[,] ... giv[ing] meaning to the loss of the object and transform[ing] the impossible object into a possible one' (McGowan 2007b, 15), in psychosis, there is no point of recovery or sense of possibility framing the object—characteristics which would denote the subject's desire (the stage that fantasy provides)—instead, the fantasy is Real, the object a is present.[10]

It is this predicament that characterizes the 'nothingness' at the heart of the psychosis of race and, specifically, the perspective of the racial other. The fact that race, and acts of racism, centre upon what is 'super-abundant and exaggerated' (Hook 2022, 44) helps to reveal how race works to transform this 'nothing' into 'something'; a 'something' that nonetheless leaves the subject in an impossible position of embracing that which is inherently 'nothing'. Thus, what is foreclosed in the psychotic fantasy is the horror it comprises. Here, '[t]he Horrible can also function as the [fantasy] screen ..., as the thing whose fascinating effect conceals something "more horrible than horror itself", the primordial void or antagonism' (Žižek 2008a, 6).

Accordingly though, in psychosis, the racial fantasy serves to reveal the horrors that reside within its perception of the other; what remains foreclosed is the horror of the fantasy itself. Indeed, as Žižek asks: 'is not the anti-Semitic demonic image of the Jew, the Jewish plot, such an evocation of the ultimate Horror, which precisely, is the phantasmic screen enabling us to avoid confrontation with the social antagonism?' (2008a, 6). What the psychotic fantasy obscures is the revelation of confronting such an antagonism.[11]

In so doing, racism serves as a diversion, a psychotic substitution, which registers social antagonism as beholden to a specific racial other and to the presence of *their* enjoyment. Racial paranoia perceives the other (and their group) as 'too seduced by pleasure to participate in the work of the social project, or too enamored of money to concern itself with the general welfare, or too violent to be tolerated, and so forth' (Rothenberg 2010, 141). In an act of racial fixing, it is not simply the case that 'the hated group seems [to] have misappropriated [the] *objet a*' (Rothenberg 2010, 141), but that *their* object *a* is itself one of misappropriation.

This goes to the heart of what Hook (2022) refers to as the 'indignation' that characterizes racism. Echoing Žižek's example of the anti-Semite, who cannot simply be told that their anti-Semitism is wrong, '[r]acism is not merely ... a set of affective responses, a collection of inter-subjective relations, or a composite array of attitudes and prejudices' but also 'involve[s] a potent "moral" dimension' (Hook 2022, 46). That is, racism is 'a type of indignation; it entails the impetus to blame and punish; and it involves a sense of laws, of norms and ideals that have been violated' (Hook 2022, 46). We can consider such forms of indignation to be directly related to the presence of the object *a* of race. It is towards the presence of this object that acts of violation are directed and it is in the presence of this object that the guarantee to blame and punish is assured.

Again, it is with regards to the certainty of the psychotic that examples of paranoia undergo a logical acceptance that speaks to the very paradoxes it evokes. Leader highlights how:

> [i]n some cases, the paranoiac's efforts are sanctioned by society as worthy, in others condemned as homicidal. Hitler's equation of the Jews with a malign stain to racial purity was—and still is—accepted by many people, just as the assassination in 1986 of the Swedish president Olof Palme was seen by some as a legitimate act supported by a moral system and by others as an unacceptable outburst of murderous violence.
>
> (2012, 79–80)

While both examples stand as acts of violence, what can be emphasized in Leader's account is how each example exhibits a misguided conviction that bears witness to the certainty of the psychotic position. Whether viewing Jews as a 'problem' that demands eradication, or whether conceiving of the assassination of a political opponent as a legitimate response, it is the paranoia behind such convictions that fundamentally 'believes' that a violent resolution can 'resolve' the antagonisms, inconsistencies, and socio-political disorders that underpin the social field. This is not to suggest that social antagonisms cannot be tackled through forms of political action, but that to consider one group or individual as *the* 'problem' to be 'resolved' is to resort to a position of psychosis that fails to recognize the inherent impossibility of a social order without antagonism.

The fantasy image: liberal and conservative approaches

With the Other's exclusion from the symbolic, we see a proliferation of others in the Real; that is, in the anxious proximity that emerges from one's 'colour' and one's racial visibility. The psychotic fantasy approaches racial visibility as grounded in the body's racial delineation. This delineation resides not just in the variances that are prescribed by the racial symbolic order, but also in its conflation with the Real. However, it is on this basis that psychotic fantasies of the racial other 'might actually pave the way for the most authentic kind of ethical encounter—an encounter in which the subject opens itself to the real dimension of the other' (McGowan 2007a, 195).[12] Certainly, the intentions of this encounter does not suggest that we freely allow the unbridled proliferation of racist fantasies (in other words, let racism run amok), nor does it imply that we simply overlook examples of racial paranoia. Rather, in its relation to the Real, the psychotic fantasy can obtain a certain ethical potential in its ability to confront the Real other, beyond any symbolic determination. Ultimately, this requires that one goes 'through' their racial paranoia in order to expose the very kernel that undergirds one's racism. In doing so, one is not merely resorting to a symbolic order of racial difference, but confronting the very limits that uphold the act of racial signification. What this confrontation works to dislodge is the fantasmatic image of the other; images that underscore both the liberal subject and the xenophobic conservative.

According to Thakur, '[n]othing appears to please liberals more than a politically correct image' (2020, 145).[13] What is key here is the image's very abstraction. Indeed, for Zalloua, 'an anti-racist stance that abstracts too much, seeing all minorities as victimized by the same out-of-control white supremacy, will obfuscate the nature of black subjection and the workings of civil society's libidinal economy' (2020, 129). While such forms of anti-racism seek to highlight and critique examples of racist discrimination, they ultimately rely upon an *image* of the racist other that functions to confirm the anti-racist's 'enlightened' separation (and, thus, their exclusion from examples of racism). As a result, McGowan notes:

> [t]he tolerant attitude that never allows itself to be jarred by the enjoying other becomes ... further from really encountering the real other than the attitude of hate and mistrust. The liberal subject who welcomes illegal immigrants as fellow citizens completely shuts down the space for the other in the real. The immigrant as fellow citizen is not the real other. The xenophobic conservative, on the other hand, constructs a fantasy that envisions the illegal immigrant awash in a linguistic and cultural enjoyment that excludes natives. This fantasy, paradoxically, permits an encounter with the real other that liberal tolerance forecloses. Of course, xenophobes retreat from this encounter and from their own enjoyment, but they do have an experience of it that liberals do not. The tolerant

liberal is open to the other but eliminates the otherness, while the xenophobic conservative is closed to the other but allows for the otherness. The ethical position thus involves sustaining the liberal's tolerance within the conservative's encounter with the real other.

(2013, 119–120)

Consequently, what is shared across both positions is an image of the other that fundamentally works to 'protect' the subject from engaging with the other—be it the racial other or the racist other. In fact, for both the tolerant liberal and xenophobic conservative it is the 'image' of the other that prevents any Real engagement. While it is the xenophobic conservative who comes closest to the other's otherness, it is in the recourse to forms of racial paranoia and racist fantasy that they psychotically divest from encountering the Real other. Under the structure of psychosis, it is the prevalence of the image that works as an imaginary form of compensation that both fixes, essentializes, and determines the other in its very presence. In fact, what is assured is that the other's image effectively renders their object *a*. It is important to note here that, outside of the structure of psychosis, 'one can only enjoy *the image of the object*, not the object itself', that is, '[t]he *objet petit a* ... is precisely what the subject misses in the image' (McGowan 2004, 19, italics in original). Subsequently, what is foreclosed in psychosis is the very recognition that what the image provides is nothing more than an imaginary composition. As a result, it is in the 'reality' of the image that the racial other becomes affixed to specific racial attributes and fantasy formations that provide the basis for one's racial paranoia.

Notes

1 Lacan would come to define paranoia 'as identifying jouissance in this place of the Other as such' (1966b, 215, cited in Vanheule 2011, 139).
2 In so doing, 'the paranoid person *observes clear signs* that the Other is driven by a malevolent plan, of which he or she as a person is the victim' (Vanheule 2011, 138, italics in original).
3 The comments were made towards Obama in light of his presidential re-election, where West added, 'it's morally obscene and spiritually profane to spend $6 billion on an election, $2 billion on a presidential election, and not have any serious discussion—poverty, trade unions being pushed against the wall dealing with stagnating and declining wages when profits are still up and the one percent are doing very well, no talk about drones dropping bombs on innocent people. So we end up with such a narrow, truncated political discourse, as the major problems—ecological catastrophe, climate change, global warming' (Cohen 2012).
4 In summarizing Obama's legacy, West has noted, 'Obama's lack of courage to confront Wall Street criminals and his lapse of character in ordering drone strikes unintentionally led to rightwing populist revolts at home and ugly Islamic fascist rebellions in the Middle East. And as deporter-in-chief—nearly 2.5 million immigrants were deported under his watch—Obama policies prefigure Trump's barbaric plans' (2017).

5 Here, Žižek clarifies: '[o]f course, the sense of menace had been ignited by genuine disorder and violence: Looting, ranging from base thievery to foraging for the necessities of life, did occur after the storm passed over New Orleans. However, the (limited) reality of crimes in no way exonerates "reports" on the total breakdown of law and order—not because these reports were "exaggerated," but for a much more radical reason. ... Even if *all* the reports on violence and rapes had proven to be factually true, the stories circulating about them would still be "pathological" and racist, since what motivated these stories were not facts, but racist prejudices' (2005, italics in original).
6 Or, in its Helegian mode, 'there is truth, but it is immanent to the symbolic process—the truth is measured not by an external standard, but by the "pragmatic contradiction," the inner (in)consistency of the discursive process, the gap between the enunciated content and its position of enunciation' (Žižek 2012, 78).
7 Seshadri-Crooks's adds: '[e]ven in identity statements such as "blacks are people of African descent" or "whites are people of European descent," though the predicates supposedly define and give the meaning of black and white, establishing the necessity of these concepts in every counter-factual situation will not be possible if only because national designations, and the notion of descent, are historically volatile and scientifically invalid respectively' (2000, 141).
8 In contrast to Braunstein, I do not believe that the 'broken' or 'absent' lozenge means that 'there is no fantasy or that the term "fantasy" would have to be redefined if we were to sustain the uncertain syntagm of "psychotic fantasy"' (2015, 91). Instead, the very use of the term 'psychotic fantasy' suggests a certain level of difference to the work of fantasy in examples of non-psychosis.
9 Khan develops this point with regard to Jacques-Alain Miller's assertion that 'the root of racism [... is] the hatred of one's own jouissance—in other words, that which is extimate to the subject' (Khan, 2018, 159). Here Miller notes how 'racism is founded on what one imagines about the Other's *jouissance*; it is hatred of the particular way, of the Other's own way, of experiencing *jouissance*' (1994, 79).
10 This offers an alternative conception to George, for whom, 'unconsciously bound to both the Real and the Symbolic, race as this illusory, impossible possession—this Imaginary *object a* that is both within and absent from the subject—ultimately directs subjective desire toward the lost being of the Real' (2014, 365). In the psychosis of race, there is no desire and, thus, no desire toward which one's sense of lost being can be directed.
11 Tied to the certitude of its conviction, there is nothing left but for the psychosis of race to confirm its racist logic, grounded in acts of racial segregation and fixed forms of racial difference.
12 Here, McGowan notes that, '[t]hrough the act of imagining the threat of the other in the real, fantasy creates the space for the part of the other that remains hidden—the other as it exists privately, when no one is looking' (2007a, 195).
13 Thakur adds, '[b]y contrast, conservatives are also attached to the image but tend to highlight the symbolic aspects of an image over everything else' (2020, 145–146).

References

Braunstein, Nestor. 2015. "'You cannot choose to go crazy'." In *Lacan on Madness: Madness, yes you can't*, edited by Patricia Gherovici and Manya Steinkoler (85–98). Hove, UK: Routledge.

Cohen, Rick. 2012. "Cornel West calls Obama a 'Rockefeller Republican in Blackface'." *The Nonprofit Quarterly (NPQ)*, November 13, https://nonprofitquarterly.org/cornel-west-calls-obama-a-rockefeller-republican-in-blackface/

DaCosta, Nia, director. 2021. *Candyman*. Universal Pictures; Metro-Goldwyn-Mayer Pictures; BRON Creative; Monkeypaw Productions.
Davis, Ossie, director. 1970. *Cotton Comes to Harlem*. Formosa Productions.
Democracy Now!2012. "Tavis Smiley, Cornel West on the 2012 election & why calling Obama 'progressive' ignores his record." November 9, https://www.democracynow.org/2012/11/9/tavis_smiley_cornel_west_on_the
Fink, Bruce. 1999. *A Clinical Introduction to Lacanian Psychoanalysis: Theory and Technique*. Cambridge, MA: Harvard University Press.
Freud, Sigmund. 1981. *The Case of Schreber, Papers on Technique, and Other Works. The Standard Edition of the Complete Psychological Works of Sigmund Freud, Volume XII, 1911–1913*. London, UK: The Hogarth Press.
George, Sheldon. 2014. "From alienation to cynicism: race and the Lacanian unconscious." *Psychoanalysis, Culture & Society* 19, no. 4: 360–378.
George, Sheldon. 2022. "The Lacanian subject of race: sexuation, the drive, and racial subjectivity." In *Lacan and Race: Racism, Identity, and Psychoanalytic Theory*, edited by Sheldon George and Derek Hook (241–262). Abingdon, UK: Routledge.
Gillota, David. 2021. "'Man, I told you not to go in that house': the humor and horror of Jordan Peele's *Get Out*." *The Journal of Popular Culture* 54, no. 5: 1031–1050.
Gordan, Lewis, and Derefe Kimarley Chevannes. 2018. "Black issues in philosophy: a conversation on *Get Out*." *Blog of the APA*, April 3, https://blog.apaonline.org/2018/04/03/black-issues-in-philosophy-a-conversation-on-get-out/
Hill, Jack, director. 1974. *Foxy Brown*. American International Pictures.
Hook, Derek. 2022. "The object of apartheid desire: a Lacanian approach to racism and ideology." In *Lacan and Race: Racism, Identity, and Psychoanalytic Theory*, edited by Sheldon George and Derek Hook (121–145). Abingdon, UK: Routledge.
Hoyt, Carlos A. 2016. *The Arc of a Bad Idea: Understanding and Transcending Race*. Oxford, UK: Oxford University Press.
Jarvis, Michael. 2018. "Anger translator: Jordan Peele's *Get Out*." *Science Fiction Film and Television* 11, no. 1: 97–109.
Khan, Azeen. 2018. "Lacan and race." In *After Lacan: Literature, Theory, and Psychoanalysis in the Twenty-First Century*, edited by Ankhi Mukherjee, 148–166. Cambridge, UK: Cambridge University Press.
Lacan, Jacques. 1997a. *The Seminar of Jacques Lacan, Book III, 1955–56: The Psychoses*, edited by Jacques-Alain Miller. London, UK: Routledge.
Lacan, Jacques. 1997b. *The Seminar of Jacques Lacan, Book VII, 1959–1960: The Ethics of Psychoanalysis*, edited by Jacques-Alain Miller and translated by Dennis Porter. New York, NY: W. W. Norton & Company.
Lacan, Jacques. 1999. *The Seminar of Jacques Lacan, Book XX, 1972–1973: On Feminine Sexuality, The Limits of Love and Knowledge*, edited by Jacques-Alain Miller and translated with notes by Bruce Fink. New York, NY: W. W. Norton & Company.
Leader, Darian. 2012. *What is Madness?*London, UK: Penguin.
McGowan, Todd. 2004. *The End of Dissatisfaction? Jacques Lacan and the Emerging Society of Enjoyment*. Albany, NY: State University of New York Press.
McGowan, Todd. 2007a. *The Real Gaze: Film Theory after Lacan*. Albany, NY: State University of New York Press.
McGowan, Todd. 2007b. *The Impossible David Lynch*. New York, NY: Columbia University Press.

McGowan, Todd. 2013. *Enjoying What We Don't Have: The Political Project of Psychoanalysis.* Lincoln, NE: University of Nebraska Press.

McGowan, Todd. 2019. "The psychosis of freedom: law in modernity." In *Lacan on Psychosis: From Theory to Praxis*, edited by Jon Mills and David L. Downing (47–76). Abingdon, UK: Routledge.

McGowan, Todd. 2021. "Cinema's paranoid tendencies." *Psychoanalytische Perspectieven* 39, no. 2: 165–186.

Miller, Jacques-Alain. 1994. "*Extimité.*" In *Lacanian Theory of Discourse*, edited by Mark Bracher, Marshall W. Alcorn Jr., Ronald J. Corthell, and Francoise Massardier-Kenney (74–87). New York, NY: New York University Press.

Parks, Gordon, director. 1971. *Shaft.* Shaft Productions.

Peele, Jordan, director. 2017. *Get Out.* Blumhouse Productions; QC Entertainment; Monkeypaw Productions.

Ragland, Ellie. 1995. *Essays on the Pleasures of Death: From Freud to Lacan.* New York, NY: Routledge.

Rothenberg, Molly Anne. 2010. *The Excessive Subject: A New Theory of Social Change.* Cambridge, UK: Polity.

Seshadri-Crooks, Kalpana. 2000. *Desiring Whiteness: A Lacanian Analysis of Race.* London, UK: Routledge.

Soler, Colette. 1995. "The subject and the Other (I)." In *Reading Seminar XI: Lacan's Four Fundamental Concepts of Psychoanalysis*, edited by Richard Feldstein, Bruce Fink, and Maire Jaanus (39–44). Albany, NY: State University of New York Press.

Thakur, Gautam Basu. 2020. *Postcolonial Lack: Identity, Culture, Surplus.* Albany, NY: State University of New York Press.

Tutt, Daniel. 2012. "Radical love and Žižek's ethics of singularity." *International Journal of Žižek Studies* 6, no. 2: 1–15.

Vanheule, Stijn. 2011. *The Subject of Psychosis: A Lacanian Perspective.* Basingstoke, UK: Palgrave Macmillan.

Wallace, Carvell. 2021. "Don't go in the basement." *The Atlantic*, August 27, https://www.theatlantic.com/magazine/archive/2021/10/candyman-horror-movie-black-pain/619825/

West, Cornel. 2017. "Pity the sad legacy of Barack Obama." *The Guardian*, January 9, https://www.theguardian.com/commentisfree/2017/jan/09/barack-obama-legacy-presidency

White, Adam. 2021. "'Black people know how scary the world is': how *Candyman* became a story of radical justice." *The Independent*, August 29, https://www.independent.co.uk/arts-entertainment/films/features/candyman-release-date-nia-dacosta-b1909815.html

Zalloua, Zahi. 2020. *Žižek on Race: Toward an Anti-Racist Future.* London, UK: Bloomsbury.

Žižek, Slavoj. 1991. *Looking Awry: An Introduction to Jacques Lacan Through Popular Culture.* Cambridge, MA: The MIT Press.

Žižek, Slavoj. 1999a. "The superego and the act: a lecture by Slavoj Žižek." *LiveJournal: Žižek*, August, https://zizek.livejournal.com/1101.html

Žižek, Slavoj. 1999b. "The seven veils of fantasy." In *Key Concepts of Lacanian Psychoanalysis*, edited by Dany Nobus (190–218). New York, NY: Other Press.

Žižek, Slavoj. 2005. "The subject supposed to loot and rape: reality and fantasy in New Orleans." *In These Times*, October 20, https://inthesetimes.com/article/the-subject-supposed-to-loot-and-rape

Žižek, Slavoj. 2008a. *The Plague of Fantasies.* London, UK: Verso.

Žižek, Slavoj. 2008b. *The Sublime Object of Ideology*. London, UK: Verso.
Žižek, Slavoj. 2012. *Less Than Nothing*. London, UK: Verso.
Zupančič, Alenka. 2019. "Love thy neighbor as thyself?!" *Problemi International* 3, no. 3: 89–108.

Part III

Ethics, lack, and doubt

Chapter 10

A space for politics

If our dependence on race and our fight against racism is to be driven by the unwavering premise that race is nothing more than a social construction, and that tackling racism requires asserting and promoting one's racial difference, then it seems that our future remains beholden to individualistic forms of anti-racist struggle that go no further than promoting an assumed racial 'melting pot'. Insofar as the promotion of one's racial experiences, one's story, and the affirming of one's racial identity revolve around the debilitations involved in routinely 'checking' one's racial privilege and affirming or assuming one's 'unconscious bias', then attempts to establish and maintain ongoing forms of collective political critique will continue to stall (Haider 2018).[1] It is for this reason that this book has turned to the work of Lacan in order to consider how his account of psychosis offers a novel approach to the prevalence of racism in contemporary society and to the continuing significance of race and racialization for the subject. When the proficiency of racism resides in what it defines, delineates, and demarcates, as well as what it degrades, then we must not remain at the level of discursive reconstruction from which the very limits of our interpretation are upheld by the ubiquity of race as an invented phenomenon. More is required if the 'construction' of race is to be assured (and critiqued).

The frustrations that abound this critique serve to move past the contention that anti-racist struggles require better interpretations and better explanations of racism, steered by the conviction that, regardless of our race, we are all the same. There is, unfortunately, no 'secret' to the racist, and, by extension, there remains no privileged particularity in one's race. There is also no secret to be found in those marginalized or disenfranchised due to the colour of their skin. Instead, the effects of racism and the racial differences that underpin the ubiquity of race work from a psychosis enacted in one's relation to language and to a conception of being that both fixes and determines one's sense of (racial) meaning. To politicize racism, is, in the first instance, to abandon any conception of race as tied to one's identity and/or personality. Race remains a fiction, yet it is a fiction that posits its own Real effects in our relations with each other and in the Symbolic frameworks that rely upon, as well as sustain, the regime of racial visibility (Seshadri-Crooks 2000).

Certainly, the argument being traced here is not one in which the representation of race can be separated from the reality of racial discrimination and inequality. Instead, the reality of race resides within the Symbolic frameworks and social institutions that maintain acts of social oppression, whereby examples of racial hatred, aggression, and violence do not simply occur, but remain ingrained in race's signification.

As noted by Seshadri-Crooks (2000), we must seek a mistrust of race while also working towards its abandonment. Equally, for Gilroy (2000), the antiquation of race remains half-finished. That is, if 'action against racial hierarchies can proceed more effectively when it has been purged of any lingering respect for the idea of "race"', then it remains clear, for Gilroy at least, that 'the growing absence of ethical considerations from what used to be termed "antiracist" thinking and action' must find its return (2000, 6). Indeed, '[r]evitalizing ethical sensibilities in this area requires moving away from antiracism's tarnished vocabulary while retaining many of the hopes to which it was tied' (Gilroy 2000, 6). In the remaining chapters, attention will be given to exploring how such ethical sensibilities can be pursued through the psychosis of race.

Ethical praxis

Interpretations of Lacan's (1997b) approach to ethics stem primarily from the subject identifying and beholding a position outside the structures that are imposed upon them. Drawing from Lacan's logic of the 'forced choice', it is '[a] subject's singular act [that] exposes the choice itself as forced and creates an inherent loophole or dimension where neither resistance nor support, but a third "singular" way out (from inside) can undermine the setup of the "forced choice" itself' (Kunkle 2008, 12).[2] It is in identifying this 'way out' that 'an "ethics without ethics"' can be pursued, one that Fimiani presents as 'an ethics without the guarantee of Aristotle's Good or Kant's "moral law within"' (2021, 3). Here, '[t]he shift ... towards becoming a subject of speech and desire requires a different "ethic", an ethic without recourse to an Ideal or the "Good"' (Fimiani 2021, 3). It is for this reason that Žižek (2008) draws upon Lacan's assertion 'that psychosis is to be "located within the register of ethics"' (Žižek 2008, 88). Indeed, *'psychosis is a mode* "not to give way as to our desire,"' insofar as 'it signals our refusal to exchange enjoyment for the Name of the Father' (Žižek 2008, 88, italics added).

As noted in Chapter 4, in the structure of psychosis there is no choice beyond that which has already been chosen. The notion of a psychotic withdrawal is premised on the fact that one's 'choice' is already chosen. Accordingly, what prevents the psychotic from following a path of subjective destitution—and thus reaching an 'end to analysis'[3]—is the foreclosure of the Name-of-the-Father and the subsequent lack of credibility afforded to Symbolic castration.[4] In light of such preventions, Fimiani asks: 'can the psychotic *accept* the limits imposed by symbolic castration without the "fiction of meaningfulness?"' (2021, 63, italics added).

What is being proposed here is not a path that seeks to absolve the racist of their racism or to ignore the paranoia, fantasies, and delusions that characterize the psychosis of race. Rather, where a path towards ethics can be found in the psychosis of race is in the very 'mode' in which it is enacted (Žižek 2008, 88). That is, it is in 'the specific knowledge (*savoir*) implicit in the psychotic experience that psychoanalysis can maintain its bearings as an "ethical praxis"' (Fimiani 2021, 1). It is this knowledge of the Law that undergirds the psychotic's disbelief in the Other. As outlined in Chapter 8, the structure of psychosis remains tethered to a belief in one's very disbelief; a disbelief that is not necessarily incorrect, but which nonetheless finds conviction in the certainty of its 'belief'. Further still, as the example of a counter-hegemonic Black paranoia in Chapter 9 considered, examples of paranoia should not be so easily dismissed as mere conspiracy—paranoia can prove justified (Zupančič 2022). Consequently, while the psychotic may not be wrong to conceive of the deception of the Symbolic order, it is in the *certainty* of their convictions that they misrecognize their relation to the Symbolic order and its fundamental requirement. Whereas the effects of the psychotic's misrecognition can prove disastrous, and, in the psychosis of race, racially oppressive, such misrecognition proves troubling when it is supplemented with the certainty of a delusional conviction. Here the psychotic 'moves from the *possibility* of becoming a desiring (split) subject to a pure object of/for the Other's enjoyment' (Fimiani 2021, 125, italics in original), thus leaving them without the 'freedom' and creativity that can be obtained from the alienating effects of desire.

Nevertheless, there remains a level of 'inventiveness' forged from the foreclosure of the Law (Name-of-the-Father) that 'yields a specific "knowledge" (*savoir*) regarding the foundation of the "Law" and the Ideals that support the rules of social coexistence' (Fimiani 2021, 4). In fact, what 'specific "knowledge"' the structure of psychosis yields rests not on the knowledge of its convictions, as well as the delusions and paranoias it perceives, but in the act of 'knowing' itself. Such 'knowing' does not look towards the knowledge that is obtained—i.e., what is 'known'—but to the responsibility 'to know': that is, to observe and to inquire. Here, the ability to know dialectically turns upon itself. This is achieved in the recognition that such a responsibility confers upon the psychotic—a shift predicated on the *doubt* that is directed towards the psychotic's certainty.

Accordingly, what underscores one's capacity 'to know' is the fact that any responsibility towards knowing requires the recognition that one's knowledge may be doubted. It is this knowledge that underscores Friedlander's (2022) critique of George's (2016) 'cynicism'. Here, George proposes 'a desire grounded in cynicism toward notions of race and racial lineage', one which 'establishes a liberating distance mutually from the alienating desire of the

Symbolic Other and from the avenging desire of the racial ancestor' (2016, 139). While the subject's desire remains a desire of the Other (Lacan 2004), it is cynicism that can allow the subject to question the Other's desire, as reflected in the articulation of the '*Che voui?*' (Lacan 2006). For George, it is '[t]his question [which] creates [a] distance between the conflated desires of the subject and the Other, allowing for the emergence of something more properly subjective and personal to the subject' (2016, 139).

The problem with this approach is the 'distance' that such cynicism relies upon, which, as Friedlander argues, can 'functio[n] as an impediment' to the separation that George (2016) seeks to evoke (Friedlander 2022, 166). Ultimately, 'cynicism entices us with the lure of "knowing better," of "seeing through" the illusion to the underlying reality' (Friedlander 2022, 116). In effect, examples of cynicism end up following the Lacanian '*les non-dupes errent*', positing a 'distance' which never fully separates from the Other, but, ultimately, requires this Other in order to constitute its cynical position (Black 2021).

In contrast to George, we can instead draw upon Friedlander's adoption of Lacan's 'ethic of skepticism', and, specifically, the importance of doubt in constituting this ethic (2022, 116, see also Lacan 2004, 224). Indeed, '[w]hereas cynicism involves a mistrust that what others say they know corresponds to what they take to be true, scepticism involves a general mistrust of all claims to knowledge' (Friedlander 2022, 116). It is through this scepticism, and its mistrust of 'knowledge', that Lacan (2004), following Descartes, was able to derive a knowledge that remained grounded in doubt. Importantly, such scepticism does not necessarily establish knowledge of the object, but, as Friedlander (2022) explains, allows Lacan to identify a 'radical suspension' in knowledge and, specifically, in the capacity 'to know' (Friedlander 2022: 117, see also Lacan 2004, 224).

Knowledge in doubt

I seek to draw a connection here between Lacan's 'radical suspension' in knowledge and the specific type of knowledge that Fimiani (2021) attributes to psychosis. It is through a Cartesian 'doubt', directed towards both the Law and its ideals, that the modern subject, and its psychotic diversions, can be found. Indeed, while examples of psychosis posit an Other of the Other, deemed to be the true authority 'behind the scenes', such diversions inevitably rely upon a questioning to know: a form of sceptical doubt that fundamentally interrogates the legitimacy of the Other's authority (McGowan 2019). Furthermore, whereas Lacan (1997a) identifies a link between the 'normal' modern subject and psychosis (McGowan 2019), and though the path of doubt can very easily resort to examples of psychosis (specifically, paranoia), there nonetheless remains a 'radical suspension' of knowledge in the very doubt that the modern subject evinces. Importantly, such radical suspension occurs not from the authority of the doubt that is professed, but from a recognition of the Other's silence. This silence underscores Lacan's (2004) account of separation, which works alongside, and in conjunction with, the alienation of the subject in language (Black 2020). According to Dolar, while 'alienation forced the subject to hold on to sense in order to retain subjectivity, then it is separation that forces him/her to abandon sense in order to sustain the Other as his/her support' (1998, 24). What separation denotes is a 'separation from sense, from the realm of signification, and in the same movement the separation from subjectivity, for it demands that the subject separates him/herself from the object' (Dolar 1998, 24).

Yet, it is important to assert that such a separation does not confine the subject to a world of senselessness, if only on the basis that no subject is ever truly separated from the Symbolic order (the Other as support). Instead, what one's separation from signification posits is a shift in the subject; a space for desire whereupon the subject's capacity to know can be founded.[5] As a result, separation 'involves a "want to know" of that which is outside structure, and beyond language and the Other', so that rather than being steered towards the Other's signifiers (which ultimately confirm the subject's alienation), 'the Other of separation is first and foremost a "lacking" Other' (Homer 2005, 72). It is this 'lacking Other' that is not tied to any authority or source of knowledge, but, rather, in a position akin to that of the analyst, demands a convergence of lack in both the subject and the Other. Here, Fimiani explains:

> [t]he analyst's offering (an 'experienced desire') consists precisely in the knowledge that there is no Sovereign Good from which the subject might derive Happiness or total satisfaction. In other words, the analyst offers the lack of such a guarantee, which is the analyst's desire to know the subject's experience of, and solutions to, absence—and lack itself. It is from the position of a *learned ignorance* (desire/lack), in the face of the subject's experience of the absence of the Good, that the analyst maintains an ethical position vis-à-vis the subject of the unconscious.
>
> (2021, 132)

It is from a position of *docta ignorantia* ('learned ignorance') that Lacan (1991) outlines a revelation of ignorance forged upon a path of not-knowing. The key to Lacan's account is not to perceive such not-knowing as encouraging forms of obvious stupidity—one predicated on some *laisseze faire* futility that simply privileges banal absurdity—but to conceive of one's ignorance as a precursor to the inherent negation that one's not-knowing prescribes. In other words, it is in acknowledging the limit within all knowledge that a position of learned ignorance confronts the silence of the Other, or 'the flaw in the symbolic' (Apollon et al. 2000, 218). In fact, for Lacan, 'to say that the analyst is in the position of a lacking Other is thus to emphasize that his role is above all to *question the savoir* of the psychotic' (Apollon et al. 2000, 222, italics in original). It is through this questioning of knowledge (*savoir*) that a position of doubt can be obtained on behalf of the psychotic. Such doubt does not result in knowledge; instead it posits a 'learned ignorance' that fully accepts the negation in knowledge itself—the *position* from which one's doubt is registered.

Therefore, what is required in examples of 'learned ignorance' is the registration of a negation on behalf of the psychotic, insofar as it is in accordance with doubt—and, thus, the capacity to know—that a recognition of lack works to dislodge the psychotic's certainty. Indeed, while '[o]ne simply cannot arrive at a symbolization of the lack in the Other through a slow process of careful conscious adjustment' (Wells 2014, 213), in psychosis, acknowledging such lack remains just as difficult. As detailed in the previous chapters, it is due to foreclosure that the psychosis of race works to obscure the subject's lack.[6]

Consequently, if there is to be an ethics in psychosis then it rests upon identifying the Other's lack beyond the obfuscation that the psychotic's convictions assuage. Put simply, if the task of Lacanian ethics prescribes a shift in the subject, then such a shift stems primarily from a recognition of lack, both in the subject and the Other. It is in relation to this lack that a separation is achieved between the subject and the Other.

This goes beyond the psychotic's simple admonishment of the Other, towards a recognition of the Other's lack. Though there is no worth outside of the Other's lack, for which the delusions and paranoias in psychosis work to obscure, there is a recourse to doubt, and, thus, to know. The underlying contention within this desire to know is that it acquires a radical suspension in meaning outside of the Symbolic order, where one's lack of knowing can be assumed. This serves to reintroduce the importance of lack on behalf of the psychotic: a lack which subsequently functions as the subject itself (Fimiani 2021). As Fimiani contests, '[t]he subject, as a gap or question mark, functions to bore a hole in delusion' (2021, 134). Where the psychotic's delusion is undermined—that is, where the capacity of the delusion to explain and/or identify an other judged responsible for one's lack is challenged—the psychotic's lack of knowledge becomes exposed.

In part, this requires a loss of the *objet a* as 'an object of knowledge' (Dolar 1991, 13); indeed, a position from which 'the subject may come to embrace the *objet a's* perpetual failure to confer subjective completion', insofar as 'the subject [comes] to position itself in the place of lack, the position previously occupied by the *objet a*' (Friedlander 2022, 114). What is described here is a traversal of the lack, which, in the psychosis of race, is hindered by the presence of the object *a* and, thus, a predetermined racial position. With the lack of any lack, there is no 'new' in psychosis. That is, there are no new instances of lack upon which the subject's capacity to name their lack can be grounded. For Fimiani, '[t]he ethical act itself requires the emergence of something new: for instance, the emergence of a potential for the reconfiguration of what *exists* (structurally)' (2021, 126, italics in original). Thus, it is in psychosis that Fimiani 'define[s] the status of the "something new" as the emergence of *lack* itself' (2021, 126, italics in original). In other words, for 'the subject ... to recognize itself as a locus of symbolic emptiness around which a new form of subjectivity takes shape' (Friedlander 2022, 114), we must return to the importance of the object *a* of race and its significance to psychosis.

The insistence of the gap

It is in the psychosis of race that one's relation to lack and the object *a* remain obscured. Through the psychotic's lack of any lack, the potential to identify the object *a*'s inherent lack—indeed, its perpetual failure to name and define what constitutes the subject—becomes obfuscated through its presence. This obfuscation refuses the very gap that remains integral to the process of signification. The problem here is that without this gap there is no political act: 'politics begins by insisting on the *gap* between the existing administered social order and the ontological lack that bolsters it' (Zalloua 2020, 16, italics in original). Insisting on such a gap thus requires a reinterpretation of the lack that helps sustain the inconsistency of the social Symbolic order. Moreover, it requires an engagement with the object *a* as that which posits one's constitutive lack with*in* the Symbolic order, as opposed to the delusions, fantasies, and paranoias that seek to obscure such lack.

Whereas it is the presence of the object *a* that determines one's racial identity, when faced with the doubt that underscores one's capacity to know, we can begin to evince a certain rupture in the certainty of the psychotic. Such rupture constitutes a level of ethical praxis on behalf of the psychotic, so that '*the* ethical choice is precisely the choice to enter into the space opened up by the rupture' (Fimiani 2021, 130, italics added). The importance of this rupture is curtailed when representation and reality are merged in examples of racism that fix one's racial ascription to one's very being. In such cases, one's position of inequality or level of social depravation is explained and defined through one's racial being. Crime and unemployment are no longer conceived as the effects of poor governance, funding, and political aptitude, but as the characteristics of one's race. The difficulty here is that the capacity to critique these racial characterizations requires a level of 'knowledge' that fundamentally produces the very characterizations that one seeks to critique. In effect, one's knowledge of the experiences and lives of those blighted by forms of racial inequality and disenfranchisement functions as the very basis from which examples of anti-racism are produced. Indeed, my point is not to critique the efforts of these endeavours, but to challenge the knowledge they require (or the presuppositions they assume). When the psychosis of race rests, in part, on the certainty it avows (a certainty maintained by the presence of the *objet a*), then it is the knowledge that underpins this certainty that the above discussion seeks to challenge. In tackling forms of racial characterization, it is in the convergence between the racial prescription and the reality of discrimination that examples of racism require the capacity to perceive 'one's identity'—be it race, gender, nationality, etc.—'not as a basis for how one knows but as a barrier to what one knows and how one acts' (McGowan 2020, 53).

Therefore, what is effectively curtailed in examples of psychosis is a recognition that one's racial identity—confined to one's racial determinants, the social structure, and the system of signification—is manifested in the particularity that one's identity provides. Here, the inconsistencies and internal dislocations that characterize the Symbolic order are obscured. While maintaining the recognition of an Other that can be doubted, ultimately, the psychosis of race does not go far enough in challenging this doubt. The task of any political intervention, a psychoanalytic one at least, is to recognize that no identity and, thus, no Symbolic authority and social structure, can work to assure or define one's racialization. This does not propose a path of unencumbered individual resistance, but instead draws attention to the social importance embedded in our capacity to doubt and, hence, to know.

A relation to lack

It is at the level of doubt that examples of anti-racism can strike at the heart of race itself; specifically, the belief that it maintains. In commenting upon Freud's 'answer to anti-Semitism', Žižek notes how Freud 'doesn't defend Jews, he strikes against Jews themselves' (1999). That is, when '[t]he Nazis believed that Jews were something special, albeit in a negative way', then, for Žižek, '[t]he true way to combat anti-Semitism is to do as Freud did, to say that "We are not what you secretly think that we are"' (Žižek 1999). Žižek's use of Freud offers a valuable insight into the psychosis of race, one in which a specific contradiction can be exposed in both the Nazi's anti-Semitism and Freud's response.

Accordingly, what Freud's example exposes is not simply the racist belief, but the *disbelief* that it relies upon. In an inverted manner, psychosis disbelieves the relative fictions and fantasies that comprise the subject's relation to the Symbolic order. While we naively 'live with' fantasies as part of our day-to-day existence, what is taken seriously in psychosis, almost to the point of dependence, is a belief in one's very disbelief—in sum, the capacity to 'see through' the Other's authority and the fictitious nature of the Symbolic order.[7] Consequently, what the Nazi anti-Semite achieves in their disbelief is the failure to ascertain the inherent fiction that frames the racist image of the Jew. Instead, for the anti-Semite, what follows their disbelief is a belief in the racist fantasy—*that* which makes the Jew 'special, albeit in a negative way'.[8]

In response to this, it is only by working against the object *a* of race—that which defines one's racial being—that Freud traces a level of doubt that can be directed at the psychosis of race itself. This doubt resides within the fact that, to a certain extent, Freud takes the Nazi's anti-Semitic belief *seriously*. What Freud challenges is not simply the racist belief, but the psychotic's lack of belief in a system of signification that nonetheless maintains one's racialization. In effect, when Freud challenges the Jewish relation to Moses, he does not merely attack the anti-Semitic assertion, he also challenges, or, rather, doubts, the anti-Semite's belief in disbelief via the position of the 'Jew' itself. In so doing, Freud strikes an act of doubt that challenges the racial definition, as well as the belief it requires. This is made not from some outside perspective, seeking a critical interpretation of anti-Semitic racism, but from a 'Jewish' position that doubts what it is that defines the 'Jew'. It is for this reason that the very *form* in which the racist fantasy resides must be taken seriously.

We observe something similar in the challenge that Malcolm X proposed when he adopted the surname 'X'. Žižek highlights how:

> [t]he gesture of Malcolm X, his act of replacing the imposed family name, the Name-of-the-Father, with the symbol of the unknown, is far more complex than it may seem. What we must avoid is getting lured into the 'search for the lost origins': we totally miss the point if we reduce the gesture of Malcolm X to a simple case of longing for the lost Origins (for the 'true' African ethnic identity, lost when blacks were torn out of their original environs by slave traders). The point is rather that this reference to the lost Origins enables the subject to elude the grasp of the imposed symbolic identity and to 'choose freedom,' the lack of fixed identity. X qua void exceeds every positive symbolic identity: the moment its gap emerges, we find ourselves in the fantasy domain of 'experimentation, danger, poison, obscenity and the drug ecstasy' that no new symbolic identity can fill out.
>
> (1993, 78–79)

If, '[t]he fundamental ethical gesture is the subject's alienation in the universality of the symbolic pact' (Žižek 2008, 90), then, returning to one's 'African past', beyond the violence enacted by slavery, would only serve to confirm the subject's racialization via the object *a*. Insofar as an adherence to this past would both fix and prescribe the subject to a '"true" African ethnic identity' (Žižek 1993, 78), the Act performed by Malcolm X is one in which a sense of doubt becomes enacted in the Symbolic dislocation he chooses to embody.[9] It is the adoption of the 'X' that subsequently stands for, and seeks a relation to, one's constitutive lack—or, the 'lack of fixed identity' (Žižek 1993, 78).

This corresponds with the work of Thakur, who draws attention to and, ultimately, critiques, postcolonial attempts to identify the epistemological limits within colonial discourse, from which 'the postcolonial exercise of filling in gaps, posed as writing back or resistance' is assumed (2020, 189). Instead, there remains an ontological impossibility (a limit) that is achieved in encountering one's lack (or what Thakur refers to as 'the anamorphic blot' [2020, 189]).[10] Importantly, this encounter is 'not about reversing the self-other hierarchy, … neither [is it] about the death of the subject (I know I am not) nor about recuperating the subject after (I know I lack therefore I am)' (Thakur 2020, 189). 'Rather', for Thakur, 'the blot as lack must be assumed as the irrevocable condition of being—I, the subject, *am* lack' (2020, 189).

What Thakur conceives as 'the irrevocable condition of being', McGowan traces in 'the Real enjoyment that derives from nonbelonging' (2022, 31). While Real enjoyment remains 'an enjoyment available to everyone, since no one truly belongs', such 'enjoyment of nonbelonging is the enjoyment of lack' (McGowan 2022, 31). This 'emerges when one embraces one's status as lacking and recognizes it as the condition of possibility for one's enjoyment and not a barrier to it' (McGowan 2022, 31). The key to such enjoyment is that it prevents one from resorting to examples of racist fantasy and the promises, or in the case of psychosis, the certainty, that it avows.

In each of these examples, lack is neither obscured nor absolved, but, rather, taken as central to the subject, existing as the very ground from which the subject's lack proves inherent to its existence and its enjoyment (Lacan 2004; 2018). It is what can be conceived in the examples of both Freud and Malcolm X, which each assume a position of lack whereupon the subject of race can doubt the psychosis of their racialization, as well as the private sense of loss, that it engenders.

A 'signifying impasse' and the space for politics

Whether we approach this lack through 'assum[ing] ... the irrevocable condition of being' (Thakur 2020, 189), or through a 'Real enjoyment' drawn from the condition of one's 'nonbelonging' (McGowan 2022, 31), we can also turn to the use of the signifier and, specifically, to the effects of the signifier in positing an alternative relation to the Other on behalf of the psychotic. In particular, Pluth has highlighted how 'signifiers do not necessarily produce meanings that one wishes to have recognized by the Other' (2007, 98). Instead, 'signifiers are used quasi-autonomously, and their use amounts to a repetition and an extension of a signifying impasse, converting an enigmatic tension into some kind of satisfaction' (Pluth 2007, 98). Whereas Pluth (2007) considers this use in relation to the Act, we can consider how a 'signifying impasse' can serve to introduce a relation to lack on behalf of the psychotic. Moreover, what the signifier represents is a political answer to the 'gap' that is required when opening a space for political action. Here, the impasse represents 'a place that is "occupied by the lack"' (Zupančič 2000, 242). Ultimately, what place the signifier posits is the 'indescribable "nothing"' (Hinton 2007, 343); indeed, that which 'can open the space for the emergence of new elements' (Hinton 2007, 444). It is in relation to this 'indescribable "nothing"' that the psychotic's lack of mediation helps to affirm the rupture that makes space for the Real.

Collectively, the 'signifying impasse' (Pluth 2007, 89), the 'place ... "occupied by the lack"' (Zupančič 2000, 242), and the 'indescribable "nothing"' (Hinton 2007, 343), can each be viewed as subscribing to a logic of the 'non-all'. In fact, when, in psychosis, the act of foreclosure results in a return of the Real, what the 'non-all' allows us to conceive is the effects of the Real as an immanent impossibility that also serves as the basis from which one's interpretative efficiencies are driven by the inconsistencies of the Symbolic order—the very impasse in signification itself. What is aimed at here is the Real, or rather, the 'impasses', the 'lack', and the 'nothing', which aver a position from which one's racialization can be challenged.

It is this position of the 'non-all' that is brought to bear in the Freud and Malcolm X examples. In both cases, each upholds a position that includes its own negation: be it Freud, with his attack against that which defines the Jew; or Malcolm X, with the Symbolic dislocation embodied in his adoption of the 'X' as subjective void. What can be considered in each position of negation is a 'zone of nonbeing', an abject condition that Fanon (2008) famously attributes to a Blackness defined by an anti-Black world. This negativity is taken up by Thakur (2022) as denoting a relation to the Real, one in which the very negativity that such a position prescribes can serve as a space for politics, the possibility of agency, and the generation of the new. It is from this position of negation that a relation to lack is founded, where lack itself stands for an 'identity' beyond the confines of one's racial prescription.

Certainly, what is disclosed here goes further than simply acknowledging the subject's constitutive lack. What remains unique to both Freud and Malcolm X is the extent to which their very positions reside within the racial fictions they seek to upend. If the psychosis of race relies upon a belief in one's very disbelief, then it is clear that such 'belief' proves even more disastrous for the fictions it upholds. In the structure of psychosis, what fails to be acknowledged is the Symbolic order's role as fiction, hence the prevalence of racial paranoia, delusion, and fantasy, all of which remain fixated upon the fictions they imply.

Nevertheless, as has been discussed, what should not be ignored is the opening of a space from which the psychotic's 'disbelief' can be channelled through the doubt it requires. Indeed, while the psychotic's disbelief 'fail[s] to accept the binding power of the Symbolic fiction' (Friedlander 2022, 117), it is within the effects of this power, as well as the doubt that can be assumed towards the power it entails, that Friedlander, in her discussion of the Act, critically outlines 'a potentially transformative engagement aimed at identifying with the very point at which the Symbolic fiction of race begins to unfurl and threatens to give way to the Real—thus undercutting the Symbolic ground for conferring identity' (2022, 117). Accordingly:

> rather than *distancing* or releasing the subject from the Other's enigmatic signifiers, the Act performs the ethical task of facilitating an impossible *identification* with both the Symbolic fiction and intrusions of the meaningless Real. Such a position resists re-incorporation into the fantasy of Symbolic closure.
>
> (Friedlander 2022, 117)

It is this resistance that serves to encapsulate a position of negation that is reflected in the examples of Freud and Malcolm X.[11] Importantly, neither Freud nor Malcolm X seek to oppose the fictions of race by distinguishing between the fiction and reality, or through proposing some greater sense of knowledge or understanding of the falsehoods of race; instead, '[f]ictions are not outside reality, they are materialized in our social interactions, in our institutions and customs' (Žižek 2022, 23), and it is on this basis of confronting the fictions at the heart of our racial relations, institutions, and customs that both Freud and Malcolm X establish their critique. By opening a space within the Symbolic fiction of race, each obtain a position that can confront the meaningless Real.

Amidst the disjunctions of the Symbolic order and the fictions it entails, it is through assuming a position of negation that the subject confronts the Other's lack as dependent upon the very fictions that sustain its avoidance of the Real (Lacan 2004). In continuing this line of inquiry, the remaining chapters will detail how such a sense of being can, for the psychotic, be further expressed in examples of creative doubt.

Notes

1 See Haider (2018) for a detailed account of how political movements can become derailed by 'identity politics' and the political fractures that are enacted through 'race'.
2 Kunkle notes: 'Bartleby did this with his "no"; Sethe in *Beloved* did this by killing the thing (her child) she treasured most; Roark in *The Fountainhead* did this by destroying his own creation, St. Paul did this with his configuration of Love beyond the Law (beyond duty, reward or punishment); Lenin did this by forming a non-socialist vanguard party, Israeli reservists did this when they refused to serve in the Occupied Territories, and so on. In this way, these subjects, entering a domain of subjective destitution, also opened a way to emerge under new coordinates vis-a-vis the inherent paradox of being' (2008, 12–13).
3 Hook details how '[s]ubjective destitution connotes the state ideally attained by the end of analysis whereby one has surrendered the *agalma*, that is, the secret treasure of "that in me more than me", Lacan's *object petit a* as object cause of desire, or, differently put, that *je ne sais quoi* property which defines what is most loveable in me. To surrender this object effectively "desubjectivizes" the subject' (2011, 500). For more on the 'end of analysis' and subjective destitution, see '"Peace at Last": Subjective Destitution and the End of Analysis in *Peaky Blinders*' (Black 2022a).
4 As highlighted in Chapter 4, it is in our encounter with castration that we 'develo[p] an ethics in response to it' (McNulty 2014, 56).
5 Here, Zupančič adds, '[t]he crucial moment of "separation" involved in psychoanalysis should be understood in this sense: not as a simple separation from the Other, from all Symbolic structures and the social mediation of the subject's being, but as the *separation of the Other* from the object that drives its structure' (2008, 34, italics in original).
6 Indeed, '[a]s the Other is structurally incomplete, lack is an inherent characteristic of the Other, but that lack is not always apparent to the subject, and even when apparent, cannot always be named' (Fink 1997, 173). In the case of psychosis, the naming of such a lack is foreclosed.

7 Do we not see something similar in the case of those who seek to identify some nefarious plot in COVID-19 and the measures brought in by national governments to help mitigate its spread? While distrusting the severity of the pandemic, as well as the information provided by national governments and international agencies, such as the World Health Organization, COVID-19 sceptics are nonetheless able to believe in a far more extravagant plot (i.e., conspiracies) regarding the virus's cause and spread. Secret organizations, government experiments, and billionaires, hellbent on some form of global control, are subsequently brought in as the Other of the Other, secretly pulling the strings.
8 It is for this reason that if one attacks the racist's belief in disbelief—that is, the very image that comprises the racial other—their whole reality disintegrates (Žižek 2022). What is attacked is the certainty that underlies their conviction and, thus, their relation to reality.
9 Similar concerns are echoed by Gilroy, who notes that, '[w]e have seen that the authoritarian and proto-fascist formations of twentieth-century black political culture have often been animated by an intense desire to recover the lost glories of the African past. The desire to restore that departed greatness has not always been matched by an equivalent enthusiasm to remedy the plight of Africa in the present. But the idea of an unsullied and original African civilization has sometimes given life to a complex archaism so powerful that it can oppose capitalism while remaining utterly alien to democracy' (2000, 333).
10 Thakur (2020) premises this argument on a critique of Spivak's (1999) 'native informant'.
11 While drawing specifically from the Act, Friedlander's (2022) analysis of the Spike Lee film, *BlacKkKlansman* (2018), can be read in accordance with an account of the 'non-all'. In the film, detectives Ron Stallworth (John David Washington) and Flip Zimmerman (Adam Driver) infiltrate the Klu Klux Klan. While speaking to the president of a local Klan chapter, Stallworth poses as White, with Zimmerman, a White Jewish colleague, impersonating Stallworth when meeting Klan members. Accordingly, rather than critiquing the illusion that sustains the Klan's racism from some 'outside' position, '[t]hey insert themselves squarely into the illusion—both identifying with and embodying its lack—and disturb the fantasy from within. Here we encounter an Act in which the Symbolic cause (the internal negativity around which the Symbolic forms and seeks to mask) enters into the Symbolic itself, disrupting the ability of the fantasy of race to function as a claim to completion—as a cover for lack' (Friedlander 2022, 119). I read this 'internal negativity' as following the logic of the 'non-all'; denoting a position which contains its own negation.

References

Apollon, Willy, Danielle Bergeron and Lucie Cantin. 2000. "The treatment of psychosis." In *The Subject of Lacan: A Lacanian Reader for Psychologists*, edited by Kareen Ror Malone and Stephen R. Friedlander (209–228). Albany, NY: State University of New York Press.
Spivak, Gayatri Chakravorty. 1999. *Critique of Postcolonial Reason*. Cambridge, MA: Harvard University Press.
Black, Jack. 2020. "On reflexive racism: disavowal, deferment and the Lacanian subject." *Diacritics* 48, no. 4: 76–101.
Black, Jack. 2021. *Race, Racism and Political Correctness in Comedy – A Psychoanalytic Exploration*. Abingdon, UK: Routledge.

Black, Jack. 2022. "'Peace at last': subjective destitution and the end of analysis in *Peaky Blinders*." *Lack: Punctual Musings*...June 17, https://lackorg.com/2022/06/17/peace-at-last-subjective-destitution-and-the-end-of-analysis-in-peaky-blinders/

Dolar, Mladen. 1991. "'I shall be with you on your wedding-night': Lacan and the uncanny." *October* 58: 5–23.

Dolar, Mladen. 1998. "Cogito as the subject of the unconscious." In *Cogito and the Unconscious, Sic 2*, edited by Slavoj Žižek (11–40). Durham, NC: Duke University Press.

Fanon, Frantz. 2008. *Black Skin, White Masks*. New York, NY: Grove Press.

Fimiani, Bret. 2021. *Psychosis and Extreme States: An Ethic for Treatment*. Champagne, CH: Palgrave Macmillan.

Fink, Bruce. 1997. *The Lacanian Subject: Between Language and Jouissance*. Princeton, NJ: Princeton University Press.

Friedlander, Jennifer. 2022. "In medium race: traversing the fantasy of post-race discourse." In *Lacan and Race: Racism, Identity, and Psychoanalytic Theory*, edited by Sheldon George and Derek Hook (105–120). Abingdon, UK: Routledge.

George, Sheldon. 2022. "The Lacanian subject of race: sexuation, the drive, and racial subjectivity." In *Lacan and Race: Racism, Identity, and Psychoanalytic Theory*, edited by Sheldon George and Derek Hook (241–262). Abingdon, UK: Routledge.

George, Sheldon. 2016. *Trauma and Race: A Lacanian Study of African American Racial Identity*. Waco, TX: Baylor University Press.

Gilroy, Paul. 2000. *Against Race: Imagining Political Culture Beyond the Color Line*. Cambridge, MA: The Belknap Press of Harvard University Press.

Haider, Asad. 2018. *Mistaken Identity: Race and Class in the Age of Trump*. London, UK: Verso.

Hinton, Ladson. 2007. "Black holes, uncanny spaces and radical shifts in awareness." *Journal of Analytical Psychology* 52: 433–447.

Homer, Sean. 2005. *Jacques Lacan*. Abingdon, UK: Routledge.

Hook, Derek. 2011. "White privilege, psychoanalytic ethics, and the limitations of political silence." *South African Journal of Philosophy* 30, no. 4: 494–501.

Kunkle, Sheila. 2008. "Embracing the paradox: Žižek's illogical logic." *International Journal of Žižek Studies* 2, no. 4: 1–21.

Lacan, Jacques. 1991. *The Seminar of Jacques Lacan, Book I, 1953–1954: Freud's Papers on Technique*, edited by Jacques-Alain Miller and translated by John Forrester. New York, NY: W. W. Norton & Company.

Lacan, Jacques. 1997a. *The Seminar of Jacques Lacan, Book III, 1955–56: The Psychoses*, edited by Jacques-Alain Miller. London, UK: Routledge.

Lacan, Jacques. 1997b. *The Seminar of Jacques Lacan, Book VII, 1959–1960: The Ethics of Psychoanalysis*, edited by Jacques-Alain Miller and translated by Dennis Porter. New York, NY: W. W. Norton & Company.

Lacan, Jacques. 2004. *The Four Fundamental Concepts of Psycho-Analysis*, edited by Jacques-Alain Miller. London, UK: Karnac.

Lacan, Jacques. 2006. "On a question preliminary to any possible treatment of psychosis." In *Écrits. The First Complete Edition in English*, translated by Bruce Fink, in collaboration with Heloise Fink and Russell Grigg (445–488). London, UK: W. W. Norton & Company.

Lee, Spike, director. 2018. *BlacKkKlansman*. Blumhouse Productions; Monkeypaw Productions; QC Entertainment; 40 Acres and a Mule Filmworks; Legendary Entertainment; Perfect World Pictures.

McGowan, Todd. 2019. "The psychosis of freedom: law in modernity." In *Lacan on Psychosis: From Theory to Praxis*, edited by Jon Mills and David L. Downing (47–76). Abingdon, UK: Routledge.
McGowan, Todd. 2020. *Universality and Identity Politics*. New York, NY: Columbia University Press.
McGowan, Todd. 2022. "The bedlam of the lynch mob: racism and enjoying through the other." In *Lacan and Race Racism, Identity, and Psychoanalytic Theory*, edited by Sheldon George and Derek Hook (19–34). Abingdon, UK: Routledge.
McNulty, Tracy. 2014. *Wrestling with the Angel: Experiments in Symbolic Life*. New York, NY: Columbia University Press.
Pluth, Ed. 2007. *Signifiers and Acts: Freedom in Lacan's Theory of the Subject*. New York, NY: State University of New York Press.
Seshadri-Crooks, Kalpana. 2000. *Desiring Whiteness: A Lacanian Analysis of Race*. London, UK: Routledge.
Thakur, Gautam Basu. 2020. *Postcolonial Lack: Identity, Culture, Surplus*. Albany, NY: State University of New York Press.
Wells, Charles. 2014. *The Subject of Liberation: Žižek, Politics, Psychoanalysis*. London, UK: Bloomsbury.
Zalloua, Zahi. 2020. *Žižek on Race: Toward an Anti-Racist Future*. London, UK: Bloomsbury.
Žižek, Slavoj. 1993. *Tarrying with the Negative: Kant, Hegel, and the Critique of Ideology*. Durham, NC: Duke University Press.
Žižek, Slavoj. 1999. "The superego and the act: a lecture by Slavoj Žižek." *LiveJournal: Žižek*, August, https://zizek.livejournal.com/1101.html
Žižek, Slavoj. 2008. *Enjoy Your Symptom! Jacques Lacan In Hollywood and Out*. London, UK: Routledge.
Žižek, Slavoj. 2022. *Surplus Enjoyment*. London, UK: Bloomsbury.
Zupančič, Alenka. 2000. *Ethics of the Real: Kant, Lacan*. London, UK: Verso.
Zupančič, Alenka. 2008. *Why Psychoanalysis? Three Interventions*. Aarhus, DK: Aarhus University Press.
Zupančič, Alenka. 2022. "A short essay on conspiracy theories." In *Objective Fictions: Philosophy, Psychoanalysis, Marxism*, edited by Adrian Johnston, Boštjan Nedoh, and Alenka Zupančič (232–249). Edinburgh, UK: Edinburgh University Press.

Chapter 11

Beyond race? The radical temporality of creative doubt

It was noted in the previous chapter that one way of challenging the psychosis of race is in the doubt that the psychotic can obtain towards the certainty of their delusions. Expressions of doubt can come in many forms, including examples of methodological doubt, such as that seen in the scientific method, and instances of existential doubt, such as that concerning the nature of one's being and the certainty of one's existence. In Lacanian terms, doubt functions alongside one's capacity to know. This posits a scepticism that acknowledges one's lack of knowledge, while also doubting the existence of an Other who knows 'the answer'. Thus, for both the subject and the Other, doubt can be perceived as encompassing a coincidence of lack. Indeed, it is at the level of doubt, and the assumption of lack, that the certainty of the psychotic structure can be challenged.

In most cases, the psychosis of race seeks the erasure of doubt in the certainty of one's racial being, a prescription endowed upon the subject via the presence of the object *a*. Where examples of doubt can prove useful, however, is in the creativity that it affords in language. While Chapter 4 detailed how the subject is alienated via its location in language, Chapter 8 highlighted that it is through language that the subject's separation 'from the realm of signification' can occur (Dolar 1998, 24). Importantly, such separation resides within 'the creative assumption of the lack in (and of) the Other'; an assumption which stands 'as the condition of language' itself (McNulty 2014, 263). In fact, rather than simply conceiving of the signifier as solely responsible for the subject's ideological interpellation, a critique Ruti (2012) applies to the work of both Badiou and Žižek, we can consider how 'the signifier [can function] as a vehicle of innovative energy' (Ruti 2012, 118). Here, Ruti explains:

> if we allow for the possibility that the signifier does not invariably obey the dictates of the big Other, and that the unruly energies of the real can regenerate, rather than merely weaken, the symbolic, it becomes apparent that the signifier is not always an instrument of ideological interpellation. While it is obvious that we are often confronted by dead signifiers—signifiers that

DOI: 10.4324/9781003414209-15

contain no trace of the real—language is by definition as much a locus of creative potential as it is of hegemonic power.

(2012, 119)

It is in light of the signifier's creative potential that we can turn to Lacan's (2018) account of the sinthome.

The sinthome's creative act

Lacan's (2018) explanation of the sinthome first appears in Seminar XXIII. Referring to that which allows the subject to establish a level of social stability, the sinthome's importance rests upon its capacity to endow the subject a *savoir faire* (know how). In effect, the sinthome is the knot that ties the Symbolic, the Imaginary, and the Real together (Lacan 2018). It is from this 'knotting' of the three orders that a 'structure' is formed from the act of knotting itself. As a result, the effect of the sinthome echoes that of the paternal metaphor, insofar as 'the *sinthome* is a signifier ... for how the paternal metaphor functions (or not)' (Ragland-Sullivan 1992, 51). What Lacan's psychoanalysis proposes, therefore, 'is [an] *identification with the sinthome*', what Žižek refers to as 'the reef on which psychoanalysis sticks' (1999, 31, italics in original).

This identification offers two unique opportunities for the subject. First, the sinthome assumes an investment on behalf of the subject—that is, an investment in the signifier itself, joining language and *jouissance* together so that the subject assumes a relation to the signifier. Though the sinthome cannot necessarily be grasped, it can be assumed as that which can be identified with—most notably, as a form of organizing one's *jouissance*. Second, the sinthome acknowledges the lack in both the Other and the subject. While the subject remains at the behest of the Other's signifiers, such acknowledgment posits that it is the Other itself—the Symbolic order—which remains inherent to its very functioning. It is in this sense that language and *jouissance* combine, so that it is the signifier that constitutes lack.

Usually, it is the paternal metaphor, the Name-of-the-Father, that occupies such lack, with the signifier of the Name-of-the-Father separating the subject from *jouissance*. By providing a metaphorical substitution, it is the Father that occupies the role of the sinthome for the subject, thus ensuring the subject's relation to the Symbolic order and its alienation. In the case of psychosis, where the Name-of-the-Father remains foreclosed, it is the sinthome that occupies this role. At its heart, therefore, the sinthome maintains an innovative function, indeed, a 'creative act' (Verhaeghe and Declercq 2016, 20), that serves at the foreclosure of the Name-of-the-Father. Already we can begin to determine the effect that this can have in the structure of psychosis: insofar as one's very lack is no longer obscured or 'lost', but is instead creatively acknowledged at the point at which it is shared with the Other. To help illustrate this, we can turn to Lacan's (2018) account of the novelist, James Joyce.

Joyce and the sinthome

Lacan's (2018) consideration of Joyce reflected broader developments within his psychoanalytic approach, and, specifically, in his understanding of psychosis. Drawing from his triadic structure of the Symbolic, Imaginary, and the Real, Lacan explored the effects of *jouissance* upon the subject, but also, with the foreclosure of the Name-of-the-Father, its effects upon the psychotic. On this basis, Joyce provided an interesting case for Lacan. Primarily, Lacan's interests in Joyce can be traced to very way in which Joyce sought to use his writing, and, particularly, his use of language as a way of managing psychosis. Joyce was not necessarily an exception to psychosis; instead, he demonstrated a level of creativity in which foreclosure did not impact upon his Symbolic functioning. Effectively, language was, for Joyce, a creative way of managing, or preventing, his psychosis.

What Joyce's identification with his sinthome ensured was a certain reinvention of language itself. Writing outside of the rules of signification, Joyce's prose reflected a relation to *jouissance* that never compromised on his sinthome. It was, instead, the particularity of Joyce's artistic innovation that reflected his relation to the sinthome (Lacan 2018). As Ruti explains, 'Lacan concludes that writing, for Joyce, is equivalent to the sinthome, that it is precisely because Joyce is infected by the "virus" of the sinthome that he is a true artist' (2012, 116). Ruti expands upon this interpretation in order to consider how 'we are not merely the passive recipients of cultural meanings, but have the power to actively reformulate these meanings' (2012, 8). While 'Lacan proposes that Joyce is a singular individual precisely to the extent that he is able to manipulate language in poetic, polysemic, and pioneering ways', it is, for Ruti, through such acts of manipulation that language serves as 'a malleable tool of counterhegemonic meaning' (2012, 8).

Importantly, Joyce's use of language, and his relation to the sinthome, can be perceived as offering a form of separation. Beyond the effects of the subject's alienation, Joyce's approach to language reflects a level of doubt that stands opposed to the confines of language itself. That is, Joyce's writing denotes a questioning—a registering of doubt—towards the absent father and the Symbolic order, reflected *in* his creative use of language. Certainly, such creativity is not beholden to great literary writers but can be reflected on an everyday level (Ruti 2012). Consider, for example, the following from Verhaeghe:

> a longstanding couple in love develops within their language an intimate speech of their own; their 'dialect' is based on the common language but contains a number of idiosyncratic choices turning it into 'their' language. The main difference with alienation as such is the fact that the subject makes a conscious choice between different possibilities in the full knowledge that not one of them is definite.
>
> (2019, 381)

Verhaeghe's example helpfully illustrates a number of important points; not least, the creativity that undergirds the idiosyncrasies in the couple's use of language. However, when making their choices, it is by acting in 'full knowledge that not one of them is definite' that some correspondence with doubt can divert the psychotic towards the lack in knowledge and, more precisely, to the knowledge of lack itself. While such doubt provides a mark against the psychotic's certainty, it also helps to establish a creative connection—a form of mediation—between the psychotic and the Symbolic order.

Furthermore, what seems to underscore Lacan's interest in Joyce is his ability to create something 'new'. In such cases, what the sinthome prescribes is an identification with the Real, from which Joyce was able to 'galvanize the real' (Ruti 2012, 116). Subsequently, what Joyce's identification with the sinthome prevented was a return *in* the Real. It is in accordance with this return that the subject succumbs to a form of psychotic withdrawal, or, in the psychosis of race, to a racial prescription that endows one's very racialization. Instead, by confronting the Real, the sinthome does not suggest that one simply resides within the psychosis of race, and, by extension, the very racism it engenders; rather, what the sinthome achieves is an animation of the signifier. Here, Ruti confirms that:

> the signifier's encounter with the real revives the signifier so that it is precisely those forms of signification that capture something of the energies of the real that remain innovative; it is only through the lively interaction between the symbolic and the real that the signifier manages to replenish itself. ... On this account, the signifier's ability to activate, incorporate, and transport morsels of the real is a precondition of creativity.
>
> (2012, 115)

Again, we can return once more to the examples of Freud and Malcolm X (discussed in Chapter 10). There is a certain innovation in both examples that can be compared with Joyce's identification with the sinthome. Within each example, neither Freud nor Malcolm X stand apart from the effects of racism, and, thus, the effects of the Real; rather, they confront the vicissitudes of racism from a position that seeks a new relation to the signifier. Indeed, if we consider that what the sinthome prescribes is a position of negation—an acknowledgement of lack that speaks from within the racial Symbolic order—then what Freud acknowledges, in his attack against the Jews, and what Malcolm X establishes, in his adoption of the 'X', is an encounter with the Real that elicits its own creative affirmation. In accordance with the example of Joyce, both Freud and Malcolm X present a path towards confronting the psychosis of race.[1]

In this regard, we can conceive of Joyce's relation towards the sinthome as occupying the position of 'the "duped who do not err"' (Balasopoulos 1997, 37). It was because of Joyce's lack of belief in the Father, and, thus, the

Symbolic order, that he was able to manage this lack via a belief in the signifier (Lacan 2018). In effect, what Joyce was able to overcome was the entrapment of a psychotic belief in one's disbelief. To remain on the side of the duped and not falter means that one is not 'trapped' by the fantasy, and, by extension, one does not commit to the error of being able to see 'beyond', or even through, one's fantasy. Instead, it is to appreciate that one's relation to the Other rests upon an enjoyment of the signifier, wherein the production of meaning, and, thus, creativity, is established. Where it is the 'duped who do not err', it is an investment in the signifier that prevails; what is enjoyed is the meaning generated by the signifier (Pluth 2007). As a result, '[o]ne can only be open to meanings because one is always-already enjoying the structure within which meaning occurs' (Hoens and Pluth 2002, 12, cited in Ruti 2012, 120). This realization helps to establish a form of Symbolic mediation on behalf of the psychotic.

Moreover, what the sinthome establishes is a relation between the Symbolic and the Real. While it has been noted that, under psychosis, what is foreclosed from the Symbolic returns in the Real, in the case of the sinthome, it is the gap itself—the presence of the Real, as such—which is established in the Symbolic.[2] For Ruti, though 'Lacan connects the sinthome to the death drive, he does not invariably regard identification with the sinthome as a matter of subjective destitution (or divine violence)' (2012, 116). Instead, '[i]n the case of Joyce, such an identification is a means of linking the symbolic and the real so as to generate fresh forms of signification' (Ruti 2012, 116). Ruti adds:

> [r]egardless of how subversive his writing gets, Joyce endeavors to awaken rather than to choke the signifier. By bringing the real in contact with the signifier, he imparts to language an unparalleled dexterity and resourcefulness. One might in fact say that Joyce's signifiers are unique precisely to the degree that they breathe to the rhythm of the real. Though there is no doubt that language is a trespasser, an intruder, in the domain of the real, Joyce reveals that it is exactly because the real makes language struggle—forces it to fight for its territory, as it were—that the encounter with the real can make language fiercely inventive. He demonstrates that even though the real as such cannot be written, one can write in such a way as to brush against it; one's signifiers can transmit energizing scraps of the real.
>
> (2012, 117)

Yet, it is important to remember that the Symbolic and the Real are not separated. In the Symbolic, the Real maintains a pervasive presence, a source of the disruption that befalls the Symbolic order. It is the gap of the Real—the inherent negation—that posits any act of signification, outside of that which race seeks to occlude (George 2014). What is assured in the case of the sinthome is the gap which guarantees that one's use of language remains 'fiercely inventive' (Ruti 2012, 117). There is, therefore, no obfuscation of the gap of creativity, as evident in psychosis, but, instead, an encounter with the Real as that which constitutes the Symbolic order. This is not to suggest that the signifier 'merely domesticates the real', rather, 'as the symbolic makes inroads into the real, the insurgence of the real within the symbolic simultaneously forces the latter to undergo a radical alteration' (Ruti 2012, 120). In so doing, '[t]he signifier and the real are *both* forced to adapt, and this is at least as much a matter of transformation as it is of violation, given that adaptation is usually a necessary precondition of renewal of any kind' (Ruti 2012, 120, italics in original). Or, as Flisfeder (2021) asserts, every negation contains its own affirmation.

Negation/affirmation and the creative betrayal

Accordingly, what the sinthome 'endeavors to awaken' is an act of negation (Ruti 2012, 177). While every act of negation posits its own affirmation, Flisfeder highlights that it is through an act of '*negation cum affirmation*, that ... we produce and open the space of subjectivity, [and] for the thought to take precedence over being' (2021, 176, italics added). It is in opening this space for subjectivity that we can begin to draw a connection between Lacan's (2018) sinthome, Ruti's (2012) focus on the creativity of language, and Flisfeder's (2021) 'negation cum affirmation'. Together, each traces the space that is required for the subject in order to enact a 'creative betrayal' (McGowan 2013, 322). McGowan notes:

> [t]he subject initially emerges through a forced choice: figures of social authority present the individual with a demand for conformity to the social law, and the individual must conform to this demand in order to become a subject. Individuals choose to comply with this demand, but one cannot accede to subjectivity without this compliance. Compliance precedes any assertion of agency on the part of the subject. Subjectivity is the result of a betrayal of oneself in the name of the social law, but the betrayal creates the very subject that one betrays. It is a creative betrayal.
> (2013, 322)

The same can also be said for psychosis. Though in psychosis the forced choice has already been made, an identification with the sinthome and the creativity of the signifier can help to posit an act of negation which elicits a level of doubt that betrays the certainty of one's psychosis—in effect, such doubt 'creates the very subject that one betrays'. While there is a return here to the dialectic of the subject, for the psychosis of race, this presents a betrayal of race itself, or, at least, the beginnings of a Symbolic framework— an awakening of the signifier (Ruti 2012)—which serves to isolate the kernel of non-sense that race relies upon. Note, this does not function to afford race its 'meaning'; that is, it does not seek to develop a knowledge of race that would, in some form or another, result in its expulsion. As argued, this would ignore the contradictions that our constructions of race—including its very critique—rely upon; instead, it is the non-sense of race that is taken seriously, so that it is *this* non-sense that is revealed.

Ultimately, in eliciting such a betrayal, we do not see a return in the Real, or, rather, we do not see a return of the racism that maintains the social oppressions which racially prescribe and determine one's sense of being. What is returned to the subject is no longer the Real, but their own lack: the non-meaning of meaning which posits the very lack that constitutes both the subject and the Other. Though the construction of race is premised on the effects of the Real, and on a racism that continues to both mask and obscure the creative betrayals that elicit the subject's relation to lack (George 2016), where the sinthome prevails is in the space (the gap) that it elicits in the psychotic structure: a space that provides a recognition of lack and the creativity therein.

A disruptive opportunity

It is in the lack of assurance that one's creativity can be ascribed. As noted by Ruti (2012), while negation presents an opportunity to approach the Real via the creativity of the signifier, what remains posited in any act of negation is the very affirmation it relies upon (Flisfeder 2021). It is this that evokes the position of the 'non-all'; a position that posits its own negativity. Where such negativity resides is in the position of enunciation that it evokes.

Indeed, this act of negation is effectively rendered in Friedlander's (2022) account of Gilroy (2000), where, in the 'planetary humanism' that he seeks to establish, Gilroy adopts a unique relation to the articulation of a post-race future. It is important to note that post-racial assertions rely, primarily, on the consideration that our societies are, today, 'post-racism'—i.e., that the effects of racism no longer obtain the significance that they once held or that the history of racism is 'in the past', and, thus, should now be ignored (approaches that clearly maintain forms of racism and White hegemony). In either instance, the prefix 'post-' denotes the end of that which it is attached to. Gilroy's account takes an alternative approach to this widely-critiqued notion. As Friedlander explains, 'Gilroy's project leverages the instability between the enunciated content of post-racial discourse and the act of its enunciation' (2022, 109). Notably:

> Gilroy seizes the disruptive opportunity already contained in the negation of the utterance by the act of saying it. … Gilroy purposefully commits to an 'over-literal' interpretation of the content of the central utterance of 'post-racial' discourse—'race no longer matters.' In particular, he wilfully ignores the open secret that the very fact of its enunciation compromises its validity.
>
> (Friedlander 2022, 109)

In effect, 'Gilroy recognizes that negation is already contained within the gap between the statement and the fact that it needs to be said (if race really did not matter, there would be no point in continuing to declare that it does not matter)' (Friedlander 2022, 109–110). Accordingly, it is by 'exploit[ing] the Symbolic efficacy of the artifice' (Friedlander 2022, 110) that Gilroy undermines the very fiction of race itself.

On this basis, we can interpret Gilroy's assertion as occupying the position of the 'duped who do not err'. For Friedlander, this is achieved by Gilroy taking the enunciated—the fiction 'race no longer matters'—*seriously*; a position that does not necessarily discount the enunciation, but accentuates it as a point of negation (if the enunciated did not matter, then there would be no need for the *position* [of enunciation] from which it is said). Thus, there is a '*disruptive opportunity* already contained in the negation of the utterance by the act of saying it' (Friedlander 2022, 109, italics added).[3] In the end, what Gilroy's negation provides is a space—a position of enunciation—that allows for a critique of race via the very discourse that maintains its significance.

Importantly, Gilroy does not 'set aside' the fiction of race, nor does he 'see through' it (Friedlander 2022, 110); instead, the position he adopts is one of negation; a position that occupies the very impasse within the fiction of race itself. Here we can consider how Gilroy meets the limitations within the 'post-race' discourse via his own 'planetary humanism': a strategic universality that critically considers the idea of race through a reimagining of the imperial and anti-imperial practices that have structured and determined who counts as 'human'. Though Gilroy's project does not propose a post-racial outlook, it nonetheless seeks an approach that moves beyond the idea of race by taking (the human) race seriously: that is, by subjecting it to a radical form of humanism that inherently subverts its Eurocentric misappropriation (one in which the conception of humanism was used to deny certain groups as much as it was used to define them). By way of elaborating on this approach, a consideration of the temporality that the 'post-' prefix provides is required.

A radical temporality: 'post-race' as an encounter with the negative

Used as a modifier, the prefix 'post-' functions to assume that something has moved 'beyond' a particular point or period of discussion. In other words, the 'post-' occurs after something else has occurred. While this focuses our attention on what has been, as well as what is due to be, it is the position from which the 'post-' is achieved that proves significant. Temporally, the 'post-' delimits a unique position between the past, present, and future. While our present may be conceived as 'post-' something—for example, some may consider that we currently reside in a period of 'post-modernity' or one may even enjoy listening to 'post-punk'—it can also refer to a past that has been left behind, and, when looking towards the future, it can prescribe a position that is yet to be achieved (a present that is to be). What this temporal ambiguity of the 'post-' prescribes, however, is a confrontation with the negative. Whether we consider the 'post-' to refer to the past or the future, in either case, it retroactively requires us to conceive of what *it is* that has been lost. In other words, it requires us to conceive of what *it is* that we have moved beyond, and, thus, what has been overcome or passed over.

This line of inquiry is effectively demonstrated in Zupančič's (2017–18) account of Maurice Blanchot's essay, 'The Apocalypse is Disappointing' (1964 [1997]). In outlining Blanchot's approach, Zupančič helpfully refers to a particular scene that she witnessed from a horror film. In the scene, a young woman is about to take her own life when, suddenly, she is attacked by a werewolf. The tropes of the scene are easily imaginable, yet it is in the actions of the woman that the scene bears its significance. Zupančič notes:

> [t]he woman who decided to commit suicide made this decision following an understanding-based insight according to which *everything* was meaningless. The surprise in the form of the 'invasion of the negative' (the werewolf) makes her start fighting for her life—the life that she never really had, and was hence ready to give up. But perhaps she will now get it, precisely through this fight. ... For the struggle for life is not the same as clinging on to life and to the *status quo*; it is much more than this, and it derives its force from the encounter with the negative, from the utmost distress which can also be a birthplace of ideas, and even truths.
>
> (2017–18, 28, italics in original)[4]

There remains a unique temporal form underlying Zupančič's example. In the act of ending her life, the woman is suddenly required to defend *that* which she wished to lose (her life). The effect here is not one in which the woman returns to her previous unhappiness, so that after defeating the werewolf she simply *accepts* her unhappiness. Instead, it is in confrontation with the negative that the woman is suddenly required to defend *what* constitutes the very life she sought to end. It was only in the encounter with the deadly werewolf and the inevitability of her impending death—a 'post-life' position—that she was able to fight for, as well as preserve, her very life. Zupančič asserts:

> if, on the one hand, we can be awakened to the idea of a whole by the possibility of losing it, that is, by the possibility of losing this *whole* (even if it doesn't yet exist), we can, on the other hand, also be woken up to it by the appearance of the *loss as such*, that is, by the cut that redoubles—and functions as a symbolic marker of—the insecurity and incompleteness of the whole (of life).
>
> (2017–18, 29, italics in original)

In effect, it was in the confrontation with the loss of life that the woman was able to conceive of the loss of this very life, even when, for her, this life was non-existent, or, at least, not worth living, hence the suicide. What is important is that it is from a position in the future—death itself—that what was lost in the present is subsequently 'awakened'.[5]

It is, therefore, through an encounter with the negative, or, rather, through an act of negation, that we affirm *that* which, from the perspective of the future (a 'post-' position), would be conceived as lost.[6] This is not to conceive of the future as fulfilling some sense of achieved satisfaction, one where our present actions are directed to some future goal or ambition. Such a critique is already made in the work of Edelman (2004), where, according to Ruti, 'Edelman is right in the sense that this vision underpins both the Christian notion of salvation and the idea that our children will somehow complete our life's mission' (2012, 65). Instead, by adopting 'a more psychoanalytic angle', Ruti acknowledges that:

> the future does not so much rescue us from the pain of the past as it allows us to engage in an (always incomplete) rewriting of this past. Because the future is, by definition, open-ended, it is not merely an illusory return to an imaginary state of wholeness where 'being' meets 'meaning,' but rather what guarantees that the two can never coincide. It does not suture our identity by closing the lack within us, but rather ensures that we keep translating this lack into ever-renewed forms of meaning; instead of offering us the 'final signifier,' it draws us into previously unencountered webs of signification that facilitate our continuous process of becoming. On this view, the future is not where we rediscover a perfect past, but rather where we take responsibility for the imperfections of this past—where we do our best to make sure that what is hurtful about the past is not repeated. This is not a matter of denying death, but merely of holding onto the possibility that between the present moment and the moment of death, we are capable of meeting the world in ways that are worthy of our passion.
>
> (2012, 65)

What underscores Ruti's account is the retroactivity it relies upon. Here, one's actions are not directed from the present but from a position in the future: a future where the loss of the past, however inconclusive, is retroactively conceived, or where the very loss of the present may be assumed. In either case, it is only by conceiving of loss from some future position that what is presently required at the level of becoming can be achieved or at least created (Black 2022). Ultimately, while loss is not overcome, it is instead conceived through the (re)writing of lack (Black 2023).

To this extent, it is in accordance with the 'post-' that one's confrontation with lack can be perceived.[7] Though it is not possible to see oneself 'in' the future (outside of the vagaries of our imagination), one can affirm a future without oneself—in fact, one can ensure this future by ending one's life in the present. Located in the position of Zupančič's (2017–18) suicidal woman, 'I' can commit to a future where 'I' no longer exist. Yet, it is at this point of negation that the temporality of the 'post-' proves significant: it is in conceiving a 'post-' position that one's relation to the present and the past can be found. It is only when 'I' no longer exist, that *I* establish the existence of this 'I'.[8] In other words, what can be conceived to be lost from the position of the 'post-' (from the position of that which has been moved beyond) can only ever be approached through an affirmation of that which has been, or will be, lost. Here, the mistakes, imperfections, and traumas of the past are conceived from a perspective that seeks to upend the effects of their resolution. As noted, there is no conclusive remedy that is provided in this retroactive position. What must be asked, however, is whether the psychosis of race can provide such a retroactive position?

Beyond race?

Referring to the case of Schreber, Millar considers whether the delusions Schreber experienced 'conjure an image for us similar to today's fantasies and speculations of artificially intelligent sex objects?' (Millar 2021, 113). She asks:

> [w]as Schreber's delusion in fact a vision of the future? Is the so called 'pornographic age' wherein the enjoying body is obscenely visible to all at every moment; a public version of Schreber's private delusion, and an attempt to construct the fantasy of an increasingly impossible sexual relation?
>
> (Millar 2021, 113)

What proves interesting in this example is how 'today's fantasies and speculations' bear a unique resemblance to Schreber's psychosis, and, specifically, his delusions. What is more, we can, in this example, consider how it is from a future position, beyond that of Schreber's initial delusions (our contemporary position), that such visions prove pertinent. In fact, whether we consider Schreber's delusions to be correct or not is beside the point; instead, what the speculation on Schreber's psychosis provides is the possibility to identify, and even refuse, such a future made present.

It is through the temporality of Millar's speculation that a space is opened where what was once past is now the future of what is present. In effect, it is through a return to the past that our discussion of any possible future (a future that is now lived) can be creatively refused or incompletely re-written (Ruti 2012). There is certainly no redemption in the delusions that plague Schreber's psychosis, nor is there any resolution in the apparent future they foreshadow. If Schreber's delusions bear any truth, and, by extension, if the delusions, paranoias, and fantasies underpinning the structure of psychosis are to be taken seriously (and, in the psychosis of race, they should be taken seriously), then identifying the (im)possibility of any future position requires a confrontation with the (impossible) Real. Thus, it is only from the position of the future (our present) that Schreber's 'impossible' delusions bear their significance (Millar 2021, 113).

Therefore, alongside the introduction of doubt, and in accordance with the creativity of the sinthome, we can outline a certain temporality in the psychosis of race. While much of the above has sought to distinguish a 'space' for which the subject can begin to 'creatively' doubt the certainty of their knowledge (the 'gap' within the Symbolic), as well as establish a relation to the sinthome that works to reintroduce the subject's constitutive lack, in each instance, it is the subject's racial prescription that is contested. That is, it is the certainty afforded to one's racial prescription that the above critique has sought to confront, insofar as it is through introducing a relation to lack that our ties to race can be doubted (and challenged).

In conjunction with Gilroy, it is not simply the case that our racism should be challenged, but that our efforts towards forging our very anti-racism must be set free from 'its ambivalent relationship to the idea of "race"' (2000, 334). Whereas Gilroy directs this endeavour towards 'a heterocultural, postanthropological, and cosmopolitan yet-to-come' (2000, 334), the same must also be said for the psychosis of race. That is, if 'we [are to] leave the century of the color line behind, we need self-consciously to become more future-oriented. We need to look toward the future and to find political languages in which it can be discussed' (Gilroy 2000, 335). Arguably, this future-orientation can be located in the temporal ambiguity of the 'post-' prefix, one that is driven by a fictional future position that affords a retroactive perspective upon the present. This can function to expose the very fiction of race—it's inherent non-sense—via an *acceptance* of the post-race fiction.

Indeed, if we are to challenge the certainty that our racial psychosis provides, then deciding what it is that we wish to move beyond proves to be of critical importance—it offers the point from which doubt can transpire; a point from which an act of interpretation can be made. It is here that the relevance of any 'post-race' assertion speaks not to our present moment, but to a future 'yet-to-come' (Gilroy 2000, 334). The significance of this future is that there is no guarantee that it will be achieved. Instead, its implications lie not in some progressive sense of inevitable accomplishment, but in the very fact that in order to conceive of such a future, we must first establish what *it is* that we wish to leave behind: what is it about race—be it the belief, the certainty, the anxiety, or paranoia it evokes—that *we* must lose? From this fictional future—a 'post-race' position—we can retroactively introduce a relation to lack at the level of our present being—an introduction of doubt that questions and undermines our present certainties in race, racism, and racialization. What these questions of doubt provide is a space in which the very certainty of our racial prescriptions become dented: a crack in the edifice of race, and our ties to it, become visible.

Thus, if we are to move beyond 'race'—beyond the delusions, paranoias, and fantasies that it exists on—then it is only through acknowledging race's inherent lack (it's very non-sense) that the psychosis of race can be critiqued. It is through the negation of the 'post-' that the obfuscations of race can be challenged and the subject's relation to, and possible embrace of, lack can be affirmed. To help conclude this account, a final precis on the relevance of this approach will be considered. Specifically, the next chapter will turn to the musician, Kendrick Lamar, where it will be argued that a relation to the 'post-' can be conceived in lyrics that aver the psychosis of race and the creativity of doubt.

Notes

1 Though George relates the work of Joyce to a path of cynicism, he builds a similar connection between the position of Joyce and African Americans when he notes that, '[u]nable to identify with the Symbolic, Joyce takes to an extreme the sense that the Symbolic and language are imposed upon the subject, the feeling, ... that is also experienced by African Americans submitted to the Symbolic's racist signifiers' (2016, 139).
2 The gap within the Symbolic order always pertains the risk of a traumatic encounter with the Real.
3 We can draw a connection here between Gilroy and the 'disruptive opportunity' of West's remarks regarding the 'Republican' Obama (discussed in Chapter 9) (Friedlander 2022, 109).
4 There is a recognition of life here that echoes the patient at the end of analysis. McGowan notes how it is 'the patient at the end of psychoanalysis who sees that "I am that": I identify myself with the traumatic object, and in doing so, I become who I always was' (2007, 24). Note the retroactivity that underscores this recognition: the patient 'becomes' what, from a position of retroactivity, it 'always' was. Similarly, Žižek notes that a failed suicide is 'the ultimate proof that being is failed non-being' (2022, 260).
5 Zupančič applies this thinking to Blanchot's take on approaching a nuclear apocalypse: '[t]he true choice is not between tolerating the Bomb (and hence running the risk of losing everything) on the one hand, and preventing the looming destruction of the world (but thereby running the risk of losing our liberal freedoms) on the other hand; the true choice is between "losing it all" and *creating what we are about to lose* (even if we lose it all in the process): only this could eventually save us, in a profound sense' (2017–18, 21).
6 In 'What's the Time? On Being Too Early or Too Late in Hegel's Philosophy', Dolar (2020) highlights the temporal significance of 'negation' in Hegel's approach to time, temporality, and retroactivity, drawing particular attention to the importance of the Lacanian Real.
7 Lack is not redeemed. In the end, 'this intrinsic impossibility—the fact that every attempt to redeem lack unavoidably falls short of its mark—is what allows us, over and again, to take up the endless process of signifying beauty' (Ruti 2008, 491).
8 Importantly, this is not a plea to fill the 'I', the subject of the 'I' is 'unknowable' (Copjec 1994). Any determination of the 'I' can always be doubted by the subject.

References

Balasopoulos, Antonis. 1997. "The demon of (racial) history: reading *Candyman*." *Gramma: Journal of Theory & Criticism* 5: 25–47.
Black, Jack. 2022. "A hole that does not speak: Covid, catastrophe and the impossible." *Philosophy World Democracy*, May 28, https://www.philosophy-world-democracy.org/articles-1/a-hole-that-does-not-speak-covid-catastrophe-and-the-impossible
Black, Jack. 2023. "Desire, drive and the melancholy of English football: 'It's (not) coming home'." In *Critical Issues in Football: A Sociological Analysis of the Beautiful Game*, edited by Will Roberts, Stuart Whigham, Alex Culvin, and Daniel Parnell (53–65). Abingdon, UK: Routledge.
Copjec, Joan. 1994. *Read My Desire: Lacan Against the Historicists*. Cambridge, MA: The MIT Press.
Dolar, Mladen. 1998. "Cogito as the subject of the unconscious." In *Cogito and the Unconscious, Sic 2*, edited by Slavoj Žižek (11–40). Durham, NC: Duke University Press.
Dolar, Mladen. 2020. "What's the time? On being too early or too late in Hegel's philosophy." *Problemi International* 4, no. 11–12: 31–49.
Edelman, Lee. 2004. *No Future: Queer Theory and the Death Drive*. Durham, N.C.: Duke University Press.
Flisfeder, Matthew. 2021. *Algorithmic Desire: Toward a New Structuralist Theory of Social Media*. Evanston, IL: Northwestern University Press.
Friedlander, Jennifer. 2022. "In medium race: traversing the fantasy of post-race discourse." In *Lacan and Race: Racism, Identity, and Psychoanalytic Theory*, edited by Sheldon George and Derek Hook (105–120). Abingdon, UK: Routledge.
George, Sheldon. 2014. "From alienation to cynicism: race and the Lacanian unconscious." *Psychoanalysis, Culture & Society* 19, no. 4: 360–378.
George, Sheldon. 2016. *Trauma and Race: A Lacanian Study of African American Racial Identity*. Waco, TX: Baylor University Press.
Gilroy, Paul. 2000. *Against Race: Imagining Political Culture Beyond the Color Line*. Cambridge, MA: The Belknap Press of Harvard University Press.
Lacan, Jacques. 2018. *The Seminar of Jacques Lacan, Book XXIII: The Sinthome*, edited by Jacques-Alain Miller. Cambridge, UK: Polity.
McGowan, Todd. 2007. *The Impossible David Lynch*. New York, NY: Columbia University Press.
McGowan, Todd. 2013. "The singularity of the cinematic object." *Continental Philosophy Review* 46: 311–325.
McNulty, Tracy. 2014. *Wrestling with the Angel: Experiments in Symbolic Life*. New York, NY: Columbia University Press.
Millar, Isabel. 2021. *The Psychoanalysis of Artificial Intelligence*. Champagne, CH: Palgrave Macmillan.
Pluth, Ed. 2007. *Signifiers and Acts: Freedom in Lacan's Theory of the Subject*. New York, NY: State University of New York Press.
Ragland-Sullivan, Ellie. 1992. "The paternal metaphor: a Lacanian theory of language." *Revue Internationale de Philosophie* 46, no. 180: 49–92.
Ruti, Mari. 2008. "The fall of fantasies: a Lacanian reading of lack." *Journal of the American Psychoanalytic Association* 56, no. 1: 483–508.

Ruti, Mari. 2012. *The Singularity of Being: Lacan and the Immortal Within*. New York, NY: Fordham University Press.
Verhaeghe, Paul. 2019. "Lacan's answer to alienation: separation." *Crisis & Critique* 6, no. 1: 365–388.
Verhaeghe, Paul and Frédéric Declercq. 2016. "Lacan's analytic goal: le sinthome or the feminine way." *Psychoanalytische Perspectieven* 34, no. 4: 1–21.
Žižek, Slavoj. 1999. "The undergrowth of enjoyment: how popular culture can serve as an introduction to Lacan." In *The Žižek Reader*, edited by Elizabeth Wright and Edmond Wright (11–36). Malden, MA: Blackwell Publishing.
Žižek, Slavoj. 2022. *Surplus Enjoyment*. London, UK: Bloomsbury.
Zupančič, Alenka. 2017–18. "The apocalypse is (still) disappointing." *S: Journal of the Circle for Lacanian Ideology Critique* 10 & 11: 16–30.

Chapter 12

Kendrick Lamar and the psychosis of race

There is nothing more mongrel than music. The study of any musical form, genre, or style very quickly delivers a multitude of competing and co-existing identities that defy a strict racial historiography. This alludes to the political significance of music, as well as the extent to which certain genres approach our relation to lack. Specifically, for George (2016), blues music offers a unique example in this regard. Indeed:

> [w]here the song of the blues artist dwells upon loss in order to transform it through aesthetics, the song is also a deep engagement with personal lack: not an effort to mask loss in a vision of complementarity but an embrace of personal fragmentation as a condition of existence. ... [T]his recognition of lack as a propelling condition of existence, ... is opened up to the musician, facilitating through lack the artistic production of something new, something revivifying.
>
> (George 2016, 72)

Undoubtedly, the production of this 'something new' does not stand apart from the trauma of race as well as 'the reality and absurdity of American slavery that occasioned this racial and cultural regeneration through music and song' (Hills 2020, 230). Instead, what it confers is a *space*—indeed, 'a deep engagement with personal lack' (George 2016, 72)—that does not ignore the absurdity of race's traumatic inflictions, but which, much like the sinthome, envisages a creative restructuring of one's experiences and certainties. It is in this sense that the psychosis of race is reproduced in the absurdity of race, as well as in the impasses and ambivalences that introduce the opportunity for doubt and a confrontation with one's racialization.

Encompassing these ambivalences and paradoxes is the hip-hop genre: an African American cultural product that bears witness to wider Caribbean and, more recently, transatlantic influences. Though the genre has proved adept at tracing the paradoxes of racial struggle and discrimination, this often sits alongside a level of marketization and commercialization that inevitably calls into question the critiques afforded to its social and political

DOI: 10.4324/9781003414209-16

commentaries. Here, a melange of resistance, appropriation, political oppression, and capitalist accedence co-align in a musical genre that remains creatively adept at examining the contradictions in contemporary society and the politics of race.

Hip-hop and the racist fantasy

For McGowan (2022), the problem with hip-hop lies not with the genre, but with the racist fantasy that it helps to sustain. Focusing on its popularity amongst White suburban teens, McGowan examines how the genre remains predicated on an enjoyment that is perpetuated *through* the racial other. It is through this racial other that the avid hip-hop fan can indulge in the misogyny, violence, and 'gangsta' lifestyle that is vivaciously portrayed across a variety of popular hip-hop songs.[1] In fact:

> [t]he affection that suburban white teens have for hip hop music shows the ability of the racist fantasy to allow people to energize themselves on the enjoyment of the other. The marginalization of hip hop stars is absolutely essential to the esteem that their white audience has for them.
> (McGowan 2022, 170)

It is from a position of nonbelonging—beyond the usual social constraints prescribed by the social order—that the marginalization of the hip-hop artist affords a level of transgression which allows the listener to subscribe to a fantasy of enjoyment that would otherwise be prohibited. In other words, it is the effects of the racist fantasy that succeeds in prescribing the racial other a level of enjoyment that fixes 'Blackness' to the 'transgressive enjoyment of nonbelonging' (McGowan 2022, 171). Consequently, by listening to hip-hop, one can remain safe in the knowledge that they are not racist: 'The fact that the singer is [often] Black enables listeners to experience themselves as utterly nonracist, which is what makes the racist fantasy so much more appealing than open displays of racism' (McGowan 2022, 172).

Certainly, McGowan does not refrain from proclaiming the obverse. Though much of his analysis rests upon a discussion of the song, 'Da Real Hoodbabies', by the Atlanta rapper and singer, Lil Gotit, he also gives reference to the Philadelphian-born rapper, Meek Mill. Echoing other hip-hop songs that 'confront white listeners with the brutality of contemporary racism and force them to address their own racism' (McGowan 2022, 172), Meek Mill's 'Championships' 'challenge[s] the association of blackness with enjoyment' by highlighting 'that guns and drugs represent a capitulation to the logic of capitalist society, not a rebellion' (McGowan 2022, 172). In fact, whereas hip-hop's political valency remains an important point of contention (a contention that, as argued below, remains integral to the genre's significance), McGowan does not suggest that we should, in view of the racist fantasy, stop listening to hip-hop.[2] Rather,

McGowan's conclusions confront the important assertion that 'the way out of an investment in the racist fantasy requires taking responsibility for one's own enjoyment, seeing this enjoyment as one's own rather than that of the racial other' (2022, 173).

Undoubtedly, while one's enjoyment cannot be found in the other, or, as seen in the case of the hip-hop artist, in the unrestrained enjoyment that the subject is denied, it is difficult to determine how such 'responsibility' could ever be acknowledged through the act of listening to hip-hop—beyond the fact that one would simply have to stop listening to it. On this basis, we can consider how the political importance of hip-hop may rest in its capacity to expose the psychosis of race in such a way that the very excesses it relies upon function to reveal the racist fantasies that constrain and delimit the genre's racialization.

Notably, in his film theory, McGowan has highlighted how examples of cinematic excess work 'not from obedience to the demands of the social order, but from adherence to and embrace of the enjoyment that exceeds that order' (2007, 57). Accordingly, in his account of the cinema of fantasy, McGowan emphasizes how it is the hidden enjoyment which underscores society that is emphatically exposed. By revealing 'too much', fantasy functions to disclose the hidden underside of Symbolic authority, as well as the 'dirty secrets' that undergird our private exchanges. Indeed, in the case of racism, films such as Spike Lee's, *Do the Right Thing* (1989) and *Bamboozled* (2000), portray the prevalence of racist fantasies in scenes that effectively bring to light the excessive enjoyment that these racist fantasies rely upon. According to McGowan, the politics of Lee's films work by exposing the racism that such fantasies allow to remain hidden. Unfortunately, Lee's politicization goes amiss in McGowan's analysis of the hip-hop genre, and subsequently overlooks the contradictions in the genre itself—contradictions that frequently underlie, but which remain integral to, the hip-hop musician and their lyrics (Cooke 2021).

It is useful here not to critique a whole genre of music based on a few well-known and popular songs. The global significance and success of hip-hop belies any simple assumption, despite its location in prevailing racist fantasies. Equally, without ignoring the importance of the racist fantasy, and its role in facilitating our enjoyment in the genre, it is through the psychosis of race that we can conceive how hip-hop offers an opportunity for both the artist and listener to 'grapple with' the constitutive fantasies that underscore our relations to the world, and, more importantly, our perceptions and representations of the other (McGowan 2007, 19).

What is brought to bear in the genre's excessive portrayals are the contradictions it creates. Here excessive forms of enjoyment, such as The Notorious B.I.G.'s (Biggie) diss track, 'Kick in the Door' (1997), sits in complete contrast to lyrics where the rapper expresses the debilitating effects of doubt, frustration, and possible suicide. In 'Suicidal Thoughts'

(1994), Biggie recites a late-night phone call to a friend, rapping openly about committing suicide by slitting his wrists and shooting himself.

Certainly, the intention here is not to laud the act of suicide as invigorating a unique insight into the effects of racism in society, or as an exclusive characteristic beholden to the genre and the venerated hip-hop artist. Instead, what these lyrics propose is that it is in such excessive displays—kicking down a door to shoot up a rival or in confiding to blow one's brain out—that the effects of a racial psychosis can be exposed and critiqued. Crucial here is identifying those examples where confrontations with lack can be averred, not just in the content of the hip-hop song, but also in a formal structure where the exposure to fantasy and excess can be creatively disclosed. With this in mind, the purpose of the following analysis is not to evaluate the relative merits of the hip-hop genre, but to draw specifically from the musical significance of one its leading proponents, Kendrick Lamar.

Paranoia and uncertainty: confronting lack in Lamar

Born Kendrick Lamar Duckworth, Lamar is a rapper and songwriter whose music has received broad critical acclaim for his lyrics, which depict a unique introspective reflection, and a broad musical style that frequently draws from a range of musical influences, such as jazz, soul, and funk. Over the course of Lamar's discography, his music has tackled issues relating to the political and social circumstances of Black Americans, with personal references and critiques of U.S. culture and society providing the bedrock to many of his most acclaimed tracks.

In fact, much of Lamar's later output suggests an emerging paranoia within U.S. politics and society, with his fourth (*DAMN.* 2017) and fifth (*Mr. Moral & the Big Steppers* 2022) albums being released post-2016. Referring specifically to Lamar's fourth album, *DAMN.*, Floyd-Thomas notes:

> [c]onfronted with [… a] drastic sea change in presidential leadership from Obama to Trump, there were millions of folks, especially young people of color, yearning to actualize a radically honest and liberating vision of intersectional politics. Reflecting on the political rise of a racist, sexist, xenophobic, narcissistic failed businessman and former reality television star to the Oval Office, Lamar's *DAMN.* is a truthful antidote to the surreal age of Trump.
>
> (2020, 88)

Criticisms of U.S. politics echo throughout Lamar's wider work, with both his lyrics and musical approach drawing heavily from his experiences of growing up in Compton, California (a city with its own rich musical heritage, such as the influential, N.W.A. ['Niggaz Wit Attitudes'], who formed in the late 1980s). Accordingly, while Lamar's preference for releasing concept albums has allowed him to discuss and dissect his relation to U.S. politics, as well as the historical significance of race relations in contemporary U.S. society, much of his work serves to explore and reflect upon these themes in relation to his Compton upbringing.

In particular, Lamar's lyrics can be conceived as eliciting a psychosis of race, with examples of delusion and paranoia being expressed (Key 2020). Where his lyrics allude to confrontations with members of the civil rights movement, or, as Lamar explains, their 'spirits',[3] such artistic licence affords him the opportunity to reference and recite the delusional encounters he has experienced with both Martin Luther King and Malcolm X ('HiiiPoWeR' 2011). In the same song, Lamar refers explicitly to conspiracy theories regarding the relationship between the Illuminati and hip-hop musicians (specifically, himself). Key notes:

> [c]onspiracy theories have long held a prominent place in hip-hop as forms of counter knowledge. It has elements of what anthropologist John L. Jackson Jr. regards as the racial skepticism that cannot take at face value the pronouncements of mainstream society. He argues that this paranoia informs how hip-hop spirituality creates its own authoritative sources. Counter knowledge or hidden knowledge often is compatible with black religious traditions that suppose themselves to be in possession of the true knowledge and the true identity of African Americans.
>
> (2020, 307)

Certainly, the relative success of using conspiracy theories as a form of 'counter knowledge' works in stark contrast to the psychotic underpinnings that this knowledge relies upon and the paranoia it engenders. Notably, it is the degree to which these conspiracies endow a certainty of knowledge—indeed, a 'possession of the *true knowledge* and the *true identity* of African Americans'—that the psychosis of race confines the subject to forms of racial delimitation just as much as it seeks to challenge the very authorities who seek to dispel such 'knowledge'. While Lamar's lyrics evidence a psychosis of race at play, it is in those instances where this relation to psychosis is challenged that Lamar's confessional rap style offers a unique opportunity to explore the difficulties and inhibitions that underlie his music.

Specifically, it is in relation to a number of key themes within Lamar's work that we can begin to decipher a challenge to psychosis. This occurs not just in his use of language, but also in the space he establishes, through which opportunities for lack and doubt can be expressed. In songs, such as 'U' (2015), Lamar displays an anxiety towards the fame and fortune that his hip-hop career has accumulated. Recited in a confessional mode, Lamar explores how his very successes—sold-out stadiums, significant record sales—are all, beyond that of his own selfishness, ephemeral achievements that only compound his sense of lack and disillusionment. On the edge of suicide, the song expounds a sense of lack deriving from Lamar's sudden confrontation with the death of a close friend that he remembers while on tour. Depression, anxiety, melancholy, and paranoia permeate Lamar's highly charged emotional deliverance as he reflects on his own 'failures'. Though the song's inherent negativity stands apart from more positive reflections, such as that expressed in the song 'i' (2015), it nonetheless echoes the very contradictions that underpin Lamar's pride and the sense of empowerment that such a 'sin' (his success) can entail.

Undoubtedly, such an assessment may stand opposed to the religious undertones that permeate much of Lamar's work. This is clearly emphasized on the album *To Pimp a Butterfly* (2015), wherein Lamar frequently acknowledges his faith in God, while also imploring his listeners to do the same. Yet, the fact that this remains a reoccurring theme throughout Lamar's music speaks more to the lack of any clear guarantee. As a result, Lamar is continually, and often distressingly, confronting a learned ignorance within, as well as through, his musical delivery. What Lamar's songs observe is an absence of knowledge and a (re)introducing of lack into the surety of his convictions and experiences, religion included.

It is in view of this lack that songs, such as 'Momma' (2015), revolve around Lamar concluding that, despite his assurances, in the end, he knows nothing. This lack of knowledge is derived from Lamar's return from a trip to South Africa in 2014. In 'Momma', Lamar refers to meeting a young boy who reminds him of his younger self. Here, it is in the juxtaposition that Lamar establishes between South Africa and his home, Compton, that he laments upon the Black diaspora. Commenting upon the song, Winters highlights that while the notion 'come back home' alludes to a return to some form of Africa as a point of origin—a 'home' for Black Americans that offers allusions to the Middle Passage—it is in the formal break which follows 'the refrain "come back home" [... that] a split, or gap, between Compton and South Africa' is registered (2020, 223). Such a 'gap' bears witness to an absence in Lamar's own reflections, one transposed in the relation between Compton and South Africa as well as his own lack of knowledge upon returning home.

This highlights how Lamar's lyrics expose a certain level of doubt that is brought to bear in the contradictions and paradoxes which underlie his reflections on race and the Black diaspora. Importantly, the sense of lack and absence that Lamar's lyrical confessions provide elicit the very space through which a relation to doubt, and the capacity to know, can afford a critical reflection on the psychosis of race. Whereas for Lacan, Joyce's art allowed him to stave off death through a language style that weaved his creativity in the impossibility of language, Lamar's music affords an equally insightful inquiry. In what follows, the lyrical content and formal structure of two specific songs will be considered: 'Sing About Me, I'm Dying of Thirst', from Lamar's second album, *good kid, m.A.A.d city* (2012); and, 'Mortal Man', from his third album, *To Pimp a Butterfly* (2015).

'Sing About Me, I'm Dying of Thirst'

Lamar's 'Sing About Me, I'm Dying of Thirst' ('Sing About Me') is divided into three parts, with the first part involving three lyrical subsections. Referring explicitly to themes of salvation, religious conversion, and the love of Christ, the song speaks to Lamar's reflections upon death and remembrance. Over the course of the song, Lamar laments his own lyrical output, while also contemplating a more mournful account of life in Compton. These deliberations are conceived, in the first part of the song, over three verses which Lamar raps from three perspectives. In the first verse, Lamar raps from the perspective of a brother of a friend, recently shot, who reflects on the violence and brutality of gang life in Compton. The second verse, again rapped by Lamar, recites the anger and frustrations of a sister of one's Lamar's friends, Keisha, a former prostitute, who was raped and killed. The sister refers explicitly to a previous song by Lamar, 'Keisha's Song (Her Pain)' (2011), where, according to the sister, he unfavourably frames Keisha's life choices without considering the material circumstances that led her to prostitution. Like the first verse, it seems as if both the sister and the brother are following the paths of their siblings. The third verse involves Lamar responding to verses one and two.

The first part of the song deals explicitly with examples of loss, as well as the angst and anxiety Lamar perceives in reflecting upon these stories. This sense of loss is formally rendered within the structure of Lamar's lyrics. While finishing the first verse, the brother is suddenly cut off, midsentence, as the sound of gunshots ring out. This is echoed in the second verse, where the sister slowly fades into silence. While the first verse relays the certainty that the brother is killed, in the case of the sister we are left reflecting on the sister's anger as her life, and possible death, echo that of Keisha. To this end, the third verse serves as a prism of loss, with Lamar reflecting on his friends' experiences, as well as his role in representing them through his music.

Critically, we can consider how 'As an identity, blackness is always supposed to tell us something about race or racism, or about America, or violence and struggle and triumph or poverty and hopefulness' (Quashie 2012, 4). Here, 'the politics of representation' (Quashie 2012, 4), which is played out in the second verse, echoes this critique, with the sister confronting Lamar on his representation of Keisha and the possibility that his music would in any way help. In contrast to the brother in the first verse, the sister goes so far as to ask Lamar not to be included in his album. Notably, it is not simply the case that Lamar's representation of the Black female experience is challenged, but that these critiques are performed by the originator of these representations—Lamar himself. As Goldstein highlights: 'Lamar is not simply telling the story of others' but is, in fact, telling us his own story through that very representation' (2015, 75). On this basis:

> we cannot simply read this as a portrayal of gendered navigation of the ghetto, but must also ask where Lamar is situating himself in this narrative matrix, as well as what the track does for him; in other words, if the actual narrators of the two verses (whose words, it must be noted, we do not actually hear in an unmediated form) speak in order to both represent and resist their circumstances, what is being performed by Lamar's representation of those representations?
> (Goldstein 2015, 75)

For Goldstein, the fact that 'Kendrick embodies the narration of a gang member (who, in this very verse, admits to killing a rival gang member) and, later, a prostitute, demonstrates that his intent is not to moralize, but rather to humanize' (2015, 79, n.20).

We can go further here and elaborate on how Lamar's position in both verses plays with the instability between the enunciated and the position of enunciation. By strategically adopting the position of both the brother and the sister in his performance, and then reflecting on these performances in the third verse, Lamar introduces an element of doubt in *his* position as the performer. It is through this doubt that Lamar critically reflects upon the effects of representation, thus opening a space in which his representations can be critiqued both in and through the act of representation itself. Here, Lamar is not some omnipresent narrator, dispatching the tragic stories of particular Black individuals, all for the aim of accentuating their social and political importance; instead, Lamar's representation brings into contention the very *position* from which they are relayed: his *position* as performer (enunciation), and his role in representing each story, as reflected through the *content* of both the sister and brother's perspectives (enunciated). By taking this position into account, and in introducing a certain 'instability' between the enunciated and enunciation, Lamar exploits the 'gap' within the representations he presents. This draws attention to the tensions that underly any form of interpretation or expression which seeks to represent the experiences of a particular group or individual (Friedlander 2022). In so doing, the gap between the enunciated content and the position of enunciation is creatively used as part of the song's narrative structure.

It is through this gap that the psychosis of race can be contested; a gap which Lamar puts to further use in the song's formal structure. For example, any critical perspective could very easily evaluate and critique the merits of the representations provided, as Lamar does from the perspective of both the brother and the sister. In this sense, the experiences Lamar describes are not unique, and you would be hard-pressed to find anyone who finds the song's narrative uniquely shocking—in the end, our knowledge of these experiences is, unfortunately, widely known and frequently confirmed. While the third verse sees Lamar reflect upon his ability to represent these experiences, *his* position within the song remains ambiguous. This is confirmed when we consider the hook which opens the song, and which is then later used as the song's chorus. With the 'unknown' narrator imploring his audience to sing about them when they're gone, the significance of these lines is that the position from which they are said remains vague. In fact, whether it is the speaker or the recipient, the ambiguity of the position of enunciation—that is, the position from which these lines are spoken from—functions to introduce a gap within the song's formal narrative. With Lamar rapping verses one, two, and three from the perspective of the brother, the sister, and himself, it is difficult to determine where this plea is spoken from, and, more importantly, by whom. Whether it is the voice of Lamar who speaks, and whether it is Lamar, or us, the audience, who are the recipients of the chorus's plea, it is through the position of enunciation that Lamar introduces a 'gap' within the song's narrative, indeed, a space through which the psychosis of race can be challenged.

Accordingly, what is outlined in this space is the disparity, or, rather, the instability, that is involved in representing the representation of others through the very act of representation itself. In other words, the song affords the very space in which the act of representation is disrupted. Here, external standards, through which one would judge these representations, are waylaid, and, instead, the relative 'success' of Lamar's ability to represent the lives of others in his lyrics forms an immanent part of the song's narrative structure.

More importantly, what Lamar performs in the song is the subject's self-division; a self-division that is obscured in accounts of psychosis, but which proves constitutive of the song's structure. This self-division is exemplified in the gap between the enunciated content and the position of enunciation. What this gap provides is a certain negativity—an act of negation—that is performed within the third verse, and from which the act of representation is itself critiqued through the representation of this very critique. It can be said that, as the song's performer, the position Lamar occupies is that of the 'not-all': a position that lies not outside the representations provided, reflecting upon the totality of the experiences presented, but as a point of view that is itself situated within the song's narrative—a narrative that includes its own point of negativity. Consequently, though the third verse finishes on Lamar validating his decision to draw from the experiences of his dead friend and Keisha, his certainty is suffused with a sense of doubt; one compounded by the fact that these experiences are relayed throughout the song from another perspective and not the perspective of the victims themselves.

In the final lines of the verse, Lamar further interrogates his surety through questions that re-align with the song's chorus, questioning his own worth and whether the work he has put in will allow him to be sung about and remembered when he's gone. In these lines, there is none of the certainty that characterizes the structure of psychosis; instead, there is a creative disruption of the very position in which they are told, one that exposes the limit in the song's representations. Indeed, while, for Copjec, the subject does not 'transcen[d] the signifier but ... inhabits it *as limit*', it is within the discrepancies of this limit that the subject is defined: '[t]his subject, radically unknowable, radically incalculable, is the only guarantee we have against racism' (1994, 209, italics in original). Such a radically unknowable subject is brought to bear through the absence of the subject who speaks the lines of the chorus. In fact, whenever one seeks the subject of each verse, the speaker remains elsewhere; an 'elsewhere' that is confirmed *in* the song's chorus. While the speaker refers explicitly to acts of memorialization after death and the fact that they seek a promise to be remembered, the position of this speaker remains ambiguous, despite the line returning throughout the song.

Furthermore, whereas a level of temporality underscores the entirety of the song—the brother reflects upon his brother's death in light of his *present* life; the sister reflects upon Keisha's life and its similarities to her *present* situation—it is in accordance with the speaker's plea that the 'radically unknowable, radically incalculable' subject (Copjec 1994, 209) serves as a 'witness for the future' (Bouretz 2010, cited in Goldstein 2015, 78).[4] Indeed, 'without legitimizing the present on the basis of the future's possibility' (Goldstein 2015, 78), it is in the temporality afforded to such a witness that the act of looking from the future bears upon the present.

For example, in verses one and two it is the present lives of both the brother and sister that are undoubtedly cut short; or, in the case of the sister, lost to a future fated by their present circumstances. Before being abruptly cut off by gunshots, we can assume that the brother's final lines relay that of the chorus, with the brother referencing the possibility of his own death before the release of the album—a death confirmed by the proceeding gunshots. Though the line draws upon the fact that one should not be forgotten, its wider significance emanates in establishing a space from which the subject, who is to be 'remembered', can be conceived. As Goldstein elaborates, '[t]he desire to have one's story retold does not, in this instance, stem from vanity, but rather from the (perhaps unspoken) conviction that to be forgotten would be to reinforce the system responsible for one's death' (2015, 75). What the witness for the future prescribes, therefore, is a retroactive temporality that conceives of one's present from a future-position, looking back.

Notably, the subject that is expressed by such a witness is based upon defining *that* which is to be lost amidst a present system of inequality and discrimination. The radical unknowability of the subject is that it is left waiting to be defined, as opposed to simply being determined as forgotten. This is implied by the fact that the promise is made from some irreducible position that retroactively speaks from some future perspective that is looking back on one's present. It is by retroactively conceiving of this present from the future—a future where the subject will be remembered and memorialized—that the promise is sought. More importantly, if we suppose that the making of the promise is delivered from someone in the present, then their death is yet to occur. It is, then, the 'promise' itself that draws attention to the very 'subject' that is to be sung about. It is not that any definite 'subject' is defined, but that in the promise of the act a space for a 'subject' and an engagement with the subject's lack is conferred. In the end, the act of defining (and deciding) this subject through one's lack is afforded.

On this basis, we can consider how the radical temporality that is at play within the song works from the contradiction it displays within the position of enunciation. This is evident in the extent to which Lamar changes the perspective of this position throughout each verse and to the compounding absence of a narrator who speaks as a witness to their future fatality—a 'non-position'; an absence or gap certified by the act of death itself. This gap in enunciation is formally rendered in the third part of the song where the second part abruptly ends, and we hear a group of men discussing what they are going to do (we can assume from the conversation that the men are discussing whether to violently retaliate against the death of the brother in the first verse). In this concluding part, the listener hears the voice of the poet and civil rights activist, Maya Angelou. Again, speaking from a position that is difficult to decipher, Angelou's words can be heard as part of the song, but, presumably, she now occupies a unique spectral position that allows her to speak to the group of men as they contemplate retaliation. Angelou encourages the boys to curtail their pain through a recital of the 'Sinner's Prayer'. The messianic tones that underpin this part of the song are undeniable. Included as an accompaniment to the song's first and second parts, the prayer functions as a form of salvation for Lamar, for which the present day is marked as the start of something new.

Throughout each part of 'Sing About Me' Lamar remains a non-linear and ambiguous narrator reflecting on how his past representations impact upon those in the present, while also alluding to some future position that retroactively draws attention to the importance of this present—a 'post-' position.

Attitudes towards race are not openly expressed within the song, but a challenge towards the psychosis of race is enacted in the representations Lamar provides and through the act of negation and creative affirmation that he produces. Here, the obfuscation of the gap between the enunciated content and the position of enunciation, which underpins the psychotic structure, is derailed, with the gap itself forming a constitutive feature of the song's formal narrative via the lack of any clear delineation between past-present-future. We know from earlier songs on the album that the men do in fact retaliate against the murder of their friend, leaving us once more in an ambiguous and uncertain position as to the success of Angelou's intervention (is the intervention a form of time-travel, undoing the retaliation that happens, before it happens?).[5] Assured convictions are not required however, as it is the sense of doubt, forged through a retroactive temporality *in the present*, which proves relevant to challenging the psychosis of race. This is given further consideration in the song, 'Mortal Man'.

'Mortal Man'

Appearing as the final song on Lamar's, *To Pimp a Butterfly* (2015), 'Mortal Man' involves Lamar rapping across several verses before concluding the song with an interview with the deceased Tupac '2Pac' Shakur (Pac). An influential hip-hop artist, killed in 1996, Pac remains a major influence for Lamar, with many of his songs paying homage to the dead musician. Accordingly, what remains unique about 'Mortal Man' is how it adapts a 1994 interview with Pac. Through the use of clever editing, Pac's replies are interpellated into the song, with Lamar asking his own questions, to which Pac's original interview responses are then used. The song's technical achievements help establish an intimacy between the two men, with their discussion referencing and commenting upon politics and philosophy, as well as the morality of race and the Black experience. Listening to the song, it is hard not to imagine the interview taking place in the present, with many of the themes they discuss, as well as Pac's responses, maintaining a contemporary relevance. As noted by Miller, 'a technologically resurrected Pac speaks a transhistorical, yet no less contingent, word on "what's next"' (2020, 159).

This sense of 'what's next' proves an essential feature of the song. Though Lamar is able to share his experiences with Pac, while also relaying his concerns and frustrations, it is in the song's temporal disunity that the psychosis of race is challenged. That is, what the song essentially provides is a delusional encounter for Lamar—a discussion with a dead hip-hop artist, who he is able to question as a source of knowledge, indeed, as a subject supposed to know. Where this delusion is disrupted, however, is in the temporal disunity that it presents. This disunity is not simply obscured via the song's technical sampling, but is reproduced in Lamar's final question and Pac's silence. After reading Pac a poem,

Lamar asks for Pac's perspective, to which Pac does not respond. A frantic Lamar is left repeating Pac's name for a response, again, with no reply. Pac's silence lingers as we are left waiting for his answer. In accordance with Pac's silence, we are suddenly reminded that, in Pac's case, 'the dead can't speak' (Miller 2020, 171). Echoing the silence that befalls both the brother and the sister in 'Sing About Me', the formal significance of Pac's silence helps to afford Lamar's question an atemporal permanence, introducing a level of doubt upon the exchange. Was the artistry that was employed merely a delusional experience, another ghost, another dead homie, haunting Lamar?

The significance of the silence is emphasized by Wert, who 'read[s] the song as raising a question, not resolving it' (2017, 118). They note:

> It is important to recognize, as speech about music inevitably tends to forget, that the song does not end with the lyrics. Indeed, there is almost an entire minute of floating jazz after the lyrical conclusion, creating space—a sort of aftermath—for pondering the bold message of the song.
> (Wert 2017, 118)

While 'Sing About Me' offers a retroactive perspective, drawn from the future to help reflect upon the present, 'Mortal Man' proposes no retroactive resignification. Instead, both Lamar and the listener are without the transcription of Pac's response. Left with the Jazz outro, we experience a space from which the lack of any Symbolic transcription bears a relation to 'the empty place of the Real' (Žižek 2008, 195). Here, there is no attempt to give meaning to the past, nor is the past afforded any direction or cause towards progress. In effect, it seems as if the lack of resolution at the end of the interview serves only to draw attention to Pac's previous responses. Much like the analytic session, Pac's position of 'learned ignorance' avers the lack of any guarantee: in effect, Pac's posthumous presence in the song is one that embodies a confrontation with lack. It is from this position that Pac's silence introduces an absence, as well as the lack of any solution or experience that could answer Lamar's question. Instead, the only answer that can be given to this 'empty place of the Real' is the subject itself: 'we can inscribe, encircle the void place of the subject through the failure of his symbolization, because the subject is nothing but the failure of the process of his symbolic representation' (Žižek 2008, 195). In this regard, Pac's silence, compounded by the 'empty place' that the song's outro provides, 'succeeds' through its very failure to offer any 'symbolic representation' (i.e., a final answer to Lamar's question), leaving only a space for the subject.

Moreover, Pac's silence avers the gap that belies any act of remembrance. The task here is not to avail such forms of remembrance in narratives of progress and overcoming. This can, as previously noted, serve just as much to forget and ignore the very systems that result in such acts of remembrance being required (Goldstein 2015). Referring to the murder of George Perry

Floyd Jr., Gray (2022) emphasizes how Floyd's death was made a 'cause', indeed, an 'event', for political and national 'progress'. For Gray, 'Floyd's "death" matters *to the extent that it can be overcome, that it can be made into a symbol of progress*' (2022, 8, italics in original), and, thus, forgotten. What we see in 'Mortal Man', however, is a detour from such re-symbolization towards the very lack which abounds one's Symbolic inscription. There may not necessarily be an answer in confronting such lack, but there is the space through which to 'think' what has been lost.

Echoing the importance of the temporality that Lamar achieves in 'Sing About Me', 'Mortal Man' formally emphasizes a confrontation with lack; one echoed by the 'cut' and the fade in the first two verses of 'Sing About Me' and Pac's lack of reply in 'Mortal Man'. In each instance, it is through a sense of insecurity and incompleteness that the psychosis of race, and the certainties afforded to the process of racialization, become challenged. While 'Sing About Me' looks towards a 'post-' position—a future where one hopes that one's present will be remembered—'Mortal Man' proposes a future without answer. Here, the doubt that Lamar registers and the lack of any answer—as evident in his critique of representation ('Sing About Me') and the answers he seeks in his discussion with Pac ('Mortal Man')—provide the creative possibility of introducing both a 'cut' and a relation to lack in the psychosis of race.

It is in experimenting with temporality that Lamar is able to develop a certain space within his lyrics and music that can allow us to confront the psychosis of race, not from some external position of understanding or higher knowledge (an anti-racism driven by ensuring that one can be educated out of the racism they expel), but through 'the energies of the Real' (Ruti 2012, 1). Through a re-structuring of the psychotic's relation to language new forms of mediation can be achieved. It is for this reason that Joyce's writing proves invaluable to Lacan, offering the means through which Joyce was able to challenge the rigidities of the Symbolic order and the lack of mediation afforded to the psychotic. Indeed, for Ruti:

> language that makes us question our assumptions, allows us to think in original ways, disrupts the monotony of the status quo, moves us emotionally, makes us sit up and pay attention, or exhibits the kind of creative suppleness that allows us to reinvent a slice of the world, is singularizing. Such language, by definition, avoids resolution. Inasmuch as it allows the 'immortal' vitality of the real to infect its structure, it incessantly pushes aside fossilized forms of meaning in order to elude being subsumed by the dominant symbolic; it, as it were, harnesses the destructiveness of the death drive for the purposes of new life.
>
> (2012, 126)

The above analysis has sought to uncover a temporal dimension to this originality; one that can challenge the rigid confines of psychosis and the fixity of our racialization in the psychosis of race. If we are to be serious about challenging racism, as well as upending the racial determinants that structure and manage our relations to race, then eroding our very belief in race must remain a central tenet of our anti-racism—specifically, we must determine what it is about race that we wish to overcome. The registering of doubt and the capacity to know offer opportunities to develop an ethical praxis within the structure of psychosis; opportunities that can, in accordance with Lacan's account of the sinthome, afford the capacity to creatively develop a relation to the Real. It is, however, through an act of temporal framing—that is, by retroactively acting from some assumed future position—that one's questioning both determines, as well as challenges, what it is that we wish to negate (as posed through the affirmation of the question itself).

Far more than a simple construction, race defines, determines, and prescribes what one is by establishing a psychosis that psychically and socially confines the human subject. It is only by acknowledging and exploring the psychosis of race that a recognition of lack can serve to challenge the fixity that this psychosis prescribes.

Notes

1 The 'reality' of such fantasy is not lost on McGowan, but it is the 'demands' levelled by an audience that remain readily open to the 'graphic enactment of prohibited enjoyment' that maintains the racist fantasy (2022, 170). Here, '[t]he toll that it takes on the artists themselves—many are gunned down at an incredibly young age—bespeaks the role of the racist fantasy in doling out life and death' (McGowan 2022, 170).
2 With regard to hip-hop's anti-racism and its White listeners, Dashiell Neroni may be correct (see McGowan 2022, 230, n.7).
3 Incidentally, Lamar's 'Alright' (2015) has become an important protest song for the Black Lives Matter movement.
4 Goldstein draws upon this phrase from Pierre Bouretz's, *Witnesses For The Future: Philosophy and Messianism* (2010). The phrase is taken from a letter Benjamin wrote to Gershom Scholem (see Goldstein 2015, 80, n.37).
5 The recital of the prayer is also used in the intro to the album's opening track, 'Sherane a.k.a Master Splinter's Daughter'. Consequently, if listening to the album in chronological order, then the listener has already heard this prayer, before it happens ('Sing About Me, I'm Dying of Thirst' is track 10 on the album).

References

Bouretz, Pierre. 2010. *Witnesses for the Future: Philosophy and Messianism*, translated by Michael B. Smith. Baltimore, MD: The John Hopkins University Press.
Cooke, Sekou. 2021. *Hip-Hop Architecture*. London, UK: Bloomsbury.
Copjec, Joan. 1994. *Read My Desire: Lacan Against the Historicists*. Cambridge, MA: The MIT Press.
Floyd-Thomas, Juan M. 2020. "The good, the m.A.A.d, and the holy: Kendrick Lamar's meditations on sin and moral agency in the post-gangsta era." In *Kendrick*

Lamar and the Making of Black Meaning, edited by Christopher M. Driscoll, Anthony B. Pinn, and Monica R. Miller (69–98). London, UK: Routledge.

Friedlander, Jennifer. 2022. "In medium race: traversing the fantasy of post-race discourse." In *Lacan and Race: Racism, Identity, and Psychoanalytic Theory*, edited by Sheldon George and Derek Hook (105–120). Abingdon, UK: Routledge.

George, Sheldon. 2016. *Trauma and Race: A Lacanian Study of African American Racial Identity*. Waco, TX: Baylor University Press.

Goldstein, Evan. 2015. "Performing redemption: Metzian theology in the art of Kendrick Lamar." *Elements* 11, no. 2: 72–81.

Gray, Biko Mandela. 2022. "Now it is always now." *Political Theology*. DOI: doi:10.1080/1462317X.2022.2093693

Hills, Darrius D. 2020. "'We gon' be alright': Kendrick Lamar and the theology of affirmation." In *Beyond Christian Hip Hop: A Move Towards Christians and Hip Hop*, edited by Erika Gault and Travis Harris (228–248). London, UK: Routledge.

Key, Andre E. 2020. "Damnation, identity, and truth: vocabularies of suffering in Kendrick Lamar's DAMN." In *Kendrick Lamar and the Making of Black Meaning*, edited by Christopher M. Driscoll, Anthony B. Pinn, and Monica R. Miller (300–320). London, UK: Routledge.

Lee, Spike, director. 1989. *Do the Right Thing*. 40 Acres and a Mule; Filmworks.

Lee, Spike, director. 2000. *Bamboozled*. 40 Acres and a Mule; Filmworks.

Lamar, Kendrick. 2011. 'Keisha's Song (Her Pain) (Featuring Ashtrobot)', *Section.80*. Top Dawg.

Lamar, Kendrick. 2011. 'HiiiPower', *Section.80*. Top Dawg.

Lamar, Kendrick. 2012. 'Sing About Me, I'm Dying of Thirst', *good kid, m.A.A.d city*. TDE; Aftermath; Interscope.

Lamar, Kendrick. 2015. 'U', *To Pimp a Butterfly*. TDE; Aftermath; Interscope.

Lamar, Kendrick. 2015. 'Momma', *To Pimp a Butterfly*. TDE; Aftermath; Interscope.

Lamar, Kendrick. 2015. 'i', *To Pimp a Butterfly*. TDE; Aftermath; Interscope.

Lamar, Kendrick. 2015. 'Mortal Man', *To Pimp a Butterfly*. TDE; Aftermath; Interscope.

Lamar, Kendrick. 2017. *DAMN*. TDE; Aftermath; Interscope.

Lamar, Kendrick. 2022. *Mr. Morale & the Big Steppers*. PGLang; TDE; Aftermath; Interscope.

McGowan, Todd. 2007. *The Real Gaze: Film Theory after Lacan*. Albany, NY: State University of New York Press.

McGowan, Todd. 2022. *The Racist Fantasy: Unconscious Roots of Hatred*. New York, NY: Bloomsbury.

Meek Mill. 2018. 'Championships', *Championships*. Atlantic; Maybach Music.

Miller, Monica R. 2020. "Can dead homies speak? The spirit and flesh of black meaning." In *Kendrick Lamar and the Making of Black Meaning*, edited by Christopher M. Driscoll, Anthony B. Pinn, and Monica R. Miller (159–174). London, UK: Routledge.

The Notorious B.I.G. 1994. 'Suicidal Thoughts', *Ready to Die*. Bad Boy; Arista.

The Notorious B.I.G. 1997. 'Kick in the Door', *Life After Death*. Bad Boy; Arista.

Quashie, Kevin. 2012. *The Sovereignty of Quiet: Beyond Resistance in Black Culture*. New Brunswick, CA: Rutgers University Press.

Ruti, Mari. 2012. *The Singularity of Being: Lacan and the Immortal Within*. New York, NY: Fordham University Press.

Wert, Adam. 2017. "Tensions and ambiguity: Paul Tillich and Kendrick Lamar on courage and faith." *Toronto Journal of Theology* 33, no. 1: 113–121.
Winters, Joseph. 2020. "Beyond flight and containment: Kendrick Lamar, black study, and an ethics of the wound." In *Kendrick Lamar and the Making of Black Meaning*, edited by Christopher M. Driscoll, Anthony B. Pinn, and Monica R. Miller (212–228). London, UK: Routledge.
Žižek, Slavoj. 2008. *The Sublime Object of Ideology*. London, UK: Verso.

Index

Act 185–186
Alienation/separation 178–179, 186n5, 190, 192–193 *see also* Psychosis (and alienation)
Ambassadors, The 69–70
Angelou, M. 215
Andrews, K.: on psychosis of Whiteness 10
Anxiety *see* Lacan, J. (on anxiety); Psychosis (and anxiety)
Anti-racism 2, 4, 6, 13, 29–30, 32, 49, 106, 175, 182, 218–219
Anti-Semitism 110, 150, 164–165 *see also* Freud, S. (on Jews and anti-Semitism)
Bamboozled 207

Belief *see* Psychosis (belief in disbelief)
big Other, the 7, 8, 100, 146n2; diversification of 138, 150–151; *jouissance* 149, 151–152, 154–155, 160, 161, 177 *see also* Desire (the Other's desire); Lack (and the Other); Psychosis (and the Other); Psychosis (and the Other of the Other)
Black minstrelsy 161
BlacKkKlansman 187n11
Blaxploitation genre 161–162
Blanchot, M. 198 *see also* Zupancic, A. (on Blanchot)

Candyman (1992) 142–146
Candyman (2021) 152–153, 154
Castration 43, 73, 80n17, 85, 116–117 *see also* Psychosis (and castration)
Cause and effect *see* Lacan, J. (Lacanian Cause); Racism (effect-cause)
Cognitive mapping *see* Jameson F. (cognitive mapping)

Colour-blindness 4, 122, 126–127
Conspiracy theories 108, 138, 140
Constitutive lack *see* Lack (and the subject)
Cooper, A. 1–2
Cottom Comes to Harlem 162
Cynicism 140 *see also* George, S. (on cynicism)

Descartes, R. 74, 77, 178
Desire: 94–95, 100, 177; the Other's desire 116, 117, 118, 129–130, 137
Deutsch, H.: 'as-if mechanisms' 67, 75, 125
Do the Right Thing 207
Dolezal, R.A. 78
Doubt *see* Psychosis (doubt)
Duarte, A. 2
Du Bois, W.E.B. 105–106, 128–129

Empty set 103
Enunciated and enunciation 48, 197, 212–214, 216
Extimate/extimacy 35, 36–37 *see also* Race (and extimacy); Real, the (exitmate)

Fascism 91–92
Fanon, F. 26, 49, 87, 105, 185
Fantasy *see* Psychosis (and fantasy); Racist fantasy
Fields, K. and Fields, B.: racecraft 6, 51–55, 56, 58n4, 124
Flisfeder, M.: affirmation/negation 195–196
Floyd Jr., G.P. 217–218
Foreclosure *see* Name-of-the-Father (and foreclosure); Psychosis (and foreclosure)

Forced choice *see* Psychosis (and forced choice)
Foxy Brown 162
Freud, S.: on Jews and anti-Semitism 182–183, 185–186, 193; *Fort-da* game 73–74
Fundamentalism 122–123

Gaze *see also* Objet petit a (and gaze)
George, S.: on blues music 205; on cynicism 177–178; on Joyce 202n1; para-being 107; on race and lack 47, 78, 101, 106–107, 129–130, 137, 196, 205; on Whiteness 41–43; Whiteness as phallus 117–118
Get Out 104, 126, 153–154
Gilroy, P.: 58n6; planetary humanism 196–197; on race 4–5, 176, 201; raciology 5, 50–51
Guattari, F. 75

Halsell, G. 3, 131n17
Hip-hop 205–208
Hook, D.: on racism 165
Hurricane Katrina 156–157

Identity politics 79n9
Imaginary, the 17n14, 33n2, 76; and the Symbolic 79n9 *see also* Psychosis (and the Imaginary)

Jameson, F.: cognitive mapping 8
Jeepers Creepers 89–90
Jouissance *see* big Other (*jouissance*); other, the (*jouissance*); Psychosis (*jouissance*); Sinthome, the (*jouissance*)
Joyce, J. *see* George, S. (on Joyce); Lacan (on Joyce, J.); Sinthome, the (and Joyce)

Kendrick Lamar 208–209; 'Alright' 219n3; *DAMN.* 208–209; 'HiiiPoWeR' 209; 'i' 210; 'Keisha's Song (Her Pain)' 211; 'Momma' 210; 'Mortal Man' 216–219; and paranoia 208–210; 'Sherane a.k.a Master Splinter's Daughter' 219n5; 'Sing About Me, I'm Dying of Thirst' 211–216; and temporality 214–219; *To Pimp a Butterfly* 210; 'U' 209–210

Lacan, J.: on anxiety 85–86; ethic of skepticism 178; on ethics 176;

Lacanian Cause 30–31, 37–38, 55; neighbour, the 149; not-all 35; on Joyce, J. 64, 79n4, 192–193, 210–211, 218; on psychosis 43–44n1, 63–66 *see also* big Other, the; Sinthome, the (and Joyce)
Lack 90, 117, 139, 190, 192–193, 199–200, 202n7, 205, 209–210, 217–219; lack of a lack 86–89, 91, 107, 110, 116, 117, 159, 180–181; and the Other 125, 179, 180, 186, 190, 191, 196; and the subject 38, 40, 43, 72, 90–91, 100, 101–102, 107, 109, 110, 121, 125, 130, 131n14, 155, 180, 183–184, 185, 191, 196, 201, 215 *see also* George, S. (on race and lack); Phallus, the (lack); Race (positivized lack); Symbolic, the (and lack); Zupancic, A. (on lack/negativity)
Law *see* Name-of-the-Father (and the Law)
Learned ignorance (*docta ignorantia*) 179–180, 217
Lil Gotit 206–207

Madness *see* Psychosis (and madness)
Malcolm X 183, 185–186, 193
Master-signifier 39, 45n11, 121–122 *see also* Missing signifier; Psychosis (and master-signifier); Race (and master-signifier); Whiteness (as master-signifier)
McGowan, T.: cinema of fantasy 207; on hip-hop 206–208; on nonbelonging 184, 206
McIntosh, P.: invisible knapsack 123–124
Meek Mill 206–207
Metaphor *see* Name-of-the-Father (and paternal metaphor); Slavery (and delusional metaphor)
Mirror stage 17n14, 68–71, 93
Missing signifier 43, 109
Morrison, T.: *Beloved* 137; *The Bluest Eye* 131–132n19; *God Help the Child* 111
Multicultural diversity 123–125

Name-of-the-Father: 16–17n13, 37, 79n8, 80n16, 141, 176, 191–192; and foreclosure 115, 116, 119–120, 127–129, 136, 163, 176–177; and the Law 114, 115, 118; and paternal metaphor 114, 115, 127–129, 191; and the phallus 115–116; and racism 120 *see also* Psychosis (and authority)

Negativity *see* Lack; *Objet petit a* (positivized negativity); Zupancic, A. (on lack/negativity)

Non-all 184–185, 187n11, 196, 213–214

Non-duped err, the (*les non-dupes errant*) 142–146, 178; duped who do not err 142–146; 193–194, 197

Non-sense *see* Psychosis (non-sense); Race (non-sense)

Notorious B.I.G. (Biggie), The 207–208

N.W.A. ('Niggaz With Attitudes') 208–209

Obama, B. 155–157, 202n3 *see also* West, C. (on Obama)

Objet petit a 11–12, 64, 69, 74, 136, 180–181; and gaze 69–70; phobic object 87; positivized negativity 91; *see also* Phallus, the (and object *a*); Psychosis (and object *a*); Race (object *a* of race); Whiteness (as object *a*)

One-drop rule 28

other, the 100, 102, 104–105, 108, 115, 138–139, 150; and conservatism 166–167; and liberalism 166–167; *jouissance* 163 *see also* Real (other)

Paternal metaphor *see* Name-of-the-Father (and paternal metaphor)

Paranoia: counter-hegemonic back paranoia 153–154, 177; racial paranoia 43, 91–92, 149, 150, 151, 155, 160, 165, 166–167, 185 *see also* Psychosis (paranoia)

Peinovich, M.E. 103

Peterson, J. 131n12

Phallus, the: 115–118; lack 116; and object *a* 116–117 *see also* George, S. (whiteness as phallus); Name-of-the-father (and the phallus)

Political correctness 124

Postcolonialism *see* Thakur G.B. (on postcolonialism)

Post-race *see* Race (post-race)

Primordial signifier 119

Psycho 136–137

Psychosis: and alienation 70–71, 72–73, 74–78, 97, 100, 103, 106, 134–135, 136; and anxiety 85–88, 115, 138–139; and authority 65, 68, 135–136, 140, 141–142, 146n2, 150, 151, 178–179; belief in disbelief 140–142, 145, 177, 182–183, 185, 193–194; and castration 72–74, 100–101, 162; certainty 107–109, 111, 150, 177, 181–182, 193; and desire 94, 136–137, 168n10; and doubt 177–183, 185–186, 190, 201, 209–211, 216, 219; and ethics 176–178, 180, 181; and fantasy 139, 146, 157–161, 164; and forced choice 74–75, 76, 77, 80n19, 97, 100–101, 130n3, 137, 176–177; and foreclosure 43, 102, 107, 109, 114, 121, 134, 138, 167, 180; and the Imaginary 67–69, 71, 72; *jouissance* 118, 136, 139, 161–163; and madness 64–68, 79n6, 79n7; and master-signifier 43; non-sense 109; ordinary psychosis 67–68; and object *a* 71, 90–91, 104, 151, 157, 163, 164; and the Other 101, 122–123, 134–146, 150; and the Other of the Other 122–123, 138, 140, 150–151, 178–179, 187n7; paranoia 67–68, 140, 149, 177, 178–179; and the Real 137, 139, 155, 184–185; schizophrenia 149; and the signifier 68, 75–76, 78, 97, 100–101, 115–116, 122, 123, 134–135, 138, 141–142, 148n1, 155, 159–160; and the Symbolic 65, 67, 68, 70, 74, 78, 88, 97, 101, 102, 103, 106, 109, 110, 114, 116, 119–120, 122, 125, 150, 155, 193 *see also* Andrews (on psychosis of whiteness); Name-of-the-Father; Schreber D.

Race: banality of 94; and biology 32, 56–57, 87, 103; contradiction in 29–30, 37, 55–57, 93; and discourse 37; and extimacy 48–51; and genetics 28, 52–53, 93, 95–96; and master-signifier 41–43; non-sense of 9, 10, 38–43, 48, 50, 134, 195–196, 201–202; object *a* of race 14, 85–97, 103, 105, 106–108, 110–111, 116–117, 118, 122, 130, 152, 154–155, 157–158, 165, 180–181, 182–183, 190; post-race 56–57, 196–200, 215–216, 218; positivized lack 105, 117; and the signifier 9–10, 32, 38–41, 48, 49, 50, 53, 78, 92, 101, 102, 106, 108–109; and temporality 200–202 *see also* George, S. (on race and lack); Gilroy (on race);

Seshadri, K. (on whiteness); Symbolic, the (and race)
Racecraft *see* Fields, K. & Fields, B. (racecraft)
Racialization 8, 14–15, 16n8, 35, 56–57, 85–86, 87, 91–94, 97, 103, 104, 107, 108, 110, 129–130, 145–146, 151, 154–155, 159, 161, 163, 182–183, 184–185, 201, 205, 207; and national identity 28
Racial identity 1, 3, 6, 14–15, 25, 28, 29, 41–42, 50, 56–57, 75–76, 93, 102, 104, 109, 175, 182
Racial realism 103
Racial segregation 95, 120, 121, 150
Racial symbolic order *see* Symbolic, the (racial symbolic order)
Racial visibility 15, 38, 41, 52, 54, 85–88, 93–94, 96–97, 105, 117, 121, 166, 175
Racism: banality of 25–26; effect-case 54–55; fetishistic disavowal 26; rational racism 125–127 *see also* Hook, D. (on racism); Real, the (and racism)
Racist fantasy 102, 110, 139, 159–161, 166–167, 185, 206–208
Real, the: 9, 17n14, 37, 151, 184–185, 186, 193, 217, 218; extimate 35, 49–50, 52, 55; other 139, 164, 167; and racism 38, 48, 51, 91–92, 94–95, 160; and the signifier 35–37, 39, 48, 122, 137–138; and the Symbolic 6, 9, 35, 37, 48, 49–50, 51, 55–56, 57n1, 58n2, 64, 91–92, 110, 137–138 *see also* Psychosis (and the Real); Symbolic, the (and the Real)
Ruti, M.: on language 194–195, 218

Schreber, D. 63–64, 80n11, 107–108, 117, 130–131n9, 131n10, 135, 141–141, 159, 200–201
Seshadri, K.: on whiteness 41–43, 44–45n10, 117–118
Shaft 162
Signifier, the: 27–28, 44n8, 58n2, 64, 71, 72, 74, 103, 109, 114, 134, 136, 163, 184, 190–191; and the sinthome 191, 193 *see also* Lacan, J. (Lacanian Cause); Psychosis (and the signifier); Primordial signifier; Subject (and the signifier); Symbolic, the (and the signifier); Race (and the signifier); Real (and the signifier)

Sinthome, the 64, 191, 193, 201, 205, 219; and *jouissance* 191–192; and Joyce 192–195; symbolic and the Real 194–195 *see also* Signifier, the (and the sinthome)
Slave/slavery: 75–76, 96–97, 205; and delusional metaphor 127–130; and psychosis 106–107
Subject: gap 100–101; Lacanian subject 44n3; and the signifier 27–28, 37, 101, 134, 141–142, 214; subjective destitution 176–177, 186n3
Surplus enjoyment 108
Symbolic, the: 7, 8, 9, 16n9, 30, 31–32, 35, 43, 73, 74, 100, 181; extimate 36–37, 50; and lack 32, 40, 49, 90–91, 101, 121; and race 9–10, 15, 40, 43, 49, 50–51, 55–56, 78, 93, 103, 108–110, 134, 176; racial symbolic order 10, 38, 42–43, 49, 50, 52, 54–55, 56–57, 92, 103–104, 105, 111, 129–130, 137, 145; and the Real 6, 9, 35, 37, 48, 49, 50, 51, 55, 56, 57n1, 58n2, 64, 91–92, 110, 137–138; and the signifier 37, 40, 48, 64 *see also* Psychosis (and the Symbolic)

Temporality *see* Kendrick Lamar (and temporality); Race (and temporality)
Thakur, G.B.: on decolonization 49; on postcolonialism 30, 183–184
Thing, the (*das Ding*) 149
Tupac '2Pac' Shakur (Pac) 216–219

Unconscious 71–72
Unconscious bias 26, 175

Void 103–104

West, C.: on Obama 155–157
White guilt 124–125
White privilege 123–124
Whiteness: as master-signifier 41–52, 117–118, 121–122; as object *a* 33n2 *see also* Andrews (on psychosis of whiteness); George, S. (on Whiteness); George, S. (Whiteness as phallus); Seshadri, K. (on Whiteness)

Zizek, S.: 'subject supposed to loot and rape' 156–157
Zupancic, A.: on Blanchot 198–200; on lack/negativity 90

For Product Safety Concerns and Information please contact our EU representative GPSR@taylorandfrancis.com
Taylor & Francis Verlag GmbH, Kaufingerstraße 24, 80331 München, Germany

www.ingramcontent.com/pod-product-compliance
Lightning Source LLC
Chambersburg PA
CBHW050533300426
44113CB00012B/2071